THAT WAS
HOLLYWOOD
THE
1930s

THAT WAS
HOLLYWOOD
THE
1930s

ALLEN EYLES

B.T. BATSFORD
LONDON

Title page: *The Sign of the Cross* – Fredric March, Claudette Colbert; this page: *Manhattan Melodrama* – Leo Carrillo, William Powell, Clark Gable. Execution day.

ISBN 0 7134 5735 X

Produced by the Justin Knowles Publishing Group, 9 Colleton Crescent, Exeter, Devon, England.

Typeset by Typesetters (Birmingham) Ltd and printed in Hong Kong by Mandarin Offset Ltd for the publishers B. T. Batsford Ltd 4 Fitzhardinge Street London W1H 0AH

CONTENTS

INTRODUCTION

There have been many critical surveys of the Hollywood films of the 1930s. This is not another one. Instead, this is a book that sets out to provide some of the information that, as a film historian, I've always wanted to see; the precise order in which films appeared, what films were competing with each other, how well or badly they did. The major trends and events that were making the present and shaping the future are also discussed year by year – the hopeful beginning of the decade, the harsh battering of the Depression and the subsequent recovery, through to the triumphant debut of *Gone with the Wind* in the very last month of the decade; technological developments, like the arrival of perfected Technicolor; and outside factors, like the crusade of the Legion of Decency.

The Hollywood film industry was a business like any other, seeking to make money. To understand what was made and why, it is necessary to know what was successful.

This book is very largely a record of the films that were the most popular with American audiences in each month – the hits and the smash hits. Hollywood was never inspired by failure, and it is the films highlighted in these pages that explain its evolution in the 1930s, for better or worse. They are also a record of the tastes and preferences of American moviegoers as a whole. Their favourites are often not the films that are held in highest esteem today, but the fact that they were popular once makes them of interest, as a reflection of the period, even if only in trying to fathom out just why some of them could ever have been liked so much!

This book further records the motion pictures that were held in highest esteem critically, thanks to the *Film Daily*'s annual poll of several hundred American reviewers. Again, the choices often jar considerably with those that would be made today. It is noticeable how often the films chosen as the 10 best were also among the most popular with audiences. Probably this is not so much because the critics persuaded moviegoers to see these films, but simply that the taste of such a broad canvas of critics (most of them presumably not too concerned with films as an art form) came close to matching the preferences of the general public.

However, the weight of critical approval was an encouragement to film executives and particularly to the actual film-makers, and it is another important factor in accounting for the

Director Wesley Ruggles and crew at work on *Are These Our Children?* (1931).

way Hollywood developed in the 1930s – for, much as Hollywood loved profit, it also relished prestige.

The Academy Awards offered the denizens of the film capital an opportunity to rate their own efforts. The Awards were the industry's choice of its best work to set beside the critics' choice and the public's choice. The annual prize-giving ceremony, initially for local consumption only, soon came to interest the whole country. In fact, the Awards and the nominations of the 1930s are of greatest significance in reflecting the preferences of the industry at the time. Today the choices often seem perverse and ridiculous (particularly when it is noted what was completely overlooked), but the Academy's changing rules and regulations sometimes need to be recalled – with years in which there was a very low number of voters or in which each studio had the right to nominate one of its own films in certain categories. There are also instances of studio pressure on employees to vote for its films as a matter of loyalty. There is little evidence that the winning choices did much to stimulate attendances at the films involved, as they had usually completed their run some time before.

The Metro-Goldwyn-Mayer studios at Culver City. The colonnaded building on Washington Boulevard was the main entrance (with gates at the side, entered by passing between the final four columns). In the aerial view, the columns can be seen at the left-hand corner. The back lot with its standing sets extends to the right. In the late 1930s the ultra-modern Irving Thalberg building, named after the late producer, was opened as the main office building. MGM was indisputably the top studio of the 1930s – its parent company, Loew's, was the only one to make profits throughout the troubled decade, and MGM had far more of the smash hits of the decade than any other studio.

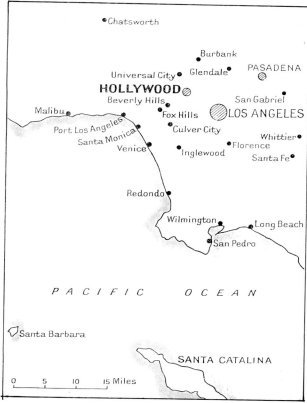

Vintage maps of Hollywood in 1933, published in that year's *The World Film Encyclopedia* edited by Clarence Winchester.

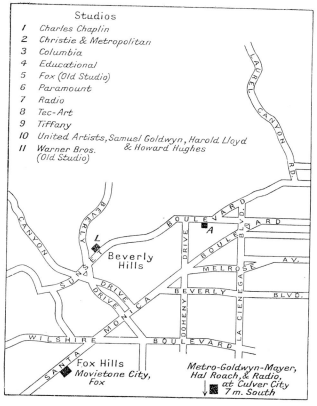

Studios
1 Charles Chaplin
2 Christie & Metropolitan
3 Columbia
4 Educational
5 Fox (Old Studio)
6 Paramount
7 Radio
8 Tec-Art
9 Tiffany
10 United Artists, Samuel Goldwyn, Harold Lloyd & Howard Hughes
11 Warner Bros. (Old Studio)

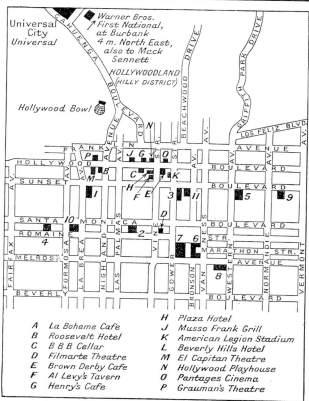

A La Boheme Cafe
B Roosevelt Hotel
C B B B Cellar
D Filmarte Theatre
E Brown Derby Cafe
F Al Levy's Tavern
G Henry's Cafe
H Plaza Hotel
J Musso Frank Grill
K American Legion Stadium
L Beverly Hills Hotel
M El Capitan Theatre
N Hollywood Playhouse
O Pantages Cinema
P Grauman's Theatre

The MGM production machine at work on
Dancing Lady (1933). Right, the director
Robert Z. Leonard watches Clark Gable
and Joan Crawford at work. Below, filming
an elaborate musical number on one of the
sound stages.

Finding the hit films

For much of the decade, the important weekly
trade paper, the *Motion Picture Herald*, listed
the six or more box-office champions of the
month, sometimes in order of box-office
receipts, sometimes alphabetically. These
formed a starting point for the films listed in this
book, but the selections are also based on other
trade comment in *Variety*, on information from
some of the more thoroughly researched and
knowledgeable histories of the period (see the
Select Bibliography) and, where necessary, on
my own reading of box-office takings reported
in the various trade periodicals. Out of just over
5,000 American-made productions released
during the decade, some 500 – the top 10 per
cent – have been picked out as the hit films.

These selections are normally based on performance in the key cities (and a few other
locations reported in the trade press) but
success was rarely patchy and was generally
repeated in all large towns. (A few of the films
may not have retained the same appeal in
smaller towns and neighbourhoods.)

The films for each month are ranked in order
of overall popularity, with those at the top
being the biggest attractions. A smash hit may
appear low down in one month before coming
first the following month. Some films were
initially released as road shows – reserved-seat,
separate-performance attractions at advanced
prices – and enjoyed two separate periods of
great popularity, the second when they went
into general release at normal prices.

The month for which a film is first listed is

very often *not* the month in which it was first shown. Some runs (especially New York and Los Angeles) may have started in the preceding month (if much earlier, this is generally noted in the text). In particular, many films would make their debut as Christmas attractions. These are listed for December if they were shown sufficiently to register among the top attractions of that month but often do not appear until January when they were being more widely booked.

New releases did not always play in all the big cities at or around the same time – for example, they often arrived belatedly in Chicago because of local censorship delays and the dominance of one particularly stubborn theatre chain there – and occasionally films (*Topper*, for example) had a very staggered release, and this is noted in the text.

Where exact figures of production costs and gross income (totals remitted by theatres to the distributor as its share of the box-office take) have been reliably established, these are quoted in the text; such precise accounting is, however, impossible for the majority of titles.

Foreign income was, of course, a significant factor, and where there is information on the overseas response to films this is given as well. Broadly speaking, films that were successful in the American market repeated that success overseas, but some exceptions are noted. Certain films, like *Cavalcade*, did even better abroad than on the domestic market and others, like some of Garbo's later films, had their biggest box-office potential in the foreign market.

Not all the films picked out in each year's hits were profitable. In many cases, as indicated in the text, they cost more than they recouped at the time. Nor did the successful films always deserve to do so well – skilful advertising campaigns sometimes did the trick – but, generally, favourable word-of-mouth was essential for a film to become a really big hit. The time of year when a film was released also had an effect, although big hits survived even the worst conditions of heat or cold. Some movies may have suffered from facing too much other strong competition, but other films – *Navy Blue and Gold*, for example – which might have been buried in a flood of hits, stand out because they drew audiences in a slack period. The film's distributor also made a difference. It was more difficult for Columbia, Universal and United Artists to succeed because these companies did not own huge theatre chains to ensure prime booking time, and even their biggest hits were reckoned to end up grossing less than they would have done in the hands of MGM or another cinema-owning producer.

Other movies besides those listed in this book will have been profitable in a minor way. B pictures and low-budgeted A pictures (including many in the horror category) returned a small but reliable profit most of the time, while some A pictures were made or released without expectation of making big profits to fill screens in the bad periods of the year (pre-Christmas, hot weeks in June and July) and to meet contractual obligations, or to test the appeal of new young talent. (In the 1930s, movie theatres and chains generally contracted to show the whole season's output of a particular studio, and, except for the releases of United Artists and very big attractions like *Gone with the Wind*, it was rare for pictures to be booked individually. Theatres left with a few clear weeks contracted for part of another studio's output.)

For each film listed there is a record of its subject matter, stars, studio, director and writers. Other factors of particular interest and significance are added, relating to the background circumstances of production, how films were launched, reasons why they did well and so on. I have usually omitted mention of any Academy Award nominations and victories because these came after their release and were not a factor in their initial reception. In addition, and as indicated earlier, nominations vary in significance from year to year: sometimes as many as 12 productions were nominated as Best Picture, while the number of Best Actor nominees went as low as three. The Academy Awards are dealt with as a separate, later historical event, when all the principal winners are named. (Readers interested in all the nominations will find the information in other books solely concerned with the history of the Oscars.)

Lack of space prevents the regular inclusion of more information on individual films, in particular the names of producers, although these – along with cameramen, art directors, composers, etc. – have been given in pertinent cases. I regret that writers' names have generally had to be restricted to the official screenplay credit when often many others are known to have worked on particular films. I have also quite deliberately omitted references to the loan-out of stars by one studio to another except in particularly interesting cases, since this happened so often and was so routine as not to be noteworthy. I have also refrained from listing most of the cast changes made before production started as it was a matter of routine for stars' assignments to be swapped around and was normally of no great moment.

Enough of explanations! I hope this book will entertain all those who were there to see the films of the 1930s when they first came out . . . and all those who wish they had been!

1930

All Quiet on the Western Front
Lew Ayres
Raymond Griffith

This was the year the talkies took full hold of the American cinema. The studios began the year issuing their films in both silent and talking versions; by the end of it, silents had been almost entirely dropped. Sound-on-film established itself over sound-on-disc. Even Warner Bros. was forced to offer its releases with soundtracks on prints while persevering with Vitaphone, the sound-on-disc process with which it had triggered the sound revolution. (With Vitaphone, it was difficult to keep the film running through the projector in synchronization with the disc on its turntable: the disc needle could jump or the film could be damaged and lose frames, putting the image ahead of the sound. A soundtrack on the film itself was obviously preferable, although Warners maintained that the quality of sound from a disc was superior. The disc system was abandoned in 1932.) Western Electric had wired up nearly half the 10,234 American movie theatres with sound in the summer of 1930, with RCA Photophone the most popular of the rival systems. A total of 13,128 theatres had sound at the year's end. Most of the remaining movie houses were unsuitable for conversion to sound and later closed.

It was a year of anxiety for the film industry. The huge Fox Film Corporation, which had control of Loew's, the parent company of MGM (Metro-Goldwyn-Mayer), was in deep financial difficulties as a result of the Wall Street Crash in October 1929, not helped by William Fox's enforced absence to recover from an automobile accident. He and production head Winfield Sheehan supported different re-financing schemes. In April, Fox sold out for $18 million to the group supported by Sheehan. Fears that Hollywood generally might lose the faith of investors were averted. Various company mergers (including Fox and MGM) seemed likely to follow Warner Bros.' takeover of First National in November 1929, but the only new one to occur was RKO's takeover of Pathé, consummated on 29 January 1931. Loew's repurchased its shares from the Fox company, and MGM regained its independence.

Sunny Side Up: Charles Farrell and Janet Gaynor were America's leading screen sweethearts in 1930.

During 1930 it became clear that the movie business was headed for trouble. The big circuit-owning companies continued their wild scramble to add new theatres until June when caution took over. (The count was approximately 1,500 theatres controlled by Paramount; 1,000 by Fox; 400 by Warner Bros.; 185 by Loew's; and 175 by RKO Radio.)

Attendances declined from the record level of 1929 as the country's economic woes cut spending power. The big downtown movie palaces suffered particularly as neighbourhood theatres added sound and as audiences began to save money on tickets and travel by waiting for films' second runs on their doorsteps. Seats were costing from 25¢ to 75¢ in big city centres, with a top price for reserved seat attractions on Broadway of $2. Admissions fell from an average 95 million per week in 1929 to 90 million in 1930. (At the time, figures of 115 to 120 million were being estimated, perhaps from wishful thinking or cheerful optimism. Had they been true, that would have represented an average of one visit per week per American, as the United States population was 122.7 million.) The amount passed on from theatres to Hollywood dropped by $200 million to $1,100 million.

Whoopee!: The huge success of this musical extravaganza launched Eddie Cantor (seen with Ethel Shutta) on an annual series of musicals for Samuel Goldwyn.

There were colossal box-office successes – *Sunny Side Up, Whoopee!, All Quiet on the Western Front* – but moviegoers' tastes seemed to be changing alarmingly. In particular, they had tired of musical revues with little or no plots. Warners' *The Show of Shows*, first seen in late 1929, was doing disappointing business in 1930. Universal's lavish *The King of Jazz*, which cost nearly $2 million, was a big flop. *Paramount on Parade*, although considered by far the best of the all-star studio extravaganzas, came too late and ran into widespread audience antipathy. MGM cut up its forthcoming revue

The March of Time into six separate shorts instead of releasing it as a feature. Paramount's *The Love Parade* was advertised as "Not a Revue" in an attempt to avoid the curse, but even this did not prevent it from being less successful than had been anticipated.

Likewise, expensive operettas like *The Rogue Song* and *The Vagabond King* were well received but still not big enough hits to encourage more of their kind. Attempts to launch opera singers like Lawrence Tibbett, Dennis King and John McCormack were unsuccessful. Backstage musicals like *Chasing Rainbows* were unwanted, and Al Jolson wore out his welcome with overly-familiar stuff: his last two films under his Warner contract, *Mammy* and *Big Boy*, were box-office disasters.

Westerns, too, were a let-down. After the success in 1929 of *In Old Arizona* and *The Virginian*, Hollywood churned out a horde of outdoor spectaculars. MGM's high-budgeted *Billy the Kid* and Fox's very expensive pioneering epic *The Big Trail* (with an unknown lead, John Wayne) were both losers. The nation also seemed fed up with gangster and crime films. For a few months, Americans seemed to prefer playing miniature golf to watching movies, but this alarming fad soon peaked and faded. There was still a big market for films that promised sexy or sensational scenes, particularly when local censors publicized them by making cuts, restricting admission to adults or issuing condemnations. The studios accepted new guidelines to acceptable screen content (known as the Hays Code), and these met with some short-lived compliance but failed to curb advertising excesses.

There was no easy answer to keeping up attendances. Many large downtown theatres offered supporting variety shows with big-name guest stars to lure audiences long distances, but the extra takings did not always cover the additional cost of the live artists. After the colour boom of 1929, the two-colour Technicolor process did not seem to guarantee larger audiences, and it took so long to manufacture prints that the release of a film could be delayed by as much as eight months, during which time its subject matter could go out of fashion or be poached by another studio in a black-and-white film. Moreover, it was expensive – $300,000 was added to the cost of making *The King of Jazz*. Fox thought that audiences would flock to widescreen films, and test features were made and shown during 1930, but it was not the right time.

Hollywood was also concerned about holding its overseas markets. Although some films were simply subtitled, the studios re-made the dialogue scenes of their big films using imported foreign artists, French, German, Spanish and

Swedish versions being most frequently undertaken. These foreign-language sequences might be shot at night using the same sets as the main production, but often they were shot months later. To save money, sometimes only one camera would be allowed, compared with the four or more used simultaneously in the original shooting to provide variety of camera set-ups.

Overseas audiences wanted sound but rejected many of these cheaply made versions, showing a worrying tendency to prefer sound pictures with original stories made in their own countries. Paramount began shooting multilingual versions in Paris, achieving a considerable saving in costs and a more acceptable end-product. The company was fortunate in having as stars Maurice Chevalier and Claudette Colbert, who could speak both French and English. The career of another French speaker, Adolphe Menjou, was in such decline that he was glad to take over Clive Brook's role in the French version of *Slightly Scarlet*, shot in Hollywood and called *L'Enigmatique M. Parkes*, but he then had so much success starring in a native French production, *Mon Gosse de Père*, that he revitalized his career in American films.

Foreigners preferred the big Hollywood stars to the less charismatic substitutes engaged by Hollywood, even if they did speak the language. The long-term answer was beginning to emerge – to keep the American stars but to dub their voices for each tongue. (Fox, though, was still shooting Spanish versions as late as 1935.)

Even television was beginning to raise its ugly head. The first experimental public broadcast took place on 22 May, when images of a vaudeville troupe performing in the General Electric plant at Schenectady, New York State, were transmitted on to a screen at the RKO Proctor Theater a mile away. The quality was so poor that much more development work was obviously necessary. In 1930, a more immediate threat to film exhibition seemed to be Western Electric's plan to market 16mm projectors with sound for use in the home.

Among the artistic films of the year, Rouben Mamoulian's *Applause* and D. W. Griffith's *Abraham Lincoln* were commercial flops, the latter having some moderate success but nowhere near enough to recover its costs or to reinstate Griffith as a major force. There were expensive write-offs when *Queen Kelly* with Gloria Swanson was abandoned and Mary Pickford decided to scrap her production of *Forever Young*.

WIDER SCREENS MEAN BIGGER BUSINESS?

Despite its financial problems, the Fox company remained highly active and was intent on launching the wide screen in 1930. It had acquired a 70mm process, which it called Grandeur and first demonstrated in 1929. This used stock twice as wide as the conventional 35mm film and gave a 2:1 screen ratio. Several big films were shot with both 70mm and conventional 35mm cameras. The first was the musical revue *Happy Days* with which the Grandeur process was launched on 14 February at the Roxy, New York. Suitable projection equipment was installed here and in a few more cities.

Other companies like Warner Bros. began shooting films with systems using a 65mm width of film and there was no agreement on standardization. Estimates in the trade press of the cost of changing over to the wide screen, coming as they did so soon after the enormous expenditure on sound installation and with attendances declining, frightened theatre owners, and there was considerable pressure

Panoramic western spectacle in *The Big Trail* failed to enthuse audiences in 1930, and unknown leading man John Wayne (on horseback above) had to wait until *Stagecoach* (1939) to achieve front-rank stardom. The bearded gentleman driving the wagon is Tyrone Power Sr.

on the studios to proceed slowly. The industry agreed to restrict its experiments with wide screen exhibition to 10 large cities.

Already in use was another big screen system in which a magnifying lens was placed in front of the projector and an enlarged image shown on a bigger screen: this was used to blow up spectacular sequences within a conventional film and had various names, including Magnascope and Magnavision.

Grandeur was re-launched in October with *The Big Trail* and MGM's *Billy the Kid*, the latter shot with Grandeur cameras but reduced to 35mm prints and shown through a special lens that spread the picture out on a wide screen. MGM called this system Realife, and it had the advantage that a portable lens could be attached to the existing projectors whereas Grandeur required special projection heads to be fitted to show its wide prints. Neither of these westerns was a big success. RKO put out *Danger Lights*, a railroad melodrama in the 65mm Spoor-Berggren Natural Vision process, on a trial booking in Chicago. Warner Bros. released the

musical *Kismet* with Otis Skinner in its 65mm Vitascope process but did not promote the added width in advertising; it also shot versions of *A Soldier's Plaything* and *The Lash* in Vitascope, but decided to release the films in conventional 35mm prints only. United Artists put out *The Bat Whispers* in a wide screen process called Magnafilm, which emulated MGM's method of spreading 35mm prints on to a wide screen.

It was perhaps unfortunate that Grandeur was not tested with more popular subjects, but it clearly did not draw appreciable audiences of its own accord. Exhibitors were relieved. There were also artistic objections – directors were worried about the awkward shape of the wide screen – and so it was dropped, although Fox had invested some $2 million. The company had a long memory and, over thirty years later, it remembered the Grandeur process and set about popularizing the wide screen all over again, this time with lasting success when it was known as CinemaScope.

THE HAYS CODE

These guidelines, written by trade publisher Martin Quigley and the Jesuit priest Daniel A. Lord, formed a new Motion Picture Production Code, which replaced earlier, less detailed advice offered to producers in the silent era. The Code was put before the industry by Will Hays in February and officially adopted by the Association of Motion Picture Producers, which represented the major studios, from 31 March. It had the immediate effect of making MGM drop its plans to film *A Farewell to Arms* and *Oliver Twist*, but before long many of its provisions were honoured more in the breach, until the Legion of Decency forced strict adherence from 1934. The rules applied only to domestic release, and studios often made alternative versions with nudity and bedroom scenes for foreign release. The Hays Code read as follows:

General Principles

No picture shall be produced which will lower the moral standards of those who see it. Hence the sympathy of the audience should never be thrown to the side of crime, wrongdoing, evil or sin.

Correct standards of life, subject only to the requirements of drama and entertainment, shall be presented.

Law, natural or human, shall not be ridiculed, nor shall sympathy be created for its violation.

Particular Applications

Crimes against the law:
These shall never be presented in such a way as to throw sympathy with the crime as against law and justice or to inspire others with a desire for imitation.
Murder:
The technique of murder must be presented in a way that will not inspire imitation. Brutal killings are not

to be presented in detail. Revenge in modern times shall not be justified.
Methods of crime should not be explicitly presented:
Theft, robbery, safecracking, and dynamiting of trains, mines, buildings, etc., should not be detailed in method. Arson must be subject to the same safeguards.

Use of firearms should be restricted to essentials. Methods of smuggling should not be presented. Illegal drug traffic must never be presented.

The use of liquor in American life, when not required by the plot or for proper characterization, will not be shown.
Sex:
The sanctity of the institution of marriage and the home shall be upheld. Pictures shall not infer that low forms of sex relationship are the accepted or common thing.

Adultery, sometimes necessary plot material, must not be explicitly treated, or justified, or presented attractively.
Scenes of passion:
They should not be introduced when not essential to the plot. Excessive and lustful kissing, lustful embraces, suggestive postures and gestures are not to be shown.

In general passion should so be treated that these scenes do not stimulate the lower and baser element.
Seduction or rape:
They should never be more than suggested, and only when essential for the plot, and even then never shown by explicit method. They are never the proper subject for comedy.

Sex perversion or any inference to it is forbidden. White slavery shall not be treated. Miscegenation is forbidden. Sex hygiene and venereal diseases are not subjects for motion pictures. Scenes of actual child birth, in fact or in silhouette, are never to be presented. Children's organs are never to be exposed.
Vulgarity:
The treatment of low, disgusting, unpleasant,

though not necessarily evil, subjects should be subject always to the dictate of good taste and a regard for the sensibilities of the audience.

Obscenity:

Obscenity in word, gesture, reference, song, joke, or by suggestion (even when likely to be understood only by part of the audience) is forbidden.

Profanity:

Pointed profanity and other profane or vulgar expression, however used, is forbidden.

Costume:

Complete nudity is never permitted. This includes nudity in fact or in silhouette, or any lecherous or licentious notice thereof by other characters in the picture.

Undressing scenes should be avoided, and never used save where essential to the plot. Indecent or undue exposure is forbidden. Dancing costumes intended to permit undue exposure or indecent movements in the dance are forbidden.

Dances:

Dances suggesting or representing sexual actions or indecent passion are forbidden. Dances which emphasize indecent movements are to be regarded as obscene.

Religion:

No film or episode may throw ridicule on any religious faith. Ministers of religion in their character as ministers of religion should not be used as comic characters or as villains. Ceremonies of any definite religion should be carefully and respectfully handled.

Locations:

The treatment of bedrooms must be governed by good taste and delicacy.

National feelings:

The use of the flag shall be consistently respectful. The history, institutions, prominent people and citizenry of other nations shall be represented fairly.

Titles:

Salacious, indecent or obscene titles shall not be used.

Repellent subjects:

The following subjects must be treated within the careful limits of good taste: actual hangings or electrocutions as legal punishments for crime; third degree methods; brutality and possible gruesomeness; branding of people or animals; apparent cruelty to children or animals; the sale of women, or a woman selling her virtue; surgical operations.

HITS OF THE YEAR

JANUARY

Sunny Side Up The immensely popular team of Janet Gaynor and Charles Farrell (co-stars in three silents) here made their first full talkie together. It was the first musical written directly for the screen (by the team of DeSylva, Brown and Henderson who also provided the songs). As a poor girl in love with a wealthy fella (Farrell), Janet sang and danced. The cheery title song was an antidote to Depression blues, and there was also "I'm a Dreamer, Aren't We All?" and "If I Had a Talking Picture of You". David Butler directed. Premiered in October 1929, the Fox picture turned into the biggest hit of 1930, racking up a world gross of $3.3 million.

The Love Parade Ernst Lubitsch added cinematic sophistication to the early talkies musical cycle, and Maurice Chevalier confirmed his appeal to American audiences. A Sylvanian romance with songs, it featured Chevalier as the great lover who marries the Queen and refuses to bend to her will. Jeanette MacDonald (in her screen debut) played the lonely ruler who surrenders to Chevalier's demands rather than lose him. Lillian Roth and Lupino Lane played servants. Ernest Vajda devised the

Sunny Side Up: Janet Gaynor proved that she could sing as well as talk, but her vocal range was rather narrow.

story and Guy Bolton wrote the libretto from a play by Leon Xanrof and Jules Chancel. The Paramount picture had been premiered in New York on 19 November 1929. Though good, the box-office response was below studio expectations, an indication of public weariness with musicals.

The Love Parade: Jeanette MacDonald, Maurice Chevalier.

Hot for Paris Victor McLaglen as a fun-loving sailor unknowingly wins a big prize and flees from officials attempting to contact him, thinking they want to apprehend him for recent misdeeds. El Brendel was his comic partner and Fifi D'Orsay a seductive Frenchwoman in Fox's comedy with songs. It was a further teaming of McLaglen with director Raoul Walsh after the colossal success of *What Price Glory* and its 1929 sequel *The Cock-Eyed World*. Walsh provided the story of *Hot for Paris*, developed by Charles J. McGuirk and William K. Wells.

Navy Blues Irrepressible William Haines made a successful transition to talkies in this comedy directed by Clarence Brown for MGM. He played a sailor with a day's shore leave who flirts with Anita Page's dancehall girl; she takes his attentions too seriously and pursues him to his ship. Raymond L. Schrock's story was adapted by Dale Van Every with dialogue by J. C. Nugent, Elliott Nugent and W. L. River.

Sally This second filming of the 1920 Broadway musical (the first was in 1925 with Colleen Moore) had sound, Technicolor and the original stage star, Marilyn Miller, recreating her role of the former waitress who makes good as a Follies dancer and wins the aristocrat she loves (Alexander Gray). Joe E. Brown lent comic support as a waiter who was once a grand duke. Waldemar Young adapted the stage work of Guy Bolton and Jerome Kern. Five new songs were added, including "Look for the Silver Lining" by B. G. DeSylva and Jerome Kern. It was First National's big money-maker of 1930.

FEBRUARY

Hit the Deck RKO's Radio picture was a follow-up to its first big musical, *Rio Rita*. Taken from the stage show of 1927 by Herbert Fields and Vincent Youmans, it again had Luther Reed adapting and directing. Jack Oakie starred as an amorous sailor opposite Polly Walker as the coffee-shop proprietress who wants to help him achieve his ambition of becoming a ship's captain. There were sequences in Technicolor. MGM re-made it under the same title in 1955.

Anna Christie: Greta Garbo, Marie Dressler.

Anna Christie "Garbo talks" – and they stood in line to listen. Frances Marion's adaptation of Eugene O'Neill's 1922 play was directed by Clarence Brown for MGM. As Anna, the waterfront woman of ill repute, Garbo seemed cold to contemporary audiences. Her now-famous first spoken words were addressed to a bartender: "Gimme a viskey, ginger ale on the side, and don't be stingy, baby." In fact, Marie Dressler, with her broad performance as the boozy old wharf rat Marthy, stole the show from Garbo. Charles Bickford also starred as the young seaman who falls in love with Anna. Garbo preferred her work in the Swedish version directed by Jacques Feyder: this was the silent version with two spoken sequences added, shot in the summer of 1930 along with a German version, also handled by Feyder.

Sunny Side Up

The Love Parade

Street of Chance Paramount's gambling melodrama, suggested by the life of the late Arnold Rothstein, starred William Powell as the Broadway card ace who cheats to teach his younger brother (Regis Toomey) a lesson and pays the price for breaking the gamblers' code. Kay Francis and Jean Arthur were the two men's wives. The unhappy ending was considered quite bold. John Cromwell directed from an Oliver H. P. Garrett

story, developed by Howard Estabrook and Lenore J. Coffee. There was a re-make in 1937, *Her Husband Lies*.

Son of the Gods Richard Barthelmess made a big comeback conveying the romantic heartbreak of a wealthy young Chinaman who has passed for white but is rejected by Constance Bennett's socialite on racial grounds (she even whips him across the face). First National's teasing with the taboo subject of miscegenation had a satisfactory ending when Barthelmess learns that he was only the adopted son of a Chinese merchant and his real parents were white. Bradley King adapted Rex Beach's 1928–9 magazine serial and Frank Lloyd directed. There were Technicolor sequences. British audiences saw it under the title *Thunder of the Gods*.

The Lone Star Ranger Helped by good reviews, Fox's modestly-scaled re-make of its 1923 Tom Mix western was a surprise hit of the year, much to the delight of movie-theatre owners who had booked it well in advance at a low fixed rental and reaped huge profits. George O'Brien starred as the wanted man who joins the Texas Rangers and rounds up cattle rustlers to demonstrate his true character. Sue Carol was the leading lady and A. F. Erickson directed. Zane Grey's story was scripted by Seton I. Miller and John Hunter Booth. The film won O'Brien a new five-year contract from Fox, which kept him busy with further Zane Grey adaptations and other brisk outdoor adventures.

The Lone Star Ranger: Sue Carol, George O'Brien. (Miss Carol later became an agent, promoted Alan Ladd to stardom and married him.)

MARCH

Anna Christie

Sarah and Son Ruth Chatterton repeated her 1929 triumph in *Madame X* with another sob-story of mother love. Here she was the opera singer who locates her lost son with the help of Fredric March's lawyer. Dorothy Arzner directed the film at Paramount from Zoë Akins' screen adaptation of a Timothy Shea novel.

The Girl Said No William Haines had another brash go-getting part in this MGM farce, directed by Sam Wood and dialogued by Charles MacArthur from a story by A. P. Younger adapted by Sarah Y. Mason. This time Haines sets out to make his fortune selling bonds, with Marie Dressler in a cameo role as a spifflicated millionairess who succumbs to his smooth talk. Leila Hyams was the girl who decided to marry someone else, only to be abducted at the altar by the persistent hero, a precursor of Dustin Hoffman in 1969's *The Graduate*.

The Cohens and Kellys in Scotland The fourth in Universal's series of Irish-Jewish ethnic comedies (inspired by *Abie's Irish Rose*) and the first of two 1930 additions. Here the comic adventures of the feuding business partners, Cohen (George Sidney) and Kelly (Charles Murray), take them to Scotland to buy plaid, anticipating that it will become the rage in American fashion. William Beaudine directed and the scriptwriter was Albert De Mond, working from a story by John McDermott.

Happy Days Fox's all-star musical revue overcame some of the prevailing antipathy towards the genre and benefited from mild interest in the 70mm Grandeur process in which it was shown at some theatres, notably in Los Angeles, where, of course, it aroused the curiosity of the film community. Benjamin Stoloff directed, assisted by Walter Catlett who also appeared. Janet Gaynor and Charles Farrell, Victor McLaglen and Edmund Lowe, Will Rogers, and Warner Baxter were among the big names who help to save a showboat from financial ruin. Future director Sidney Lanfield provided the story and Edwin Burke the dialogue.

Son of the Gods

The Rogue Song MGM's Technicolored version of Franz Lehár's 1912 musical play *Gipsy Love* introduced the Metropolitan Opera's baritone star Lawrence Tibbett to the

Sarah and Son: Philippe De Lacy, Ruth Chatterton.

THE ACADEMY AWARDS

The first Awards of the Academy of Motion Picture Arts and Sciences (founded on 11 May 1927) had been presented at a banquet on 16 May 1929 and covered films that opened between August 1927 and July 1928 inclusive for at least a week in the Los Angeles area.

The Awards for the next season's releases, from August 1928 to July 1929, were made on 3 April 1930 in the Coconut Grove at the Ambassador Hotel in Los Angeles. The winners were nominated by the Academy membership and selected by a small group of judges representing all the different branches (producers, actors, directors, writers and technicians). *The Broadway Melody* was the Best Picture; Warner Baxter the Best Actor for *In Old Arizona*; Mary Pickford the Best Actress for *Coquette*; while Frank Lloyd, nominated as director for three films, won for *The Divine Lady*. The other victors were writer Hans Kraly (for *The Patriot*); cinematographer Clyde De Vinna (for *White Shadows in the South Seas*); and art director Cedric Gibbons (for his interior decoration of *The Bridge of San Luis Rey*). The winners had been announced in advance and the ceremony made no great stir outside the movie community, being covered only by local radio with a live broadcast. However, the Awards were widely felt to have leaned in favour of the Academy's charter members and a more democratic way of choosing the winners was hurriedly announced for future occasions.

The Awards for the next period – August 1929 to July 1930 inclusive – were presented on 5 November 1930 at another banquet at the Ambassador Hotel. Each branch voted to determine the nominations in its field and the full membership of around 300 was polled by mail to determine the winners. *All Quiet on the Western Front* won the prize for Best Picture and Best Director (Lewis Milestone); George Arliss and Norma Shearer, both nominated for two performances, were victorious for *Disraeli* and *The Divorcee* respectively; Frances Marion picked up the writers' Award for *The Big House*; and Douglas Shearer, brother of Norma and head of MGM's sound department, collected the new Award for Sound Recording. The other winners were Joseph T. Rucker and Willard Van Der Veer, for their photography of the documentary *With Byrd at the South Pole*, and Herman Rosse, for the interior decoration of *The King of Jazz*.

Norma Shearer admires her statuette for *The Divorcee*, held by actor Conrad Nagel (a founder member of the Academy of Motion Picture Arts and Sciences) who was the host at the Awards Ceremony in November 1930.

screen under the direction of Lionel Barrymore (who did not appear). Only one of Lehár's songs was retained, new ones being contributed by Herbert Stothart and Clifford Grey, while Dimitri Tiomkin wrote the ballet music. The screenplay was by Frances Marion and John Colton. As a lovable bandit of the Russian mountains, Tibbett cheerfully sang one of his songs while being flogged. The film has become a key example of now-lost sound films, although some of the most missed footage has been located: two and a half minutes' worth of the comedy support supplied by Laurel and Hardy in which Ollie mistakes a bear for Stan in a fur coat.

APRIL

Montana Moon Joan Crawford's spoiled heiress marries John (later Johnny) Mack Brown's simple cowpoke in this modern western romantic comedy. Ricardo Cortez complicated matters with his interest in the bride at the wedding party. The director of the MGM picture was Malcolm St Clair, the writers Sylvia Thalberg, Frank Butler and Joe Farnham.

Ingagi Purporting to be a documentary record of "the Royal Expedition into the Heart of Africa Headed by Sir Hubert Winstead, FRGS", this Congo Pictures production was rapidly revealed as a fake. It was, in fact, based on a 1924 film record of the Lady MacKenzie expedition (originally called *Heart of Africa*) with additional footage shot in Los Angeles' Luna Park and at the Selig Zoo, using black extras and a man in a gorilla suit. The new material featured jungle tribes with vaccination marks on their arms and wild life unknown to Africa; it also showed the sacrifice of a live native virgin to gorillas, which carry her off into a thicket, as well as a lion attacking the cameraman, then falling over dead on cue. The lurid advertising drew enormous audiences to drool over the idea of gorillas mating with young women. The film was a freak success for States' rights distributors. After the Hays Office forced the studio-owned circuits to stop booking it because of its "false misrepresentation and objectionable aspects", independent theatres leapt in to reap a fortune as they had with the earlier banned *White Cargo*. Columbia followed up with *Africa Speaks*, openly admitting that there were added studio scenes. It was not long before *Ingagi* inspired a more acceptable use of its most titillating idea when Fay Wray was offered as a live sacrifice to King Kong.

High Society Blues Huge afternoon attendances and weak evening business was reported for this latest Janet Gaynor and Charles Farrell vehicle. It was a musical romance, directed by David Butler, in which the two stars sang four musical numbers by Joseph McCarthy and James F. Hanley. She for once played a girl of wealthy background, spurning the European count (Gregory Gaye) whom her snobbish parents (William Collier Sr. and Hedda Hopper) want her to marry. She prefers Farrell, the son of a successful businessman (Lucien Littlefield) who has dared set up residence among New York's exclusive set. The Dana Burnet story was scripted by Howard J. Green. Gaynor was disgusted by her feeble, undemanding role and insisted that Fox give her something better.

The Divorcee This was MGM's film version of Ursula Parrott's sensational novel about extra-marital affairs, *Ex-Wife*, published in 1929. The Hays Office forced the studio to drop the title, even from the film's credits. Tired of playing respectable women, Norma Shearer delighted in taking the leading role of the divorcee who indulges in numerous affairs. Chester Morris co-starred as the husband whose infidelities first wrecked the marriage, while Conrad Nagel and Robert Montgomery were men with whom Shearer dallied. It was one of her husband Irving G. Thalberg's productions, directed by Robert Z. Leonard and written by John Meehan.

Hold Everything Warner Bros.' version in Technicolor of the 1928 Broadway musical comedy hit (by DeSylva, Brown, Henderson and John McGowan) gave Bert Lahr's

All Quiet on the Western Front: Lew Ayres and Louis Wolheim seated at the back. Some of the grimmer scenes in the film sent women scurrying from the auditorium. The industry predicted that it would either be a huge success or a total flop.

stage role to Joe E. Brown, the rising comic with the cavernous mouth. Robert Lord did the screen adaptation for Roy Del Ruth to direct. The story was set in the boxing world, and the film co-starred former champion prizefighter turned actor Georges Carpentier, along with Sally O'Neill and Winnie Lightner.

MAY

All Quiet on the Western Front
Universal bravely spent over $1 million to shoot its film version of Erich Maria Remarque's 1929 anti-war novel. It was so effectively made and so highly praised by the critics that it drew huge audiences despite its lack of stars, grim theme, downbeat ending and running time of 140 minutes (cut to 105 when it was re-issued in 1939). (A rival World War I drama with comparable drawbacks, *Journey's End*, had a more patchy reception at the box-office.) The film not only made a profit but also, when it went on to win the Academy Award for Best Picture, provided every encouragement for Universal's new policy of concentrating on high-grade movies for the big first-run theatres. Maxwell Anderson, George Abbott and Del Andrews adapted the novel to the screen, and Lewis Milestone directed with assistance from George Cukor. The remarkable battle scenes were shot at the Irvine Ranch 50 miles south of Los Angeles and involved over 500 extras. A mile-long trench was dug, and a 1,000-yard concrete pavement was built for the camera to travel along (Arthur Edeson was the cinematographer). Lew Ayres played the young, disillusioned German soldier, while Louis Wolheim was the veteran of the ranks who befriends him. Former comedian Raymond Griffith (in his last acting job) appeared as the married French soldier who is fatally wounded by

The Cuckoos: Bert Wheeler (left), Dorothy Lee, Robert Woolsey.

Ayres and dies in front of him in a shell hole. ZaSu Pitts was cast as the mother in the silent edition but replaced by Beryl Mercer for the main talking version. Universal ran into bans on the film in Germany (after making a German-language version) and in Italy, but it was a huge success in Britain, kicking off with a record 14-week run at Leicester Square's Alhambra, and its world gross was reported at just under $2 million at the end of 1938.

The Divorcee

Hold Everything

The Cuckoos After providing the comedy relief in the 1929 hit musical *Rio Rita*, the team of Bert Wheeler and Robert Woolsey (the latter the one with glasses and cigar) were promoted by RKO to star in this screen adaptation of a musical play by Guy Bolton. The zany pair appeared as penniless fortune-tellers looking for a kidnapped heiress (June Clyde). Bert Kalmar and Harry Ruby provided most of the songs, Cyrus Wood wrote the screenplay and Paul Sloane was the director. The Radio picture had Technicolor sequences.

The Arizona Kid After his immensely-popular portrayal of the Cisco Kid in *In Old Arizona*, Warner Baxter came back as another Mexican bandit–hero in a story written by Ralph Block and directed by Alfred Santell. Fox cast Mona Maris as the leading señorita with Carole Lombard in support as a villainous girl from up north.

Ingagi

JUNE

So This is London Following his 1929 *They Had to See Paris*, Will Rogers had the same screenwriters, Owen Davis and Sonya Levien, adapt a 1922 stage comedy by Arthur Goodrich into another vehicle with a European setting for his folksy humour. He was the Anglophobe, forced to visit London on business, who discovers the British aren't such a bad lot after all when his son (Frank Albertson) insists on marrying the daughter (Maureen O'Sullivan) of a lord (Lumsden Hare). John Blystone guided the actors through Fox's picture.

So This is London: Lumsden Hare, Will Rogers.

Caught Short Using an idea from Eddie Cantor (for which he was reputedly paid $10,000), MGM experimented with starring Marie Dressler in a film of her own after her stand-out work in *Anna Christie*, re-teaming her with an old comedy partner, Polly Moran. They played landladies who dabble in the stock market. Charles F. Reisner directed with a screenplay by Willard Mack and Robert E. Hopkins. The studio shelved it at first, then found it had a big hit on its hands. Dressler had become a major star all over again.

All Quiet on the Western Front

The Devil's Holiday Rave reviews took Paramount's romantic drama, written and directed by Edmund Goulding, to box-office business above the studio's expectations. Nancy Carroll had a meaty role as a manicurist who marries young Phillips Holmes without loving him to gain revenge on his wealthy family. Also cast were James Kirkwood, Hobart Bosworth, Ned Sparks, Paul Lukas and ZaSu Pitts.

The Lady of Scandal MGM found a juicy new title for Frederick Lonsdale's play *The High Road* when it was turned into a vehicle for Ruth Chatterton, appearing as the popular actress of the London stage whose unhappy experiences of upper-crust men (played by Basil Rathbone and Ralph Forbes) make her glad to get back to the footlights. Sidney Franklin directed the romantic comedy-drama (which retained the play's title for its British release), and Hans Kraly, Claudine West and Edwin Justus Mayer wrote the adaptation.

JULY

The Big House The prominent woman screenwriter Frances Marion wrote this gritty exposé of life behind bars, inspired by recent headline–grabbing prison riots, and her husband George Hill directed for Cosmopolitan/MGM (Martin Flavin, author of the prison

The Big House: Wallace Beery.

play *The Criminal Code*, provided additional dialogue with Joe Farnham). Sharing a cell are Chester Morris, as the tough inmate reformed by love for Leila Hyams, Wallace Beery, as the king of the cons who engineers the climactic revolt, and Robert Montgomery, as the well-bred weakling who squeals to the warden (Lewis Stone). The movie's success encouraged other studios to produce similarly-patterned prison pictures, forming a distinctive sub-genre within the crime film. (French and German versions of *The Big House* were directed by Paul Fejos, whose surviving German version has been called superior to the original in detail and atmosphere. Charles Boyer was one of the players in the French version. There was also a Spanish version directed by Ward Wing.)

Let Us Be Gay Frances Marion also wrote this more characteristic MGM picture, based on Rachel Crothers' stage hit. Norma Shearer starred as another divorcee, but this time a prim and homely woman who smartens her appearance and manner so much that she attracts hordes of admirers, among them Rod La Rocque, who doesn't even recognize her as his former wife. Marie Dressler generated laughter as a wealthy, scheming dowager. Robert Z. Leonard provided the smooth direction. Gilbert Emery, Hedda Hopper and Sally Eilers were featured.

Our Blushing Brides Something of a sequel to MGM's 1928 *Our Dancing Daughters*, which made Joan Crawford a top star, this had Crawford, Anita Page and Dorothy Sebastian as flatmates who work as mannequins in a big department store. Their varied adventures with men (roles for Robert Montgomery, Raymond Hackett and John Miljan) formed the subject of the film, written by Bess Meredyth and John Howard Lawson and directed by Harry Beaumont. It was a huge matinee draw.

Lon Chaney: Centre, on the set of *The Unholy Three* (1930), his only talking picture in which he played Echo the Ventriloquist, with director Jack Conway and co-star Lila Lee. This publicity shot helped to emphasize that Chaney had spoken with his own voice in the film.

The Unholy Three MGM had a fourth concurrent success with Lon Chaney's talking debut in a re-make of his 1925 picture. It met some resistance from moviegoers, who thought that spoken dialogue had been dubbed on to the silent version and who believed that Chaney was mute like his parents. The actor signed an affidavit declaring that the vocal

impersonations accompanying the five disguises he adopted in the film were all his own work, and this was featured in the publicity. Jack Conway directed the story (adapted by J. C. Nugent and Elliott Nugent from a novel by Clarence Aaron Robbins) about a gang of crooks from a carnival with a weird assortment of skills: Chaney's ventriloquist who sells apparently talking parrots, Harry Earles' midget and Ivan Linow's strong man. It was Chaney's last film – the Man of a Thousand Faces died on 26 August, aged 47, a victim of bronchial cancer.

Romance Yet another MGM crowd-puller was Garbo's second talkie. Based on Edward Sheldon's 1913 play, it cast Greta as an Italian opera singer, with Gavin Gordon as the clergyman who will always regret he never married her because of her immoral past. Lewis Stone appeared as a wealthy admirer. Clarence Brown directed Bess Meredyth and Edwin Justus Mayer's adaptation.

For the Defense Patterned after *Street of Chance*, this melodrama cast William Powell as a criminal lawyer (suggested by the real-life William J. Fallon) who defends gangsters and mixes in high society. He breaks the professional code when he bribes a juror in an attempt to help the woman he loves (Kay Francis), and has to pay the price. In addition to the same stars as *Street of Chance*, Paramount's film retained the same director, John Cromwell, and writer, Oliver H. P. Garrett. Thomas Jackson was the persistent detective who brought about Powell's downfall.

AUGUST

Common Clay "Does one slip make a bad woman?" asked Fox's advertising. In another saga of motherly love, Constance Bennett portrayed the maid seduced by the young master of the house (Lew Ayres), who bears his child and refuses to be paid off by his parents. Fox's biggest money-maker

of the year (after *Sunny Side Up*), it was written by Jules Furthman from a 1915 stage success by Cleves Kincaid and directed by Victor Fleming.

The Dawn Patrol Richard Barthelmess topped an all-male cast in this stark drama of World War I from a story by John Monk Saunders. Like *All Quiet on the Western Front*, it proved that there was an audience for serious films without love interest. This dwelt on the stress of being responsible for sending young British flyers on dangerous missions that too often claimed their lives. Douglas Fairbanks Jr and Neil Hamilton also starred in Howard Hawks' film for First National (Warner Bros.). Hawks shared the writing credit with Dan Totheroh and Seton I. Miller. Howard Hughes tried suing for copyright infringement of his own *Hell's Angels*. *The Dawn Patrol* was closely re-made for 1938 release with Errol Flynn.

Raffles Ronald Colman starred as the debonair cricketer and jewel thief A. J. Raffles, a character devised by E. W. Hornung 30 years before and portrayed on stage and in two earlier films. Of course, Raffles is essentially a decent chap, an amateur cracksman who really indulges in crime for the sport of outwitting Scotland Yard, represented by David Torrence. Kay Francis is the society woman for whom he turns over a new leaf. Samuel Goldwyn's production for United Artists release had a script by Sidney Howard and was directed by Harry D'Arrast and George Fitzmaurice (although no director received credit on screen).

Our Blushing Brides

Manslaughter Paramount's romantic drama was a re-make of its 1922 Cecil B. DeMille picture with Leatrice Joy and Thomas Meighan. In George Abbott's re-working (he both wrote and directed), Fredric March was the upright young district attorney who

Common Clay: Beryl Mercer, Constance Bennett, Tully Marshall.

ensured that, despite his affection for her, Claudette Colbert's wealthy spoiled socialite went to prison for causing a death through reckless driving and learned her lesson. Alice Duer Miller concocted the original story.

Anybody's Woman Following *Sarah and Son* and *The Lady of Scandal*, Ruth Chatterton again drew moviegoers in this Paramount drama, playing a showgirl who marries Clive Brook's divorced attorney during one of his drunken sprees. Paul Lukas was the lawyer who almost took her away from Brook. Dorothy Arzner directed from a script by Zoë Akins and Doris Anderson, based on a Gouverneur Morris tale.

Let Us Be Gay

Hell's Angels: Douglas Gilmore, Jean Harlow, James Hall, Ben Lyon.

Hell's Angels Howard Hughes' aerial epic of two British pilots in World War I was an attempt to outdo *Wings*. His Caddo Company production started out as a silent, written by Harry Behn and Howard Estabrook and directed by Luther Reed, who was supplanted by Hughes himself. Its action sequences then had sound effects added while dialogue scenes were specially written (by Joseph Moncure March) and recorded under the direction of James Whale, with Jean Harlow receiving her big break, replacing Greta Nissen whose Scandinavian accent was deemed unsuitable. Harlow's accent was hardly ideal for playing the dazzling British socialite who captures the affections of the two airmen – the upright James Hall and his disreputable brother, Ben Lyon. (The Canadian censors objected to Lyon's British officer being shown as a coward and traitor, so a title was inserted, making the two brothers Americans, for release there and in Britain.) It was the spectacular

war-time aerial sequences, including a Zeppelin raid over London, that made the big impression – but at enormous financial outlay. The total production cost of the film (which even included sequences in Technicolor) was estimated to be a staggering $3.2 million, with a considerable additional amount required for the distributors, United Artists, to launch the picture. It was praised by critics and was an immediate box-office success on its special engagements at advanced prices and again on general release at the end of 1930. Though it came nowhere near recovering its immense cost, Hughes had his tool company fortune to bail him out.

Animal Crackers Paramount's Astoria Studios on Long Island provided another film version of a Marx Brothers stage hit, which proved an even bigger wow with picture fans than their first, *The Cocoanuts*. Again little altered for the change of medium; it featured all four of the Marxes on the rampage at a society gathering, with Groucho as the African explorer, Captain Spaulding, Zeppo as his blithely incompetent secretary, Chico as a hired musician

The Office Wife: Dorothy Mackaill, Lewis Stone, Natalie Moorhead.

Animal Crackers: Chico, Groucho and Harpo Marx, Margaret Dumont.

and Harpo as a gatecrasher. Victor Heerman directed this valuable film record of George S. Kaufman and Morrie Ryskind's play with its music and lyrics by Bert Kalmar and Harry Ruby. At one New York showing, a diligent reporter clocked 388 laughs, an average of four a minute (301 for spoken gags, 87 for situations). It was Paramount's top domestic grosser of the year. However, the film did not export too well – audiences in the north of England, for example, found its verbal humour incomprehensible.

SEPTEMBER

Animal Crackers
Anybody's Woman
The Office Wife "Ten million wives have asked this question. What goes on in the office after hours?" According to this Warner Bros.' version of a Faith Baldwin novel (adapted by Charles Kenyon), the boss is apt to go overboard for his secretary, especially when she looks like Dorothy Mackaill. Lewis Stone was the ageing executive whose interest in her breaks up his marriage. Rather surprisingly, he and Mackaill are permitted to settle down for a happy future together, although his wife (Natalie Moorhead) is shown to have been unfaithful to him. Directed by Lloyd Bacon, this became Warners' top-grossing film of 1930. The company re-made it under the same title as a "quota quickie" in England in 1934.

Holiday The Pathé studio's great asset was its trio of women stars: Ann Harding, Constance Bennett and Helen Twelvetrees. Its weakness was that it never managed to get the

bookings its best product deserved. Just before RKO Radio arranged to take over the company, it had its biggest draw of the year in this Horace Jackson adaptation of Philip Barry's play, directed by Edward H. Griffith. Ann Harding played the high society girl inspired by Robert Ames's young lawyer to throw aside conventions and enjoy life to the full. With sterling support from Edward Everett Horton and Hedda Hopper, this touching comedy had a most appealing message, one that charmed audiences all over again when Columbia put out its 1938 re-make with Katharine Hepburn and Cary Grant.
Common Clay

OCTOBER

Whoopee! Samuel Goldwyn collaborated with Broadway showman Florenz Ziegfeld in order to bring the latter's smash hit of the 1928–9 season to the screen. The Technicolor musical comedy launched the stage production's star Eddie Cantor on a new career in movies as a shy comic and brought choreographer Busby Berkeley to Hollywood to devise the routines for the newly-formed Goldwyn Girls (who included Betty Grable, Virginia Bruce and Claire Dodd), putting them into kaleidoscopic patterns and using an overhead camera. Cantor's character of "the nervous wreck" (developed through a story, straight stage comedy and musical by E. J. Rath, Owen Davis and William Anthony McGuire respectively) goes on a health cure to Arizona, where heroine Eleanor Hunt is in love with an Indian (played by Paul Gregory), who is ultimately discovered to be really a white lad and so a suitable partner after all. Cantor sang "Making Whoopee" (the only song retained from the stage show) and other musical numbers from Walter Donaldson and Gus Kahn. William Conselman did the screenplay and Thornton Freeland directed. Released by United Artists, *Whoopee!* took more money than any other film opening in 1930 in American movie theatres and went on to a world gross of well over $2.5 million.
Check and Double Check With their enormous following on radio (they had a 15-minute spot nightly), it was inevitable that dialect comedians Amos 'n' Andy would bring their routines to the screen. They played New York cab drivers looking for a missing deed in a haunted house. Sue Carol and Charles Norton were young lovers, and Duke Ellington and his Band provided a musical interlude. RKO launched a massive press and poster campaign to arouse interest in actually seeing as well as hearing the blackface duo and opened the Radio

Whoopee!: The climax to a dance number staged by Busby Berkeley with the Goldwyn Girls in Indian head-dress.

picture simultaneously at 200 theatres on 24 October. The result was the biggest week's business ever for one film in the history of the movies to that time, but the audience came all at once and attendances quickly fell off. Made for $1.1 million (the high cost in part because the team had to maintain their live radio broadcasts during production), it grossed around $2.5 million. Adapted by J. Walter Ruben from a story by Kalmar and Ruby, and directed by Melville Brown, the movie was privately recognized by RKO as being a very feeble freak attraction,

Min and Bill: Dorothy Jordan, Marie Dressler, Wallace Beery.

and the team never made another one. However, Freeman F. Gosden (Amos) and Charles J. Correll (Andy) did well enough, with a reported $¼ million fee plus half the net profits.

NOVEMBER

Min and Bill More dramatic than audiences expected with Marie Dressler heading the cast, this MGM film teamed her with Wallace Beery in the title roles. She was the hard-boiled proprietress of a ramshackle waterfront hotel who kills to protect the waif she has raised (Dorothy Jordan). Beery was Dressler's fisherman sweetheart. Frances Marion and Marion Jackson wrote the script from a Lorna Moon novel, while George Hill directed. It was MGM's most profitable film of the year and

DECEMBER

Min and Bill
Hell's Angels
Lightnin' A classic stage play of 1918 by Frank Bacon and Winchell Smith, *Lightnin'* was filmed as a silent by Fox in 1925 and now became ideal material for Will Rogers in S. N. Behrman and Sonya Levien's adaptation. It was a comedy about a drinking man's difficulties with his wife (Louise Dresser) and her problems with property sharks after their hotel. Joel McCrea was the young lawyer who helped them out and became engaged to their daughter (Helen Cohan). In his first film for Fox, director Henry King shot everything on location at Lake Tahoe, the setting for the story.
Morocco Having seen the way Josef von Sternberg handled Marlene Dietrich in the German production *The Blue Angel*, Paramount (which distributed the film in the USA) put Dietrich under contract and re-teamed her with director Josef von Sternberg for *Morocco*, hoping she would have the same appeal to American audiences as Garbo. To ease acceptance, she was co-starred with an established Hollywood name, Gary Cooper. Sternberg went well over schedule ensuring that Dietrich made exactly the visual impact he desired with the help of cinematographer Lee Garmes. She was the cabaret singer who finally threw over everything to follow barefoot into the desert after Cooper's American serving in the

cued further pairings of Dressler and Beery.
Hell's Angels
The Doorway to Hell This Warner Bros. gangster film cast Lew Ayres as the racket boss with a Napoleonic complex who attempts to retire (a little-known actor called James Cagney played his ineffective successor); when his younger brother is killed, Ayres returns to exact revenge. Robert Elliott was the shrewd and vigilant cop who engineered his downfall. Rowland Brown's original story was scripted by George Rosener, and Archie L. Mayo directed. This was the prototypical rise-and-fall-of-a-gangster picture – its success paved the way for more of its type. In Britain it was seen as *A Handful of Clouds*.
Feet First Harold Lloyd produced and starred in this example of his "thrill comedy" for Paramount release, playing a young shoe-salesman in Honolulu who climaxes a series of misadventures by hanging off the side of a skyscraper in Los Angeles. Clyde Bruckman directed from a script by Felix Adler, Lex Neal and Paul Gerard Smith.

The Doorway to Hell: Lew Ayres, Robert Elliott, James Cagney.

Morocco: Gary Cooper, Marlene Dietrich. Note how the still, like the film, favours Dietrich.

Tom Sawyer: Lucien Littlefield, Jackie Coogan, Mitzi Green.

French Foreign Legion. Adolphe Menjou was the wealthy older man she rejected. Paramount spent a fortune promoting Dietrich, and it paid off handsomely. Cooper came first in the billing and enhanced his standing as a romantic lead, being the object of such adoration.

Tom Sawyer Jackie Coogan made a big comeback at the age of 15 after three years off screen. He starred as Tom with Junior Durkin as the ragamuffin Huckleberry Finn who arranges most of their escapades in Paramount's version of the Mark Twain classic, adapted by Sam Mintz, Grover Jones and William Slavens McNutt and directed by John Cromwell. Mitzi Green and Jackie Searl were other youngsters in the cast, while Lucien Littlefield, Tully Marshall, Clara Blandick (grumbling Aunt Polly), Jane Darwell (jolly Widow Douglas) and Charles Stevens (murderous Injun Joe) played some of the grown-ups. It was a strong Christmas attraction for kids but inevitably posted poor evening attendances. There was to be another version of the story on offer from David O. Selznick in 1938.

CLOSE RUNNERS UP

The following films were also reported as doing substantially above average business and came close to being included among the hits of the year for the month indicated: *Devil-May-Care* (February), *Half Shot at Sunrise* (October), *Honey* (April), *Playboy of Paris* (October), *Sin Takes a Holiday* (November), *The Vagabond King* (March).

TEN BEST - CRITICS' CHOICE

There were 333 American critics and commentators participating in the *Film Daily*'s ninth annual nationwide poll to select the top 10 films released between 1 December 1929 and 30 November 1930 from ballot papers supplied by the trade paper listing the eligible films. The *New York Times*, which published its own "Ten Best" list, did not take part until 1934 (when chief critic Mordaunt Hall was succeeded by André Sennwald). The winners (with number of votes cast) were:

1.	*All Quiet on the Western Front*	271
2.	*Abraham Lincoln*	167
3.	*Holiday*	166
4.	*Journey's End*	151
5.	*Anna Christie*	141
6.	*The Big House*	141
7.	*With Byrd at the South Pole*	121
8.	*The Divorcee*	94
9.	*Hell's Angels*	91
10.	*Old English*	87
	Close Runners Up	
11.	*The Dawn Patrol*	78
12.	*Sarah and Son*	77
13.	*Common Clay*	73

Four of the above films – *Abraham Lincoln, Journey's End* (a British-American co-production shot in Hollywood), *Old English* and *With Byrd at the South Pole* (a documentary) – were less popular with the paying public and do not feature among the hits of the year.

1931

Dracula
Helen Chandler,
Bela Lugosi

This was the year that the Depression made an impact on the film business. There was a huge drop in the weekly attendances at American movie theatres. While there are no fully accurate statistics, it is generally accepted that admissions dropped from around 90 million in 1930 to around 75 million in 1931.

People simply didn't have as much money to spend on movie tickets, especially children (those aged between 5 and 12 represented under 5 per cent of the audience). Theatre owners tried cutting admission prices. They tried offering better value with double bills, even though there was a shortage of films and the two pictures might have been shown separately. They lamented the wasteful practice of putting two stars in the same film when one might have done. Really large theatres relied on live variety to support the films and to even out attendances, especially those on the RKO circuit that had been former vaudeville houses. Independent owners tried to cut down on projection staff and found the unions retaliating by releasing stink bombs in the auditorium and worse.

The problem of declining audiences became most serious during the summer when studios completed delivering their year's output to contracted theatres with a last few weak items. When the shortage of good films was most acute, hot weather would also arrive to keep patrons away. Many theatres simply closed down for a few weeks.

The big theatre-owning companies began finding it difficult to meet the financial obligations they had undertaken in their haste to acquire more and more theatres, and Warner Bros., RKO and Fox posted substantial losses. The construction of new movie theatres fell to its lowest level for years.

Much less money was reaching the studios. Revenue from showing films abroad had still not recovered, although dubbing was fast proving the most economical and acceptable means of putting out films in other languages, not only for export but also for showing in ethnic enclaves in the United States.

The studios were forced to trim picture budgets, institute pay cuts and reduce staffing levels. This was a time to batten down the hatches. No more attention was paid to developing wide screen, and Technicolor was hardly used on features but kept for shorts. RKO quickly abandoned its intention of running its new Pathé acquisition as a separate entity, the two companies merging under one roof with heavy job losses, especially in the exchanges (distribution branch offices) of the two companies.

Continuing efforts to restore silent stars like John Gilbert and Ramon Novarro to favour were resisted by audiences, as was Paramount's attempt to launch Tallulah Bankhead in *Tarnished Lady* and others. Paramount also had one of the year's worst flops with *The Night Angel*, starring Nancy Carroll and Fredric March, which was despised by critics and boycotted by audiences – all the more curious as the previous collaboration of Nancy Carroll with its director Edmund Goulding had resulted in the huge hit, *The Devil's Holiday*. Other disasters were suffered by Mary Pickford with *Kiki* and Clara Bow with *Kick-In*. The film industry needed more new stars like Clark Gable, fast becoming the screen's biggest male draw by year's end, and young Jackie Cooper, who put new life into kids' pictures with *Skippy*.

The industry also needed less interference from local censors, whose cuts and bans hurt the gangster and horror pictures that seemed to be the most popular with audiences. Hollywood musicals had virtually disappeared until *The Smiling Lieutenant* showed they still had some box-office pull, although the most successful foreign-language imports were musicals, mostly from Germany, that played long runs in "little theatres" (the art houses of today). This led to the importation of many of these films' leading stars to make American films.

This building at 9336 West Washington Boulevard, Culver City, is the one in the Selznick International trademark, used to introduce the company's pictures from *A Star Is Born* (1937) onwards. It apparently began life as a Southern mansion set for *Barbara Frietchie* (1924), a romantic drama set in the Civil War, although Thomas Ince founded studios here in 1919. It was adapted to become the administration building for Producers Distributing Corporation and then Pathé studios. When Pathé was taken over by RKO, the two companies continued to function separately for a short period. The illustration shows the building as the front entrance of the RKO Pathé Studios in 1931. RKO concentrated production on its own studio and this became a rental lot. Late in 1936, Selznick's company took a lease and re-named it the Selznick International Studio. The hanging sign was retained to carry the company name in the introductory trademark. The lot has most recently become the Culver Studios after many years as the Laird International Studios.

HITS OF THE YEAR

JANUARY

The Man Who Came Back This was a more dramatic subject for the Janet Gaynor/Charles Farrell team, in answer to Gaynor's demand for meatier roles from Fox after the cream puffery of *High Society Blues*. She was the café entertainer who had become a drug addict in Shanghai, he the playboy who has taken to drink. Together they haul themselves out of the seamy depths. Far from shocking audiences with its drugs theme, it was enjoyed as a creaky old melodrama, having been filmed often before (most recently by Fox as a 1924 silent with George O'Brien and Dorothy Mackaill). Edwin J. Burke handled this latest adaptation of Jules Eckert Goodman's play from a John Fleming Wilson novel, and director Raoul Walsh notched up another success.

Reducing While *Min and Bill* was still cleaning up at the box-office, MGM put Marie Dressler back with her *Caught Short* co-star Polly Moran and director Charles F. Reisner for a new farce. Here Dressler was the poor, dowdy country sister of Moran's beauty salon proprietress, who came to stay with her and created slapstick havoc around the place. Anita Page and Sally Eilers as their daughters competed for the same wealthy young man (William Collier Jr). Lucien Littlefield was Dressler's ineffectual husband. Willard Mack and Beatrice Banyard wrote the picture, its title referring to a contemporary craze for weight watching.

Paid This MGM crime drama cast Joan Crawford in the kind of tough

The Man Who Came Back: Charles Farrell, Janet Gaynor.

Paid: Joan Crawford, Marie Prevost.

Little Caesar: Douglas Fairbanks Jr (rear) and Edward G. Robinson (surreptitiously adjusting the clock face to fix an alibi).

Little Caesar The crowds literally smashed the doors in their anxiety to view this First National (Warner Bros.) gangster film on its New York premiere run. It confirmed what *The Doorway to Hell* had suggested: that films about crime did pay. As Caesar Enrico Bandello, the small-time hoodlum who becomes a crime czar, Edward G. Robinson was so effective that he made himself a big name and was forever associated with the part. His final line, "Mother of Mercy, is this the end of Rico?", as he breathes his last, has become one of the most famous screen utterances of all time. Mervyn LeRoy directed the picture, drawn from W. R. Burnett's novel and adapted by Francis E. Faragoh. Douglas Fairbanks Jr, Glenda Farrell and Thomas Jackson (as the cop who goads his man into giving himself away) were also prominent.

part that ideally suited her as a shopgirl wrongly imprisoned of crime who sets about paying back those responsible by methods that are just within the law. As part of her scheme, she marries the son (Kent Douglass) of her ex-employer. (Kent Douglass later called himself Douglass Montgomery.) Also cast were Marie Prevost and Polly Moran as other prisoners, Robert Armstrong as a big-time crook and Hale Hamilton as a district attorney. Sam Wood directed from a script by Charles MacArthur and Lucien Hubbard, based on the Bayard Veiller play *Within the Law*, previously filmed under its original title in 1917 (with Alice Joyce) and in 1923 (with Norma Talmadge), and subsequently in 1939 (with Ruth Hussey). MGM retitled this version at only the last minute, to disguise the fact that the story had been seen before, although it went out as *Within the Law* in Britain.

The Criminal Code Columbia's prison drama cast Walter Huston as the tough new warden whose daughter (Constance Cummings) falls in love with one of the inmates (Phillips Holmes). Howard Hawks directed and the script was written from Martin Flavin's 1929 play by Seton I. Miller and Fred Niblo Jr. The film benefited from good reviews. In 1939 the story reappeared as *Penitentiary* with Walter Connolly.

Hell's Angels

FEBRUARY

Cimarron RKO spent a fortune ($1,433,000) on filming Edna Ferber's epic novel, (paying a 1930s record high of $10,000 for literary rights) launched it with a massive advertising campaign at 300 theatres simultaneously (in the manner of *Check and Double Check* in 1930) and were rewarded with the year's biggest money-maker. Richard Dix returned decisively to he-man roles after a period in farce to play Yancey Cravat, the idealist and roamer who plays a key part in the historical development of Oklahoma. Irene Dunne was his patient wife and Edna May Oliver an indomitable pioneer: both gained stardom as a result of the film's popularity. Howard Estabrook wrote the screenplay and Wesley Ruggles directed. The spectacular landrush sequence cost $150,000 after a week's wait for suitable weather and with many of the 6,000 extras walking off with their costumes. The running time was 131 minutes, exceptionally long for this period. For all its comparative success, *Cimarron* fell well short of recovering the cost of production and promotion because of the sudden, unexpected general decline in attendances. Re-make rights were

The Criminal Code: Walter Huston (centre).

sold to MGM (whose 1960 version starred Glenn Ford), and RKO's original disappeared for many years, unseen on television, thought to be a lost film, but since recovered and given occasional film museum screenings.

Trader Horn Another epic based on a best-seller (running 123 minutes and costing $1,322,000 at a time when a good top feature normally cost $300,000), this was a pioneering adventure set in Africa and opened by MGM as a roadshow attraction at advanced prices. It played off much more slowly and eventually showed a considerable profit. Filming had started under W. S. Van Dyke's direction in remote areas of Central

Africa in 1929 with veteran outdoor star Harry Carey, newcomer Duncan Renaldo and the unknown Edwina Booth. Richard Schayer, Dale Van Every and John Thomas Neville had written the screen adaptation of the book by Mrs Ethelreda Lewis and Alfred Aloysius Horn. The plot concerned the rescue by Trader Horn of an English lord's daughter who has become a jungle goddess. Work in Africa took over seven months in 1929, because of illness, variable weather and numerous other problems (Booth got her role partly because she was one of the few actresses willing to undergo the hardship of an African safari). It had still not been completed when studio

Trader Horn: Edwina Booth, Duncan Renaldo, Harry Carey.

head Louis B. Mayer ordered the unit to return. Cyril Hume wrote a new screenplay based on what had been gathered. Most of the soundtrack had to be re-recorded or created in Hollywood. MGM was held up while Booth put on weight after a serious illness induced by the trip, so that further shots would match her location footage. (She later sued the company over her continuing fever ailment and received a settlement in April 1935.) Additional shooting was discreetly carried out in 1930 in somewhat more hospitable surroundings in Mexico. The interest in Africa aroused by the book and the forthcoming film had stimulated a flood of frequently specious documentaries about the Continent, including the notorious *Ingagi* as well as *Africa Speaks* and, most recently, *Rango*. The studio refused to be rushed and hoped that the cheap competition would not take the edge off its film. It did not. A three-minute introduction in which Cecil B. DeMille introduced Alfred Aloysius Horn testifying to the authenticity of the picture was deleted for a 1937 reissue. (A 1973 re-make stirred no interest at all.)

City Lights: Charles Chaplin, Virginia Cherrill.

City Lights Not even Chaplin was able wholly to resist the winds of change. His first film for three years, *City Lights* had been made as a silent, but he agreed to add sound effects and his own musical accompaniment before it was released by United Artists. Some thought that Chaplin might pave the way for a general return to non-talking films. There was initial resistance from exhibitors when Chaplin demanded half the takings from first-run engagements, but the film's appeal was demonstrated in a special New York engagement beginning in February and it went on to become

one of the year's big three hits, racking up further huge takings on reissues over the years as later generations flocked to Chaplin's timeless story of his tramp's affection for a blind girl (Virginia Cherrill) and his fluctuating relationship with a millionaire (Harry Myers) who only recognizes him when drunk. Jean Harlow was an extra in a nightclub scene.

Inspiration Garbo was the artist's model who sacrifices her own happiness rather than ruin the career of Robert Montgomery's young diplomat. MGM's film was written by Gene Markey and directed by Clarence Brown, with Lewis Stone, Marjorie Rambeau and Karen Morley in supporting roles.

Millie Helen Twelvetrees had a field day ageing 17 years as a woman of loose reputation who shoots John Halliday's elderly roué: he was one of the men who ruined her life, and she steps in when he is about to seduce her 16-year-old daughter (Anita Louise). The standard courtroom climax in the *Madame X* tradition followed. Robert Ames's reporter helped her live happily ever after. Based on a Donald Henderson Clarke novel, re-worked for the screen by Charles Kenyon, the Charles R. Rogers production was directed by John Francis Dillon and released by RKO as a Radio picture.

The Easiest Way MGM borrowed Constance Bennett from Pathé to play the lady of easy virtue (Adolphe Menjou being one of her influential lovers) who wishes she'd been better behaved when Robert Montgomery's wealthy Argentine rancher learns of her past and drops her in disgust. Audiences were disappointed when they didn't come together again. Clark Gable made his MGM debut as Bennett's brother-in-law, a

Millie: Helen Twelvetrees, Lois Jane Watkins

laundryman. Edith Ellis scripted from Eugene Walter's play, while Jack Conway directed.

MARCH

City Lights
Dracula Universal was stimulated to make this horror film by the huge success of the play based on Bram Stoker's novel. John Balderston and Hamilton Deane's stage version had opened on Broadway in 1927 and had been performed so often across America that there were fears that it might have exhausted its appeal, especially as Universal retained Bela Lugosi as the Transylvanian vampire Count as well as Edward Van Sloan and Herbert Bunston to repeat their stage roles. However, apart from

Dracula: Edward Van Sloan, Bela Lugosi.

some problems with local bans, the film did so well that it became Universal's top attraction of the year and inspired the production of a "medical melodrama" called *Frankenstein* in addition to eventual sequels beginning with *Dracula's Daughter* (1936). Apart from Lugosi's hypnotic performance, *Dracula* had memorable work from Van Sloan as Dracula's stubborn adversary, Van Helsing, and Dwight Frye as the hapless estate agent reduced to fly-eating madness. Helen Chandler and David Manners also appeared. Tod Browning directed, making good use of a roving camera (Karl Freund was the cinematographer) in some of the cobwebbed sets by Charles D. Hall. Garrett Fort and Dudley Murphy wrote the screenplay.

The Last Parade This was Columbia latching on to the interest in underworld stories with a sympathetic study of a gangster's downfall. Jack Holt, the studio's leading he-man star, and Tom Moore were war-time buddies who went different ways. Holt has become a racketeer and Moore a policeman. Holt decides to go straight and marry the girl (Constance Cummings) but not before avenging the murder of her young brother. Moore arrests him and accompanies him on the last parade to the death chamber. Erle C. Kenton directed Dorothy Howell's script from a Casey Robinson story.

East Lynne Fox had made previous films of Mrs Henry Wood's celebrated weepie with Theda Bara in 1916 and Alma Rubens in 1925. Now the studio borrowed Ann Harding from Pathé to play the Victorian lady who suffers social disgrace from an unfair divorce, then the loss of her lover (Clive Brook) and finally total blindness. Plush production values and director Frank Lloyd's skilful handling of Bradley King and Tom Barry's screenplay gained the film a large female following although it was not a success everywhere.

Unfaithful Ruth Chatterton suffered nobly as the wife unable to divorce her wretched husband (Paul Cavanagh) because he is carrying on with her sister-in-law (Juliette Compton) and she won't bring public humiliation on her brother (Donald Cook). Paul Lukas played Chatterton's artist friend. It was their third teaming, and Paramount had hopes of building Lukas into a popular romantic lead. John Cromwell was the director of Eve Unsell's script from a story by John Van Druten.

APRIL

Strangers May Kiss Norma Shearer starred in another adaptation of an Ursula Parrott novel, again playing a loose-living woman, and repeated the success of *The Divorcee*. Neil Hamilton was the man who forgave her conduct during his long absence as a war reporter, and Robert Montgomery was the childhood sweetheart who hangs around in vain. John Meehan's script was directed by George Fitzmaurice at MGM.

Skippy The big Easter attraction for kids, this film from Percy Crosby's newspaper cartoon strip cast Jackie Cooper (nine-year-old pout-lipped star of Our Gang comedies) as the lovable young scamp Skippy and Robert Coogan (brother of Jackie) as his younger friend Sooky in a story of the two boys' attempt to raise money and recover Sooky's pet dog, impounded for lacking a licence. The film seemed shrewd and unsentimental and was a hit with reviewers as well, launching Cooper as major child star and cueing an early sequel. Norman Taurog (Jackie Cooper's uncle) directed at Paramount and the many hands in the writing were those of Joseph L. Mankiewicz, Norman McLeod, Don Marquis, Sam Mintz and Percy Crosby himself.

Dishonored As in *Morocco*, Marlene Dietrich yielded top billing to an established American star, previously Gary Cooper, this time Victor McLaglen, but it was she who brought in the crowds for her second Paramount picture. Her mentor Josef von Sternberg devised the story that presented her as the prostitute turned German spy, X-27, who is destroyed by her love for McLaglen's Russian agent, H-14. Barry Norton was the callow lieutenant in charge of the firing squad she keeps waiting while she renews her lipstick. Lew Cody and Warner Oland also appeared. The absurd plot was an excuse for von Sternberg's preoccupation with visual texture and mood. Samuel N. Rubin wrote the script while Lee Garmes was the director's cinematographic collaborator.

A Connecticut Yankee Last filmed by Fox in 1921 with Harry Myers, Mark Twain's classic story *A Connecticut Yankee in King Arthur's Court* was turned by the studio into another Will Rogers vehicle, with the comedian taking the knock on the head and dreaming himself back 1,300 years to Camelot where he shows the natives a thing or two, as when he lassoes his opponent in a jousting match. Myrna Loy was a villainous sister of King Arthur, and Maureen O'Sullivan and Frank Albertson were the medieval lovers. William Conselman's adaptation was directed by David Butler. Since nobody in Britain has ever been able to spell Connecticut, retitling took place turning it into *The Yankee at King Arthur's Court*. The story became a Bing Crosby musical in 1949.

The Front Page Ben Hecht and Charles MacArthur's hit comedy-melodrama of the 1928 Broadway season retained its staccato pace in Howard Hughes' screen version, adapted by Bartlett Cormack and Charles Lederer and directed by Lewis Milestone. Pat O'Brien was the newspaperman who wanted to retire and get married, while Adolphe Menjou was the editor who ruthlessly connived to keep him on the job, covering an impending execution that goes awry when the condemned man (George E. Stone) escapes to the press room. Mae Clarke was a streetwalker friend of the prisoner and Edward Everett Horton a frustrated poet of the prints. Unlike most Hughes projects, this one was shot

The Front Page: Adolphe Menjou, Mary Brian, Pat O'Brien.

speedily and rushed into release just three weeks later by United Artists. The play was an even bigger hit as a Columbia film in 1940 (*His Girl Friday*) and was re-made again in 1974 for Universal.

MAY

The Millionaire George Arliss attracted a wider audience than usual in modern dress as the automobile magnate who retires on doctor's orders and becomes partners with young David Manners in a gas station to keep himself busy, without revealing his true identity. Arliss had the right to cast his pictures from bits to featured players, and he exercised it shrewdly in selecting pre-stardom James Cagney to play the brash insurance salesman who, in one brief but pivotal scene, persuades Arliss that he needs to remain occupied. Evalyn Knapp portrayed the tycoon's daughter. John G. Adolfi directed at Warner Bros. from Earl Derr Biggers' story "Idle Hands", which was shaped for the screen by Julian Josephson and Maude T. Powell with dialogue by Booth Tarkington. The same story became a vehicle for Sydney Greenstreet in 1947's *That Way with Women*.

The Public Enemy James Cagney seized audiences by the lapel with his vigorous portrayal of a dynamic young hood, Tom Powers, who both repelled and fascinated. The beer-and-blood saga was written by a new team from Chicago, Kubec Glasmon and John Bright, and adapted by Harvey Thew. Its most celebrated sequence shows Cagney squelching a grapefruit in his moll's face at breakfast – the actress was Mae Clarke, superseded in the film by Jean Harlow. Eddie Woods was Cagney's buddy (he started out playing Powers but had to swop places when director William A. Wellman saw how Cagney was stealing the scenes in the rushes), while Donald

Seed: Don Cox, Kenneth Selling, unidentified, Terry Cox, Lois Wilson, John Boles.

The Public Enemy: Mae Clarke, James Cagney: the citrus facewash.

Cook was Cagney's brother, a priggish war hero. The Warner Bros. picture suffered a little at the box-office from its courageously stark, gruesome finale of Cagney's trussed corpse falling headlong into frame. In Britain, the film was retitled *Enemies of the Public*.

Seed Female audiences packed the matinees to see John Boles as the writer who abandons his wife (Lois Wilson) and their five children for another woman (Genevieve Tobin). John M. Stahl directed Gladys Lehman's screen adaptation of the Charles G. Norris novel. Potentially controversial aspects relating to birth control in the novel were deleted, along with references to the church and religion, and two bishops from Chicago were allowed to vet the script. Despite this, it was Universal's

biggest hit of the year after *Dracula*. Bette Davis had one of her first roles as one of the five daughters.

JUNE

Daddy Long Legs The warm response to this whimsical Cinderella fable confirmed Janet Gaynor's pull even without Charles Farrell, although she had a strong co-star in Academy Award winner Warner Baxter. She was the orphan girl helped by a mysterious benefactor, while Baxter was the kindly bachelor in whom she confided, little knowing that he was

Daddy Long Legs: Janet Gaynor, Warner Baxter.

the guardian angel. Alfred Santell was the director; Sonya Levien and S. N. Behrman provided the script. Mary Pickford had had a huge hit in the 1919 version of Jean Webster's novel, and it was to perform well again when Fox made it with Shirley Temple (as *Curly Top*, 1935) and with Leslie Caron in 1955.

Women of All Nations Although it didn't scale the box-office heights of the first two adventures of Victor McLaglen's Sergeant Flagg and Edmund Lowe's Sergeant Quirt, *What Price Glory* and *The Cock-Eyed World*, there was still strong interest in the pair's further exploits in the Marines, pursuing women in Sweden, Nicaragua and Egypt. Raoul Walsh again directed, and Barry Connors wrote the script, while Greta Nissen, El Brendel, Fifi Dorsay, Bela Lugosi and Humphrey Bogart had supporting roles in the Fox production. Sacked from *Hell's Angels* because of her thick Norwegian accent, Miss Nissen was recovering nicely, being touted as Fox's answer to Garbo and Dietrich.

A Free Soul Based on a novel by Adela Rogers St John, this lurid melodrama had a particularly troubled gestation, being worked on by armies of writers over four years and at least once being shelved. Norma Shearer portrayed the society woman who throws over her polo-playing fiancé (Leslie Howard) in favour of Clark Gable's gambler gangster, Ace Wolfong. Gable fascinated women in the audience, too, with the brutish vitality of the character he played – audiences applauded when he shoved Shearer into a chair. Lionel Barrymore had a colourful part as Shearer's alcoholic father, a celebrated criminal lawyer who sobers up for one final court appearance to help his daughter. John Meehan and Becky Gardner won the writing credit. Clarence Brown directed. MGM re-

made it as *The Girl Who Had Everything* (1953) with Elizabeth Taylor.

JULY

A Free Soul

Night Nurse Barbara Stanwyck starred in this Warner melodrama as the nurse who prevents two young children being starved to death as part of a plot to gain an inheritance. She is assisted by Ben Lyon's bootlegger, while Clark Gable made a colourful impression as the brutish chauffeur villain who socks Stanwyck on the jaw. Scenes in which Stanwyck and Joan Blondell (as another nurse) undressed were regarded as a further attraction. There were some quirky humorous touches to relieve the grim plot of the movie, written by Oliver H. P. Garrett and Charles Kenyon from Dora Macy's novel, and directed by William A. Wellman.

The Smiling Lieutenant Not only did the re-teaming of Maurice Chevalier and director Ernst Lubitsch repeat the success of *The Love Parade*, it also proved that musicals could still draw and started Hollywood making them again. This was a lightweight operetta with only four songs, though Oscar Straus was brought from Vienna to write the music (Clifford Grey supplied the lyrics). Chevalier was the Viennese guards officer who marries Miriam Hopkins' plain-looking queen and continues his affair with Claudette Colbert's vivacious violinist. (The British censor delayed its London opening, suspecting a slur on the Austrian monarchy.) Ernest Vajda and Samson Raphaelson did the screenplay from an old operetta *The Waltz Dream* by Leopold Jacobson

Politics: Polly Moran, Marie Dressler, Roscoe Ates.

and Felix Doermann (which had been the basis of a successful 1925 German film) and from a novel by Hans Müller. The Paramount picture was shot at the Eastern (Astoria) studios where Lubitsch also made a French version with the same three stars.

AUGUST

Politics The irrepressible Marie Dressler played the widow who runs for mayor to clean up the town, with Polly Moran as her campaign manager. MGM cleaned up the picture prior to release by removing gangster sequences, fearful of the gathering backlash at the depiction of hoodlums on screen. Roscoe Ates, Karen Morley, William Bakewell and Joan Marsh were in support. Wells Root, Zelda Sears and Malcolm Stuart Boylan concocted the farce from a Robert E. Hopkins story, and MGM assigned Charles F. Reisner to direct the pair once again.

The Smiling Lieutenant

The Common Law A shrewdly chosen vehicle for Constance Bennett, this re-teamed her with the young leading man and the director of *Born to Love*, a less successful romantic tear-jerker released earlier in the year. Enabling her to play yet another woman with a shady past, the script by John Farrow and Horace Jackson (from Robert W. Chambers' 1911 novel) had her posing nude for Joel McCrea's aspiring painter on the Paris Left Bank and winning his love but being quite unacceptable as his wife in social circles back home. Also cast were Lew Cody, Robert Williams and Hedda Hopper. The director of the RKO Pathé film was Paul L. Stein. The Hays Office pruned some of its scenes before release and expressed its disapproval of the kind of common-law marriage shown. An earlier film

A Free Soul: "Aw, sit down and take it and like it!" Clark Gable, Norma Shearer (nursing a bruised arm).

The Common Law: Joel McCrea, Constance Bennett.

way into upper-crust circles and gains Ray Milland's playboy as a lover. She finds true happiness with Ben Lyon's striving writer. Constance's celebrated actor father, Richard Bennett, played her father in the film. Charles Kenyon and former actor Raymond Griffith put Harriet Henry's novel *Jackdaw's Strut* into screen shape for director Archie L. Mayo.

Young as You Feel It was Will Rogers once more, playing a respectable businessman feeling his oats and taking off on a spree with a young French girl (Fifi Dorsay, Rogers' girlfriend in 1929's *They Had to See Paris*). His irresponsible sons (Donald Dillaway and Terrance Ray) were left to run things. Edwin Burke wrote it from a George Ade play and Frank Borzage directed for Fox.

Dirigible: Ralph Graves, Jack Holt.

had been made from the novel in 1923.

Dirigible The most expensive Columbia production to date, this film was in production from July 1930 to 17 January 1931 – a record length of time for the small studio. It seemed a fairly safe bet, reuniting Jack Holt and Ralph Graves as sparring partners in a further action spectacular under Frank Capra's direction to follow *Submarine* (1928) and *Flight* (1929). The story about an aerial expedition to the South Pole was obviously inspired by the real-life flight of Admiral Byrd in 1930 but added some more dramatic twists. Graves was the reckless flyer whose plane crashes in the Antarctic wastes, and Holt played the more sober-headed airman who pilots a dirigible to rescue him and his party. Fay Wray was the woman who married Graves and loved Holt. The film's snowscapes were created on a three-acre exterior set in the San Gabriel Valley, while the scenes in the immense hangar were shot at Lakehurst, New Jersey (some other shooting was done at the pioneer Fort Lee studio in the same state). Frank Wead's story was developed by Jo Swerling and Dorothy Howell. When *Dirigible* first opened back in April at advanced prices, it was a big flop. A scene of a leg amputation and some risqué dialogue were cut. Fortunately for Columbia, *Dirigible* finally scored when put into regular release at prices the public were willing to pay.

Bought Constance Bennett delivered again, this time for Warner Bros. She was yet another loose-living, ambitious working girl who worms her

Monkey Business: Harpo, Zeppo, Chico and Groucho Marx: the four stowaways.

Huckleberry Finn Paramount
followed up its success with *Tom
Sawyer* by putting Jackie Coogan and
Junior Dorkin to work again as Tom
and Huck in another Mark Twain
adaptation, supported as before by
Mitzi Green, Jackie Searl, Clara
Blandick and Jane Darwell, and
directed by Norman Taurog. Tom and
Huck saved two helpless girls
(Charlotte V. Henry and Lillian
Harmer) from two rascals (Eugene
Pallette and Oscar Apfel). Clarence
Muse was Tom's young negro friend.
This version was scripted by Grover
Jones and William Slavens McNutt.
Paramount had previously filmed the
story in 1919 and MGM would be next
in 1939.

SEPTEMBER

Monkey Business For the shipboard
shenanigans in their first screen
original (shot at Paramount's
Hollywood studios), the four Marx
Brothers found it difficult, working
without material thoroughly pre-
tested on the stage, to know when to
leave pauses for laughter. However,
the studio editors guessed right and
they were more popular than ever.
S. J. Perelman, Will B. Johnstone and
Arthur Sheekman were the scribes
and Norman McLeod captained the
movie, which also featured Thelma
Todd as a gangster's promiscuous
wife.
Bad Girl Though misleadingly titled,
this was both a critical and popular
success, particularly pleasant for Fox
as it had cost so little to make. Sally
Eilers and James Dunn (in his screen
debut) starred as the lovers forced into
marriage who have to struggle
financially. The two stars went on to
make five other films together. Frank
Borzage directed this one from Edwin

Bad Girl: Sally Eilers, James Dunn.

Burke and Sonya Levien's adaptation
of Vina Delmar's best seller.
Merely Mary Ann Janet Gaynor was
the boarding house maidservant in
London who inherited an oil well and
gave her hand to penniless aspiring
composer Charles Farrell. The team
were guided this time by Henry King.
Also participating were Beryl Mercer
and Lorna Balfour (in her only screen
role – she died in 1932, aged 19). Jules
Furthman did the adaptation of Israel
Zangwill's story, which Fox had filmed
previously in 1916.

OCTOBER

Susan Lenox Her Fall and Rise The
torrid combination of Garbo and
Gable wooed audiences to a confused
picture (even the title seems

awkward). Garbo was the farmer's
illegitimate daughter who runs away
from an arranged marriage and lives a
life of sin, loving Gable's engineer and
finally proving herself worthy of him.
More than 22 of MGM's writing staff
slaved over the years on this project,
drawn from the novel by David
Graham Phillips: they had no problem
with Garbo's fall but they couldn't
make her rise convincing. Garbo was
critical of the script throughout the
shooting, apparently walking off six
times, and the ending was continually
re-written. Wanda Tuchock took the
script credit, with Zelda Sears and
Leon Gordon as the named dialogue
writers. Robert Z. Leonard directed.
Gable was shooting another picture,
Sporting Blood, at the same time, so
keen were Metro to build him into a
top star. Garbo never starred with
Gable again. In Britain the film was
retitled *The Rise of Helga*.
The Spirit of Notre Dame Universal's
football drama was dedicated to the
memory of Knute Rockne who died in
a plane crash while on his way to the
studio in connection with the film (he
appears in the prologue). Lew Ayres
starred as a big-headed quarterback
who learns team spirit, opposite Sally
Blane and William Bakewell, with J.
Farrell MacDonald as coach Rockne
and several celebrated Notre Dame
players. Russell Mack directed from a
script by Richard Schayer, Dale Van
Every and Walter DeLeon.
Palmy Days Sam Goldwyn's second
Eddie Cantor musical comedy was
written by Cantor himself with Morrie
Ryskind and David Freeman.
A. Edward Sutherland directed, and
Busby Berkeley staged the dances
with more of his distinctive overhead

Susan Lenox Her Fall and Rise: Greta
Garbo, Clark Gable, Ian Keith.

shots. Cantor also helped write his blackface number, "There's Nothing Too Good for My Baby". The flimsy plot had Eddie on the run from crooks (including George Raft in an early role) and hiding out in drag with the Goldwyn Girls (still including the young Betty Grable). Charlotte Greenwood was an amusing gym instructor, while Barbara Weeks was the girl of Eddie's dreams. United Artists released.

Five Star Final Based on Louis Weitzenkorn's 1930 play about the damage done by muckraking journalism, this was adapted for First National (Warner Bros.) by Robert Lord and Byron Morgan. Mervyn LeRoy directed Edward G. Robinson as the newspaper editor who reluctantly resurrects an old scandal to gain circulation. Boris Karloff stood out in a small part as a venomous defrocked clergyman called T. Vernon Isopod. Aline MacMahon was the editor's loyal but disapproving secretary. The cast also included Marian Marsh, Oscar Apfel and George E. Stone. Other films like *Scandal Sheet* with George Bancroft joined in the denunciation of the gutter press. The Hearst papers gave *Five Star Final* a roasting as a disgraceful attack on the newspaper industry and thereby whetted curiosity to see the film. The story was re-made as a programmer under the title *Two Against the World* (1936).

Monkey Business

Devotion More gallant suffering for Ann Harding as the woman who falls in love with a celebrated London barrister (Leslie Howard) and takes a post as his son's governess to be near him. Olive Tell was the wife in the way, Robert Williams was an accused

murderer being defended by the barrister, and Dudley Digges, Louise Closser Hale and O. P. Heggie were also cast. (It was Williams' last film – he died of peritonitis on 3 November, aged 32.) Graham John and Horace Jackson took the script from a Pamela Wynne novel, and Robert Milton directed for RKO Pathé.

NOVEMBER

Possessed Gable confirmed himself as the male find of the year opposite Joan Crawford in this romantic drama. She was the small-town girl drawn to the big city who becomes the back-street mistress of his wealthy New York lawyer with political ambitions. Lenore Coffee adapted Edgar Selwyn's 1920 play *The Mirage*, and Clarence Brown directed the MGM picture. Crawford's 1947 film of the same title has a completely different story.

The Sin of Madelon Claudet As a prominent stage star, Helen Hayes had been screen-tested and rejected by several studios before MGM took

The Sin of Madelon Claudet: Robert Young, Helen Hayes. The doctor takes pity on an old lady, not knowing she is his own mother.

the plunge and starred her in this shameless saga of mother love in the *Madame X* tradition. The sin of the title was having an illegitimate child. Helen Hayes' Frenchwoman has to relinquish the child and becomes a whore, but from a distance she helps her son grow up and become a successful doctor (Robert Young). It was the film version of another Edgar Selwyn play, *The Lullaby* (1923), and Selwyn also directed. Numerous writers worked on the screen adaptation, and Hayes' husband, Charles MacArthur, who was the last, took the credit. After disastrous sneak previews, the film was partially re-cast and extensively re-shot under Irving G. Thalberg's close supervision. Not only did audiences now love it, but the nation's reviewers were unstinting in their praise. Neil Hamilton, Jean Hersholt and Lewis Stone were in the supporting cast. In Britain the film took the play's title, *The Lullaby*.

Touchdown! The second successful sporting drama of the season came from Paramount and starred Richard Arlen as the coach who introduces

The Sin of Madelon Claudet: Helen Hayes.

outside talent to the college football team but finally agrees with his girl (Peggy Shannon) and the coach (J. Farrell MacDonald) that no game is worth winning dishonestly. To prove the point, the team *don't* win the big match at the end. Charles Starrett and Regis Toomey were featured, and Jack Oakie delivered the humour. Norman McLeod directed. The writers were Grover Jones and William Slavens McNutt, from the novel *Stadium* by Francis Wallace. It kicked off in British cinemas as *Playing the Game*.

Are These Our Children? A small-scale collaboration between director Wesley Ruggles and writer Howard Estabrook after their success with *Cimarron*, this was a stark study of

Five Star Final: Edward G. Robinson, Aline MacMahon.

juvenile delinquency without any star names. Eric Linden played the youth who drifts into crime, kills a delicatessen owner during a burglary, and is confident he will get away with it thanks to a false alibi. Rochelle Hudson and Arline Judge were the two contrasting women in his short life, and Beryl Mercer played his sorrowing Mum. The RKO release had no happy ending, except at the box-office.
Five Star Final

DECEMBER

Frankenstein In April Universal bought the rights to the 1930 London stage adaptation of Mary Shelley's story by Peggy Webling, which was Americanized by John L. Balderston. The studio initially envisaged Bela Lugosi as the monster after the success of *Dracula*, with George Melford as the first choice for director (he had handled the Spanish language version of *Dracula*), followed by Robert Florey, who remained on the credits as one of the three scriptwriters (with Garrett Fort and Francis Edwards Faragoh). James Whale was the director finally selected, and he brought in Colin Clive (who had starred in *Journey's End*) to play the tormented inventor, Frankenstein. Boris Karloff, of course, won the role of the creature he brings to life. Jack Pierce's make-up of Karloff, the sets by Charles D. Hall, the electrical apparatus by Kenneth Strickfaden and the agile camerawork of Arthur Edeson contributed immensely. From its first grave-robbing, the film was exceptionally graphic for its time and had some censorship problems

Frankenstein: Boris Karloff.

(especially with the scene of the creature throwing the little girl into the lake), but audiences relished being

THE ACADEMY AWARDS

In response to increasing interest in the Awards ceremony, it was moved to a larger venue, the Biltmore Hotel, where 1,800 guests could be accommodated, and the speeches were broadcast nationally. The Vice President of the United States attended, bestowing Washington's approval on the Academy and its activities. For the first time, too, the winners were not known well in advance. The Awards covered the season August 1930 to July 1931 inclusive, and the ceremony was held on 10 November. *Cimarron* was chosen as the Best Picture, the only western that has ever won the top award, while writer Howard Estabrook and designer Max Ree also won for their work on the same picture (Ree's prize was the one for art direction, which was called "interior decoration", although his most impressive work on the picture had been outdoor sets). Lionel Barrymore was adjudged Best Actor for *A Free Soul*; Marie Dressler the Best Actress for *Min and Bill*; Norman Taurog the Best Director for *Skippy*; Floyd Crosby collected the Cinematography prize for *Tabu*; the Paramount Sound Department was accoladed for the Best Recording standard; and there were several Awards in the new Scientific or Technical category.

Norma Shearer, herself a nominee for *A Free Soul*, presents the Best Actress Award to a colleague at MGM, Marie Dressler. Lionel Barrymore (at right) was presented with the Best Actor Award by George Arliss (left).

scared by it. Last-minute re-takes were ordered in the fiery climax to allow Frankenstein and his monster to be revived for a sequel. Made for only $240,000, the film went on to become Universal's biggest hit of 1932, grossing around $1.2 million on first release for the studio.
Possessed
Delicious Fox's only musical among 48 features on its 1931–2 programme, this had the box-office insurance of Janet Gaynor and Charles Farrell in their ninth feature together. It was a Christmas smash hit, and the year's biggest success at the nation's biggest

theatre: 186,000 people paid to see it in one week at the 6,200-seat Roxy in New York. It also played simultaneously at 1,962 theatres across the country, a considerable expansion of RKO's mass-release strategy with *Check and Double Check* and *Cimarron*. Gaynor was the Scots waif who smuggled herself into the United States where she is sheltered by a family of Russian musicians and falls for Farrell's millionaire polo player. Raul Roulien and Virginia Cherrill were in support, along with El Brendel, who served up laughs as a Swedish valet. George and

Delicious: Janet Gaynor, Charles Farrell.

Ira Gershwin wrote their first screen musical, and the songs included "Delishious" (which spreads its way around an ocean liner) and "The New York Rhapsody", a musical interpretation of the city as Gaynor wanders fearfully around it one evening. There was a striking dream sequence of her arrival in America. David Butler directed from a Guy Bolton and Sonya Levien script.

Sooky Paramount had this sequel to *Skippy* ready for the festive season with the same young stars, Jackie Cooper and Bobby [Robert] Coogan. The death of Sooky's ailing mother (Helen Jerome Eddy) at the end corresponded to the sad fate of the dog in the earlier film. Sam Mintz, Joseph L. Mankiewicz and Norman Z. McLeod wrote the script from Percy Crosby's comic strip *Dear Sooky* and Norman Taurog again directed.

The Champ: Wallace Beery, Jackie Cooper.

The Champ MGM had noted Jackie Cooper's appeal in *Skippy* and fashioned its own vehicle for the young actor, including another sad ending. He played the son of a washed-up ex-fighter (played by Wallace Beery); his shining faith in his father encourages the old derelict to attempt a comeback. Originally he lost his fight and died, but producer Irving G. Thalberg realized that the film needed a more positive ending, so once again MGM doctored a production, having Beery win the match before dropping dead. Leonard Praskins and Frances Marion wrote it, and King Vidor directed. The studio was next trying to figure out a way to team Jackie with Marie Dressler. *The Champ* was re-made as *The Clown* with Red Skelton and released in 1952.

TEN BEST-CRITICS' CHOICE

A total of 340 of the nation's critics, reviewers and entertainment editors responded to the *Film Daily* poll and decided that the year's top 10 motion pictures were (with number of votes cast):

1.	*Cimarron*	273
2.	*Street Scene*	200
3.	*Skippy*	178
4.	*Bad Girl*	172
5.	*Min and Bill*	164
6.	*The Front Page*	162
7.	*Five Star Final*	138
8.	*City Lights*	128
9.	*A Free Soul*	114
10.	*The Sin of Madelon Claudet*	99
	Close Runners Up	
11.	*Little Caesar*	97
12.	*The Smiling Lieutenant*	91
13.	*Trader Horn*	88

All of the above films were also well received at the box-office. *The Champ*, which was a big hit in December 1931, ranked second in the 1932 results.

CLOSE RUNNERS UP

16 more films also seemed very popular with audiences and were narrowly omitted from the hits of the year for the month or months indicated: *Alexander Hamilton* (October), *Ambassador Bill* (November), *An American Tragedy* (September), *City Streets* (April), *Dance, Fools, Dance* (February), *The Devil to Pay* (February), *Donovan's Kid* (May, June), *Free Love* (January), *Indiscreet* (May, June), *Laughing Sinners* (June), *Private Lives* (December), *The Right to Love* (January), *Smart Money* (June), *The Star Witness* (August), *Street Scene* (September), *This Modern Age* (September).

1932

Red Dust
Clark Gable,
Jean Harlow

If 1931 had been bad, 1932 was much worse. Weekly attendances at America's movie theatres crashed by another 15 million to around 60 million. A tax was imposed on all but the cheapest tickets, and this was added to admission prices, making movie-goers more selective and less frequent in their visits. Many theatres started to offer double bills for 10¢ and to resort to gimmicks – lotteries with prizes of automobiles, refrigerators, furniture, sets of linen; or free items of chinaware to build up a set by regular attendance. The building of new theatres ceased.

As a sign of the times, the nation's largest movie theatre, the Roxy in New York, was forced to close at the end of June, leaving the staff unpaid for their last week's work. It re-opened under new management with lower prices in August, still supporting an orchestra of 70, a ballet company of 24 and 32 Roxyettes, but it continued to lose money for the rest of the year. Grauman's Chinese in Hollywood went dark for periods when there were no promising attractions available. In fact, large theatres were closing temporarily in all the principal cities to alleviate the film shortage and concentrate what business there was on the remaining halls.

According to one trade calculation, the average film was now costing $250,000 to make or $420,000 to release (adding the distribution sector's cost of prints, selling and handling), but was only bringing in around $300,000 from the principal bookings.

Hollywood was compelled to act. Prices for play and book rights dropped. Pay cuts were enforced on regular employees at most studios and on stars and other contract talent when their options came up for renewal. Will Rogers, for instance, reduced his fee per picture to $100,000 when renewing with Fox. Others were less co-operative: director Dorothy Arzner refused to take a cut on the next option period of her Paramount contract and was dropped. Highly paid artists were also affected by new income tax rates, a dozen or so losing half their income and a further three dozen (on *Variety*'s estimate) losing a third of their pay. The companies became more agreeable about loaning out players to their rivals than they had been in the past. A star could be sent to another studio that needed him for a fee above his normal salary, the difference being pocketed as profit by the studio that loaned him out. It was better than having the player idle on his home lot or miscast to keep him occupied, and, if he improved his popularity in another company's picture, his home studio would benefit from his increased drawing power when he returned.

The studios' financial reports showed that Warner Bros., RKO Radio and Fox had increased losses, while Universal and United Artists were now bathed in red ink as well. Paramount was doing so badly that it spent the year trying to avoid bankruptcy. Only Loew's with its string of hit MGM pictures and more soundly-based involvement in theatre operation showed a huge (though reduced) profit, and Columbia made a very small surplus. In 1932, major company productions dropped to the lowest total of the decade, 300 American-made features (compared with 379 in 1929), while independent production was virtually at its peak with 189 feature releases, evidently aimed at filling the product shortage.

This was the year that the all-star drama was tried and the huge success of MGM's *Grand Hotel* encouraged Paramount's *If I Had a Million*. Exhibitors named as the top money-making stars of the season ending in July: Marie Dressler, Janet Gaynor, Joan Crawford, Charles Farrell, Greta Garbo, Norma Shearer, Wallace Beery, Clark Gable, Will Rogers and Joe E. Brown. No fewer than six of these were MGM stars. The company had another top name by the year's end: Jean Harlow.

HITS OF THE YEAR

JANUARY

Emma Writer Frances Marion created this sentimental drama as a star vehicle for Marie Dressler. She played the faithful housekeeper and nanny who marries her employer (Jean Hersholt) after he becomes a widower, much to the consternation of the snobbish children she once raised. The spoiled eldest daughter (Myrna Loy) subsequently accuses her of causing his death to inherit the family fortune. Leonard Praskins and Zelda Sears wrote the screenplay from Marion's story, and Clarence Brown directed. Richard Cromwell played another of the offspring in the MGM picture, and Mickey Rooney made one of his earliest, unbilled screen appearances.

Hell Divers MGM's drama of the Naval Air Force, based on a story by Lt Comdr Frank Wead, teamed Wallace Beery and Clark Gable as feuding rivals in the Quirt-Flagg tradition established by *What Price Glory*, ultimately favouring Gable by killing off Beery's character. Dorothy Jordan was Gable's girl, dropped early on to emphasize the action. George Hill directed from the screenplay by Harvey Gates and Malcolm Stuart Boylan.

Dr Jekyll and Mr Hyde With its amazing transformation scenes (done without dissolves by an ingenious use of filters), Paramount's film version of the Robert Louis Stevenson novel was a classy addition to the horror cycle and a big career boost for Fredric March in the celebrated dual role, played by John Barrymore in Paramount's 1920 version. Rouben Mamoulian's inventive direction gave the story real force, contrasting Rose Hobart's cool and respectable fiancée with Miriam Hopkins' earthily available working girl. Samuel Hoffenstein and Percy Heath wrote the screenplay, and Karl Struss was the cameraman. Spencer Tracy tackled Jekyll and Hyde for MGM in 1941.

Mata Hari MGM's answer to

Mata Hari: Greta Garbo (costume by Adrian), Lionel Barrymore.

Dr Jekyll and Mr Hyde: Holmes Herbert, Fredric March.

Dietrich's glamorous spy of *Dishonored* was Greta Garbo in this pictorially accomplished, very similar story in which the famous German agent, an exotic dancer, loses her heart to Ramon Novarro's Russian lieutenant and goes to the firing squad. William Daniels was Garbo's cameraman as usual, and George Fitzmaurice handled the direction from a script by Benjamin Glazer and Leo Birinski with dialogue by Doris Anderson and Gilbert Emery. Also cast were Lionel Barrymore as a Russian general, Lewis Stone as a spymaster and Karen Morley as a rival agent.

Delicious

FEBRUARY

Hell Divers

Emma

Arrowsmith Director John Ford had been dropped by Fox after 10 years and landed this uncharacteristic assignment with Samuel Goldwyn – the film version of the 1925 Sinclair Lewis novel with Ronald Colman as the dedicated doctor, Martin Arrowsmith, who loses his wife (Helen Hayes) during an epidemic in the tropics. Myrna Loy was a woman who put temptation in the medic's way. Sidney Howard did the adaptation and United Artists was the distributor.

Lady with a Past Such a title almost demanded Constance Bennett and yet it was misleading, for in this RKO Pathé comedy she played against type

as a timid wallflower who invents a colourful past and transforms herself into the most popular woman in Paris and New York social circles. Ben Lyon (borrowed from Warner Bros. to take over the part intended for the late Robert Williams), played the gigolo who helped Bennett achieve the transformation, and David Manners was the nice young man who was suitably impressed. Edward H. Griffith directed Horace Jackson's screenplay from a Harriet Henry novel. British audiences saw it under the title *Reputation*.

High Pressure One of several stars that Warner Bros. poached from Paramount, William Powell was cast as the fast-talking promoter of artificial rubber with George Sidney as his crackpot inventor accomplice and Evelyn Brent as his patient girlfriend. Evalyn Knapp, Guy Kibbee and Frank McHugh were among those in support. Mervyn LeRoy directed the comedy, which Joseph Jackson scripted from a play by Aben Kandel.

The Man Who Played God George Arliss played the concert pianist who becomes deaf and gains meaning from life by using binoculars to lip-read conversations in Central Park and help unfortunates out of their difficulties. Arliss had also starred in the 1922 version. Having shrewdly cast Cagney in *The Millionaire*, he showed the same acumen in giving Bette Davis the choice role of his fiancée who falls for a younger man (Donald Cook). John G. Adolfi directed. Julien Josephson and Maude Howell based their screenplay on a Gouverneur Morris story and a play by Jules Eckert Goodman called *The*

The Man Who Played God: George Arliss, Bette Davis.

Silent Voice (which title was used for the film's British release). The same story was dished up with Liberace as *Sincerely Yours* (1955).

MARCH

One Hour With You Ernst Lubitsch began supervising this re-make of his 1924 comedy *The Marriage Circle* as part of his general duties of overseeing the Paramount studio's output, then took over from director George Cukor to finish it. Maurice Chevalier was the Frenchman, married to Jeanette MacDonald, who strays with Genevieve Tobin, whose husband Roland Young finds out and forces Chevalier to confess all to

MacDonald, who then takes up with an admirer, Charles Ruggles, to teach her husband a lesson. . . . The film introduced the rather daring device of Chevalier periodically breaking off to address the ladies and gentlemen of the audience in confidential asides regarding his amorous difficulties (this was a technique employed, of course, on stage in *Strange Interlude* for serious purposes and earlier satirized by Groucho Marx in *Animal Crackers*). The original source was Lothar Goldschmidt's play *Nur ein Traum*, and Samson Raphaelson did the adaptation. Lubitsch directed a French-language version with Chevalier and MacDonald. She had become hugely popular with French audiences and was then much more of a favourite in Europe generally than she was in North America.

The Lost Squadron Leading stunt flyer Dick Grace concocted this extravagant story of three veteran combat flyers (Richard Dix, Robert Armstrong, Joel McCrea) working on an aerial movie for a maniacal director (clever casting of Erich von Stroheim) who causes, directly and indirectly, the deaths of two of them. RKO Radio assembled squadrons of aircraft and included some spectacular flying stunts. Wallace Smith wrote the screenplay from Grace's story, and George Archainbaud directed. RKO's new production chief David O. Selznick took a close interest in it and ordered Paul Sloane to re-shoot much of the action for greater impact. The studio did a follow-up drama of Hollywood stuntmen called *Lucky Devils* (1933).

Shanghai Express This visually striking, richly atmospheric drama gave Josef von Sternberg more scope than *An American Tragedy* for his pictorial preoccupations. Marlene

Arrowsmith: Ronald Colman, Helen Hayes.

Shanghai Express: Marlene Dietrich, Clive Brook.

Dietrich was the notorious "white flower" of China ("It took more than one man to change my name to Shanghai Lily"), who meets an old lover (Clive Brook) on the Shanghai express, and Warner Oland played the war lord who holds captive the passengers (including Eugene Pallette, Louise Closser Hale and Anna May Wong). With the help of art director Hans Dreier and cameraman Lee Garmes, Sternberg made railroad lines and stations in California evoke the hectic bustle of life in China. Jules Furthman wrote the script from Harry Hervey's story. Paramount did a loose re-make called *Night Plane from Chungking* (1942) and one with Corinne Calvet called *Peking Express* (1951).

The Man Who Played God
Lady with a Past
Tarzan, The Ape Man MGM took Hollywood by surprise when, after an intensive hunt for a suitable performer, it settled on Olympic champion swimmer Johnny Weissmuller to be its king of the jungle. Following the success of *Trader Horn*, MGM had great hopes of another jungle adventure and bought rights to the Tarzan character from author Edgar Rice Burroughs. Cyril Hume and Ivor Novello fashioned the screenplay and *Trader Horn*'s W. S. Van Dyke again took the megaphone. The film emphasized the romance between Tarzan and the English girl (Maureen O'Sullivan) whom he carries off to his tree-top world, but there was a spectacular climax of elephants racing to the rescue. Shooting was done in the Toluca Lake area of north Hollywood, while spare background footage from *Trader Horn* was used. It became MGM's biggest money-spinner of the year after *Grand Hotel*. Because the author refused to sell exclusive film rights, other companies were able to make Tarzan follow-ups.

Business and Pleasure Another of Will Rogers' comic adventures in foreign parts, this Fox vehicle cast him as the razor-blade king from Oklahoma who goes with his wife (Dorothy Peterson) and daughter (Peggy Ross) on a voyage to Algeria and Syria and is the only man on board unperturbed by a storm at sea. Jetta Goudal was an exotic spy engaged by business rivals, and Joel McCrea was the love interest for the daughter. David Butler directed, and William Conselman wrote it from the 1930 Broadway play *The Plutocrat* by Arthur Goodrich which had starred Charles Coburn. The play came from a Booth Tarkington novel.

APRIL

Tarzan, The Ape Man
One Hour With You
Alias the Doctor Richard Barthelmess was the star attraction of this medical drama, playing an Austrian orphan brought up by a farming family. He and his foster brother (Norman Foster) both study medicine, and Barthelmess nobly shoulders the blame when the other carries out an illegal operation on a girl. Marian Marsh was the childhood sweetheart who stood by the hero. Houston Branch and Charles Kenyon adapted a play by Emric Foeldes, while Lloyd Bacon and Michael Curtiz split the direction for First National (Warner Bros.).

The Crowd Roars James Cagney played the racing-car driver who tried to deter his younger brother (Eric Linden) from following in his footsteps. Ann Dvorak and Joan Blondell were the women in their lives. Howard Hawks created the storyline and directed the Warner Bros. picture, while Kubec Glasmon, John Bright, Niven Busch and Seton I. Miller provided the screenplay. Many Indianapolis winners drove in the racing scenes, which were filmed at the Ventura and Ascot tracks. Warner Bros. did an economical re-make, *Indianapolis Speedway* (1939), re-using the action footage.

Shopworn In this saga of suffering and ultimate happiness, Barbara Stanwyck was the waitress jailed on false immorality charges by Oscar Apfel's cruel judge in order to break up her romance with Regis Toomey's young medical student, while his selfish, socially prominent mother packs him off to study in Vienna. When next they meet, he is a doctor and she is a notorious actress. (Those familiar with Regis Toomey as a character actor in later years must find it hard to imagine him as a romantic lead.) ZaSu Pitts and Lucien Littlefield brought humorous relief as owners of a cheap eating-house. Nicholas Grinde directed the Columbia picture with dialogue by Jo Swerling and Robert Riskin from a story by Sarah Y. Mason.

MAY

Grand Hotel MGM had invested in the

Alias the Doctor: Richard Barthelmess, Marian Marsh.

Tarzan, the Ape Man: Maureen O'Sullivan, Johnny Weissmuller.

American stage production of a German play adapted by Vicki Baum from her novel and made a huge profit when it became the toast of the 1930–1 Broadway season. For the film version, the studio spent $695,000 and made it the first all-star drama – with Greta Garbo as the bored ballerina (who says "I vant to be alone"), Joan Crawford as the ambitious hotel stenographer, Wallace Beery as the crooked industrialist, John Barrymore as a sophisticated jewel thief, Lionel Barrymore as a dying book-keeper having a last fling in unaccustomed style and comfort, Lewis Stone as the hotel doctor and Jean Hersholt as a porter. William A. Drake, who had so successfully adapted Baum's material for Broadway, revised it for the screen (with much uncredited assistance) and Edmund Goulding directed. The film ran 115 minutes and started off as a roadshow attraction at increased prices. It was the top box-office hit of 1932. The 1945 re-make was called *Weekend at the Waldorf*.

Letty Lynton MGM had another hit when John Meehan and Wanda

Tuchock adapted Marie Belloc Lowndes' novel, based on a famous British murder trial, into a Joan Crawford vehicle: her Letty Lynton is

Letty Lynton: Nils Asther, Joan Crawford. Set design by Cedric Gibbons.

a wealthy New York socialite who falls in love with Robert Montgomery and unintentionally poisons an old lover (Nils Asther) after he threatens to wreck her marriage plans. May Robson had a key supporting role as her formidable mother. The director was Clarence Brown. A popular play, *Dishonored Lady*, had also been based on the same original murder case and its authors successfully claimed that their copyright had been infringed by MGM's movie. The amount of damages was contested in lengthy court proceedings. In December 1938, a judge declared himself legally obliged to award the entire net profits of the film, $587,604, to the authors and their attorneys even

though he felt that 25 per cent would have been more fitting, given that the skill of the director and the drawing power of the stars had contributed heavily to its success. MGM appealed, the case went to the Supreme Court, and the plaintiffs finally received $167,528 in 1940. *Letty Lynton* had to be permanently withdrawn from circulation. (*Dishonored Lady* became a 1947 film with Hedy Lamarr.)

The Rich Are Always With Us Ruth Chatterton was another big Paramount star who moved to Warner Bros. and First National. Her first movie at her new home was this Park Avenue comedy in which she was the wealthy woman who vacillates between her ex-husband (John Miljan), who is in financial difficulties, and George Brent's dashing writer whose repertoire of tricks includes lighting two cigarettes, one for her and one for himself, long before *Now, Voyager* made the routine famous. In real life, as in the film, Chatterton chose Brent, and married him. Envisaged as the studio's answer to Clark Gable, he was just beginning his starring career after playing some bits. Bette Davis had a supporting role in the film as the rival for Brent's affections. Austin Parker's screenplay was based on a novel by E. Pettit. Alfred E. Green directed.

Scarface (known also as *Scarface, The Shame of the Nation*) There was so much opposition to gangster films and their alleged glorification of crime that Howard Hughes' production had to be considerably toned down before it could be released by United Artists, almost a year after it finished shooting. Thus it gained both the

Scarface: George Raft, Paul Muni.

Grand Hotel: Greta Garbo, John Barrymore.

Grand Hotel: Looking down on the lobby set. Art direction by Cedric Gibbons.

subtitle *The Shame of the Nation* and an awkward scene in which an editor denounces organized crime to a group of citizens (and by extension the audience), proposing that martial law should be declared to deal with the gangster menace and that the volunteered aid of the Army and American Legion should be accepted. As many as fifty overall changes were reported as having been made. The title *Scarface* came from a novel by the late Armitage Trail, but the film was suggested by the life of Al Capone, and, to provide a more sophisticated treatment of now familiar subject matter, the approach adopted by director Howard Hawks and his writers Ben Hecht, Seton I. Miller, John Lee Mahin and W. R. Burnett was to cast their gang boss, called Tony Camonte, as a modern-day Borgia with a childish zest for living. In Paul Muni's hands, he became both fascinating and repellent (this was the real start of Muni's film career after an earlier attempt at Fox). Ann Dvorak played the sister who introduced an element of Borgian incest, George Raft was the coin-flipping henchman and Osgood Perkins was the displaced gang leader, while Boris Karloff, prior to making *Frankenstein*, was a rival mobster wiped out in a bowling alley. It was vivid, exciting stuff, surprisingly well received by the critics. Many state and local censorship boards attempted to ban the film, and Hughes took legal action. He was forced to provide an alternative ending for New York State in which Muni's downfall was given extra emphasis when he is hanged instead of being shot down by the police. (In Chicago, Capone's home city, the film didn't open until 20 November 1941.) The uproar aroused the curiosity of audiences but ensured that it was the last gangster movie of this type. Howard Hughes decided that he had had enough and quit film-making for the next few years.

State's Attorney There was a meaty part for John Barrymore, rivalling his brother Lionel's work in *A Free Soul*, as the criminal lawyer involved with the underworld who falls in love with a client (Helen Twelvetrees) after winning her an acquittal in court. RKO's drama was the most popular of a batch of competing criminal lawyer movies that included Warners' *The Mouthpiece* with Warren William and Columbia's *Attorney for the Defense* with Edmund Lowe. Louis Stevens' story was scripted by Gene Fowler and Rowland Brown. George Archainbaud directed. *Cardigan's Last Case* was its title for British showing.

Merrily We Go to Hell: Cary Grant, Sylvia Sidney, Fredric March.

JUNE

As You Desire Me Pirandello fever had gripped Hollywood in 1930 when three of his works were bought for the screen, two by Universal and this one by MGM. Gene Markey's adaptation preserved the author's concern over problems of identity, with Greta Garbo as the amnesiac who falls in love with Melvyn Douglas as the man who claims to have been her husband. Erich von Stroheim was her lover and protector who wouldn't give her up. George Fitzmaurice directed. Audiences were tickled rather than baffled by the film's ambiguities, enjoyed seeing Garbo in a platinum blonde wig for part of the movie and also went because it might be the last film she would make: her contract with MGM had expired and she was threatening to retire to her farm in Sweden.

Merrily We Go to Hell A not-so-merry drama from Paramount, handled by Dorothy Arzner, Hollywood's only woman director of the period. Sylvia Sidney's heiress marries Fredric March's writer on a whim, discovers that he has a drinking problem and a prickly temperament, and returns to the family mansion. Cary Grant had a bit part as an actor in a stage play. Edwin Justus Mayer did the adaptation of a Cleo Lucas novel.

Two Seconds In the two seconds it takes him to die in the electric chair, Edward G. Robinson's convicted murderer recalls the circumstances that brought him there. He had been the sap who married a dance-hall floozie (Vivienne Osborne), accidentally killed his best friend (Preston Foster) in a row over her and then bumped her off for betraying

him. It was a typically tough, working-class drama from First National (Warner Bros.). Harvey Thew's adaptation of an Elliott Lester play was directed by Mervyn LeRoy.

Letty Lynton

Grand Hotel

Red-Headed Woman The Platinum Blonde changed her hair colour, went into her first big opportunity at MGM and came out a star, playing a woman who uses her charms freely to get the best out of life. Jean Harlow tricked socially prominent Chester Morris into marriage, later takes a pay-off from his wealthy father (Lewis Stone), blackmails a leading businessman (Henry Stephenson) into introducing her to high society and plays around with the chauffeur (Charles Boyer, in a minor role) for amorous relief. Harlow made the outrageous material funny under Jack Conway's direction, and was even left unreformed at the

Two Seconds: Edward G. Robinson, Vivienne Osborne.

Red-Headed Woman: Lewis Stone, Jean Harlow. Receiving a pay-off.

JULY

Bring 'Em Back Alive RKO Radio successfully mounted another of its massive publicity campaigns for this documentary narrated by and starring famous hunter Frank Buck. It was suggested by his popular book, and audiences saw the wild life of the Malayan jungle in all its raw variety. Clyde E. Elliott was the director for the Van Beuren Corporation. Its huge success put it ahead of rival attractions: Fox's *Congorilla*, Columbia's *Blond Captive* and Universal's *Igloo*. Buck went on to provide RKO with further real-life camera expeditions called *Wild Cargo* (1934) and *Fang and Claw* (1935).

Red-Headed Woman

What Price Hollywood? Constance Bennett was the movie-mad waitress who becomes a star, while the alcoholic director (Lowell Sherman) who discovered her turns into a has-been and commits suicide. Gregory Ratoff played the studio head, Neil Hamilton the wealthy polo player she briefly marries. Its bold dramatic contrasts helped make it one of the few inside-Hollywood stories to draw big audiences (fortunately so, since it had been expensive to make at $600,000). Adela Rogers St Johns and John Hyland provided the original story, adapted by Rowland Brown and Gene Fowler and scripted by Jane Murfin and Ben Markson. George Cukor directed and David O. Selznick produced for RKO Pathé. When he became an independent producer,

end. Anita Loos adapted the Katharine Brush novel, and Harlow's future husband Hal Rosson photographed.

Selznick used a very similar story for *A Star Is Born* (1937).

Winner Take All James Cagney became a cocky prizefighter who got too big for his gloves in this Warner Bros. comedy-drama written by Wilson Mizner and Robert Lord from a Gerald Beaumont story and directed by Roy Del Ruth. Virginia Bruce was the disloyal society blonde he kicked in the rear end, while Marian Nixon was the simple girl who loved him, broken nose and all. Former boxer Harvey Perry coached Cagney for his scenes in the ring and also took a small part.

AUGUST

Horse Feathers Campus capers from the Marx Brothers. Groucho is the new college head, Professor Quincey Adams Wagstaff, while Chico (the iceman) and Harpo (the dog-catcher) become football-playing students, and Zeppo romances Thelma Todd as the

voluptuous college widow. This is the one with the speakeasy scene (in which the password is "Swordfish") and the wild football match at the end. Bert Kalmar, Harry Ruby, S. J. Perelman and Will B. Johnstone were the writers, and Norman Z. McLeod directed for Paramount.

The First Year Janet Gaynor and Charles Farrell were the newly-weds struggling through the first year of married life. There was a scene in which they put on a disastrous dinner to impress important guests that prefigured similar calamities in *Alice Adams* (1935) and *Made for Each Other* (1939). Actor-writer Frank Craven's 1920 play had already been a 1926 Fox picture with Kathryn Perry and Matt Moore. Lynn Starling wrote the script for Fox's new version, directed by William K. Howard.

Guilty as Hell Victor McLaglen and Edmund Lowe were teamed again as a tough police captain and hard-drinking newshound respectively in a comedy thriller of crime detection – of the type in which the villain is known to the audience and the suspense lies in preventing the execution of the wrong man. Richard Arlen appeared as the victim of a frame-up, and Adrienne Ames was his sister. It had been a play on Broadway earlier in the year, *Riddle Me This* by Daniel N. Rubin, when it had starred Thomas Mitchell and Frank Craven. Paramount's screen version was written by Frank Partos and Arthur Kober and directed by Erle C. Kenton. The last word of its title was unacceptable in England where it became *Guilty As Charged*. A loose

Horse Feathers: Harpo orders a drink in a speakeasy – this big. With Groucho and Chico Marx, Vince Barnett (next to Chico), Edgar Dearing (bartender).

re-make of 1937 was entitled *Night Club Scandal*.

Bring 'Em Back Alive

American Madness Walter Huston starred in Frank Capra's drama as the dedicated banker whose faith is tested when there is a run on his bank by the small investors after a robbery and when his neglected wife (Kay Johnson) turns out to know one of the robbers. Though it showed the system returning to normal, Capra's images of the mob storming the bank were strong stuff in the Depression era when banks were collapsing all around. Pat O'Brien and Constance Cummings also starred. This was the director's first collaboration with writer Robert Riskin and Columbia's leading picture of the year.

Doctor X First National (Warner Bros.) came up with this zestful story of dangerous laboratory experiments and a murderer who strangles his victims on the nights of the full moon. Lionel Atwill was the head doctor at a medical academy for surgical research where all the staff are prime suspects, while Fay Wray had a chance to scream when the killer attacks her, and Lee Tracy was the persistent newspaper reporter with the wisecracks who comes to the rescue in the nick of time. The film's "synthetic flesh", an invention to restore a missing limb, was created by the Max Factor Company. *Doctor X* was one of the year's few productions in the current two-colour Technicolor process (photographed by Ray Rennahan and Richard Towers), but outside the big cities it was released in more economical black and white. Michael Curtiz directed, and Robert Tasker and Earl Baldwin adapted the

Doctor X: A controlled experiment to reveal the cannibalistic killer that goes wrong. Set design by Anton Grot.

Guilty as Hell: Victor McLaglen, Henry Stephenson, Edmund Lowe.

1931 stage play of the same name by Howard Warren Comstock and Allen C. Miller.

SEPTEMBER

Grand Hotel (On wider release at normal prices.)

70,000 Witnesses Paramount's mystery drama dealt with the murder of a star player on the football field during a game. Phillips Holmes (prime suspect), Lew Cody (his gangster brother), Charlie Ruggles (bibulous reporter), Dorothy Jordan (attractive heroine) and David Landau (persistent detective) appeared with Johnny Mack Brown (star player). Ralph Murphy directed, and the screenplay from a Courtland Fitzsimmons novel was by Garrett

Fort, Robert N. Lee, P. J. Wolfson and Allen Rivkin.

Bird of Paradise Joel McCrea and Dolores Del Rio starred in this South Seas romance from this famous 1912 play by Richard Walton Tully. Wells Root, Wanda Tuchock and Leonard Praskins were credited with the screen adaptation. McCrea was the American adventurer who falls in love with Del Rio's native princess. Producer David O. Selznick, wanting this to be a big picture, persuaded King Vidor to direct and sent a huge unit on location to Hawaii where bad weather made it impossible to complete the work. It was finished in California, and the total cost of $850,000 made it RKO's most expensive film since *Cimarron*. Thanks to Vidor's sensual treatment of the love scenes and an exotic score by Max Steiner, the film turned out well – especially abroad, where its strong visual appeal and limited

Bird of Paradise: Dolores Del Rio, Joel McCrea.

amount of dialogue were an asset –
but it failed to recoup its cost, and
plans to team the same two stars in
another exotic classic of romance,
Green Mansions, were dropped.
There was a Fox re-make of *Bird of
Paradise* in 1951 with Jeff Chandler
and Debra Paget.

Back Street Universal proved there
were still tears to be jerked by a good
soap opera. "Waiting – always waiting
– in the shadows of the back street . . .
longing for the man she loves . . .
asking nothing, receiving nothing – yet
content to sacrifice all for him.
WHY?" asked the adverts. (A
mystery indeed to modern audiences,
apt to wonder how the stiff John Boles
came to be regarded as an irresistible
ladykiller in so many pictures of this
type.) Irene Dunne was borrowed
from RKO to star as the patient
mistress, happy with the occasional
crumbs of companionship that Boles's

Love Me Tonight: Jeanette MacDonald,
Maurice Chevalier.

Back Street: Irene Dunne, John Boles.

wealthy banker provides when his job
and marriage permit. The film
confirmed Dunne as an important new
star and gave Universal its biggest hit
since *All Quiet*. Gladys Lehman and
Lynn Starling handled the screen
adaptation of Fannie Hurst's novel
and John M. Stahl directed. Re-makes
starred Margaret Sullavan in 1941 and
Susan Hayward in 1961.

Love Me Tonight As Lubitsch was
busy, Rouben Mamoulian was
assigned the task of a follow-up
picture for Maurice Chevalier and
Jeanette MacDonald after the success
of *The Love Parade*. His adventurous
approach fully integrated the songs by
Richard Rodgers and Lorenz Hart
("Isn't It Romantic?", "Mimi" and
others) into the fairy-tale romance and

included many daring and successful
stylistic touches such as slow motion
and an early use of the zoom.
Chevalier was the tailor mistaken for a
baron, and MacDonald the haughty
Princess who finds she loves him
anyway. Sophisticated, often risqué
and always imaginative, the film
liberated the musical from its
stultifying conventions and was widely
praised at the time. It came from a
play by Leopold Marchand and Paul
Armont and was written by Samuel
Hoffenstein, Waldemar Young and
George Marion Jr. The supporting
cast included Charlie Ruggles,
Charles Butterworth, Myrna Loy and
C. Aubrey Smith, not forgetting
Elizabeth Patterson, Blanche
Frederici and Ethel Griffies as the
three aunts.

Tiger Shark Edward G. Robinson was
again the unfortunate in love as the

exuberant Portuguese tuna fisherman
with one arm who marries a young,
attractive woman (Zita Johann) and
loses her to his best friend (Richard
Arlen). Howard Hawks directed First
National's drama, written by Wells
Root from a story by Houston Branch.
The plot was so simple and effective
that Bryan Foy, head of B pictures at
Warner Bros., frequently re-used it in
different settings for such minor films
as *Bengal Tiger* (1936) and *King of the
Lumberjacks* (1942). It was also
unofficially remade (with Edward G.
Robinson again, opposite Marlene
Dietrich and George Raft) as
Manpower (1941).

OCTOBER

Smilin' Through This celebrated
sentimental romance, which actress
Jane Cowl originally co-authored with
Jane Murfin as a starring role for
herself in 1919, had been a big Norma
Talmadge film of 1922. Now it became
Norma Shearer's turn to play the dual
role of the woman who is shot dead by
a rebuffed suitor on her wedding day
and her grown-up niece who falls in
love with the son of the killer.
Fredric March played both these
male parts while Leslie Howard co-
starred as the man who loses his
beloved in this world but is reunited
with her in the next. Sidney Franklin
directed MGM's picture and Ernest
Vajda, Claudine West, Donald Ogden
Stewart and James Bernard Fagan
came up with the script. It would be
filmed again in 1941 with Jeanette
MacDonald.

The Big Broadcast Even though
Paramount had re-invented the
musical with *Love Me Tonight*, the

studio also revived the old-fashioned all-star revue format in a successful attempt to woo radio audiences out to the theatres actually to see the favourites of the airwaves. Not only did it launch Bing Crosby as a star singing such Ralph Rainger/Leo Robin numbers as "Please" and his future theme song, "Where the Blue of the Night Meets the Gold of the Day", but it also featured George Burns and Gracie Allen, Kate Smith, Arthur Tracy, the Mills Brothers, the Boswell Sisters, Donald Novis, the Vincent Lopez Orchestra and Cab Calloway. There was a slim plot, about a Texan millionaire (Stuart Erwin) saving a radio station, in the script by George Marion Jr from a play by William Ford Manley that Paramount had backed. Frank Tuttle directed. Further *Big Broadcasts* would follow in 1936, 1937 and 1938.

A Bill of Divorcement Katharine Hepburn made her screen debut opposite John Barrymore in this

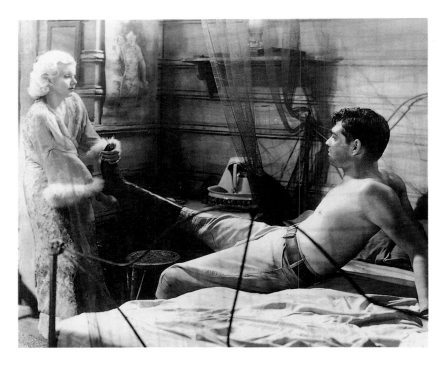

Red Dust: Jean Harlow, Clark Gable.

A Bill of Divorcement: John Barrymore, Katharine Hepburn.

tender drama from the Clemence Dane play. He was the man released from a mental home and she was his daughter, who comes to know him for the first time and to realize that she may have inherited his streak of insanity. George Cukor directed the RKO Radio picture from the adaptation by Howard Estabrook and Harry Wagstaff Gribble. The play had been made into a British film of 1922, and would be re-made by RKO as a 1940 release starring Maureen O'Hara and Adolphe Menjou.

Grand Hotel

The Phantom of Crestwood This RKO Radio picture gave radio listeners the solution to a mystery serial, which had been deliberately broadcast without an ending (there was a contest with prizes for the best one sent in by the audience). Which of five ex-lovers

killed blackmailing Karen Morley with a dart? Numerous flashbacks led to the truth as private detective Ricardo Cortez winkled out the guilty man. The huge publicity derived from the radio tie-in gave the routine thriller a considerable box-office boost. Bartlett Cormack wrote the screenplay, and J. Walter Ruben directed from a story they devised jointly.

NOVEMBER

Red Dust The torrid box-office combination of Clark Gable and Jean Harlow and a skilful script by John

Lee Mahin turned a failed 1928 play by Wilson Collison into potent screen material. The suicide of Harlow's current husband, producer Paul Bern, had interrupted production and heightened interest in her. She played the prostitute who becomes involved with Gable as the manager of a remote rubber plantation in Indo-China; Mary Astor was the more refined married woman who also interests him and Gene Raymond was the engineer husband. Besides humour and vitality, Harlow brought an affecting

I Am a Fugitive From a Chain Gang: Paul Muni (about to have his shackles hammered on the rail by black convict behind).

sensitivity to the part of the fallen lady. Much was also due to Victor Fleming's direction of the MGM film, re-made as *Congo Maisie* (1940) and (with Gable again) as *Mogambo* (1953).

I Am a Fugitive from a Chain Gang
This Warner Bros. film was inspired by the headline-grabbing revelation of conditions in a Florida prison camp, particularly the use of the "sweatbox", in the autobiography of escaped convict Robert E. Burns, who served as the film's technical adviser and was still at liberty when it was made and first shown but who was dramatically recaptured in New Jersey in

I Am a Fugitive From a Chain Gang: Paul Muni. Under arrest.

December. (RKO had earlier put a Richard Dix prison melodrama, *Hell's Highway*, back into production to add a sweatbox scene, but that movie was not a big success.) Paul Muni portrayed an innocent man sentenced to 10 years hard labour on the chain gang who escapes and establishes a new life in Chicago as a successful and respected engineer. Lured by false promises into returning to prison, he again escapes and, in one of the decade's most memorable endings, has a brief reunion with his girl (Helen Vinson) in a garage one night. She asks him how he manages to live, and his chilling reply as he withdraws into the darkness closes the picture: "I steal!" Glenda Farrell appeared as a landlady who blackmails him into marriage, and Edward J. McNamara was the brutal warden. Mervyn LeRoy directed, and Sheridan Gibney and Brown Holmes wrote the screenplay.

Prosperity Marie Dressler co-starred with Polly Moran for what proved to be the last of eight times in this Depression-conscious MGM comedy-drama directed by Sam Wood. Dressler was the widowed mother and president of a small-town bank that

THE ACADEMY AWARDS

The Awards covered the season from August 1931 to July 1932 and were presented at the Ambassador Hotel on 18 November. *Grand Hotel* was voted Best Picture. Fredric March picked up most votes for Best Actor for *Dr Jekyll and Mr Hyde*, but Wallace Beery was only one vote behind for *The Champ* and under the rules of that time this meant that both actors won. Helen Hayes was the winner for Best Actress for her debut in *The Sin of Madelon Claudet*. *Bad Girl* brought Academy Awards to its director Frank Borzage and adapter Edwin Burke, while Frances Marion won for the Best Original Story which she devised for *The Champ*. For Best Cinematography, Lee Garmes of *Shanghai Express* was the winner, and for Best Interior Decoration it was Gordon Wiles of *Transatlantic*. Paramount again collected the award for Sound Recording. To mark the recognition of Short Subjects as worthy of honour, Walt Disney was given a special Academy Award for the creation of Mickey Mouse and won another in the new cartoon category for *Flowers and Trees*. In the new Short Comedy category, Laurel and Hardy's *The Music Box* won, and there was an Award to *Wrestling Swordfish* in the Novelty field. Technicolor were honoured in the Scientific or Technical category for their "colour cartoon process", which was the new three-strip full colour system of much improved Technicolor first used on *Flowers and Trees*.

Wallace Beery and Fredric March, joint Best Actors, flank Lionel Barrymore (who presented the Best Actress Award) and Conrad Nagel.

Academy President and Awards host Conrad Nagel with the initial winner for Best Actor, Fredric March. It was later discovered that Wallace Beery had come so close that he was entitled to be the joint winner.

Once in a Lifetime: Waiting to see the head of the studio – but "Mr. Glogauer Is In Conference". Onslow Stevens, Aline MacMahon, Jack Oakie, Russell Hopton.

goes bust, making her live on charity and attempt suicide. Moran was her best friend whose loose tongue precipitated the run on the bank. This was one of several MGM films that prospered after a disastrous preview, thanks to extensive re-writing (by four staff scribes) and re-takes. The screenplay credit was given to Zelda Sears and Eve Greene and the story attributed to Frank Butler and Sylvia Thalberg. Anita Page and Norman Foster were featured as the two ladies' children.

Washington Merry-Go-Round A dramatic addition to a cycle of unflattering portraits of American political life, this was timed to coincide with the climax of the presidential contest between Roosevelt and Hoover (won by the former on 10 November). It had been preceded at the box-office by two satires, Warner Bros. *The Dark Horse* and Paramount's *The Phantom President* (with George M. Cohan), as well as the MGM drama *Washington Masquerade* with Lionel Barrymore. This one presented Lee Tracy as the gabby, idiotic-seeming young Congressman crusading against the big crooks (led by Alan Dinehart) who secretly manipulate the government. Walter Connolly was a senior senator unwittingly involved in corruption and Constance Cummings played his grand-daughter. With some pre-echoes of *Mr Smith Goes to Washington*, this earlier Columbia picture was scripted by Jo Swerling from a Maxwell Anderson story and directed by James Cruze.

Once in a Lifetime Moss Hart and George S. Kaufman's crude but uproarious comedy about filmland inanities during the transition to sound was such a colossal hit on Broadway in 1930 that it was bound to be filmed – Hollywood could take a joke, especially if it might make some money and was part of history – but that didn't stop Universal's head, Carl Laemmle, appending a message at the start of the film version congratulating himself on his own courage in filming it. Jack Oakie was the most dimwitted of three vaudeville artistes (the other two played by Aline MacMahon and Russell Hopton) who are put out of work by the talkies and go west, hoping to become voice trainers in the film colony: he becomes a director and accidentally makes a masterpiece, or at least that's what the critics call it. Gregory Ratoff played the studio tycoon Herman Glogauer, and Sidney Fox, Russell Hopton, ZaSu Pitts,

Louise Fazenda and Onslow Stevens were also featured. Russell Mack directed the Universal picture, and Seton I. Miller adapted the play for the screen.

DECEMBER

Prosperity

Call Her Savage Clara Bow made a tremendous comeback after her career had been blighted by various scandals blown up in the press. She had been given up by Paramount and shot this at Fox, where she had to lose weight before production could start. In a lively melodrama, she was the wildcat with an Indian mother who tries to get her revenge on society after being scorned by the family of the man she recklessly marries (Anthony Jowitt). Taking up streetwalking to feed her child, she eventually finds happiness with another half-breed (Gilbert Roland). The film put her in a vivid brawl with Thelma Todd. It was written by Edwin Burke from Tiffany Thayer's 1931 best-seller and directed by John Francis Dillon.

Rockabye This RKO Pathé weepie was shot with Constance Bennett, Phillips Holmes and Laura Hope Crews under the direction of George Fitzmaurice at a cost of $465,000. Executive producer David O. Selznick found the result so deplorable that he

Call Her Savage: Clara Bow.

brought in George Cukor to substantially re-shoot the picture with Joel McCrea and Jobyna Howland as new co-stars for Bennett, adding another $200,000 to the cost. She played the Broadway star who craved a child but, out of respect for the sanctity of motherhood, dispatched her young lover, McCrea's playwright, back to his wife and their baby. Howland was an alcoholic actress friend of Bennett, Walter Pidgeon a crooked politician, and Paul Lukas the theatrical agent whose love for her was some consolation. Jane Murfin was credited with the screenplay, taken from a Lucia Bronder play. Though the film did well, it had become far too expensive and led to Selznick's contract with the studio not being renewed. *Rockabye* was the last RKO film to carry the Pathé name.

If I Had a Million Paramount's answer to Depression woes and to MGM's all-star *Grand Hotel* was this multi-story feature about various individuals' reactions to being given a cheque for $1 million. Episodes starred Charles Laughton as a humble clerk who delivers a "Bronx cheer" to the company president before walking out (directed by Lubitsch); Charlie Ruggles as the shop assistant who smashes up the china shop where he works (directed by Norman Z. McLeod); W. C. Fields and Alison Skipworth as the leaders of a convoy of secondhand cars which attack roadhogs (directed by Norman Taurog); Gene Raymond as a man about to die in the electric chair (directed by Bruce Humberstone); and Wynne Gibson as the prostitute who buys a night of luxury in a hotel bed all on her own (another directed by Lubitsch). Further stars involved were George Raft, Gary Cooper, Jack Oakie, Mary Boland and, in the final story, May Robson who buys the old-folks' home in which she is living and turns it into a place of luxury. Other directors were Stephen Roberts, James Cruze and William A. Seiter. Eighteen writers elaborated on Robert D. Andrews' basic story: Claude Binyon, Whitney Bolton, Malcolm Stuart Boylan, John Bright, Sidney Buchman, Lester Cole, Isabel Dawn, Boyce DeGaw, Walter DeLeon, Oliver H. P. Garrett, Harvey Gates, Grover Jones, Ernst Lubitsch, Lawton Mackaill, Joseph L. Mankiewicz, William Slavens McNutt, Seton I. Miller and Tiffany Thayer.

Strange Interlude In 1931, MGM spent $82,000 buying the rights to Eugene O'Neill's five-hour play, a huge Broadway hit of 1928, intending to reunite its star Lynn Fontanne with her husband Alfred Lunt in a film version. But the tepid response to these stage luminaries in their first MGM picture, *The Guardsman*, determined a safer course of action, giving it to Norma Shearer and Clark Gable in the hope of attracting their strong following. Screenwriters Bess Meredyth and C. Gardner Sullivan whittled the play down with considerable fidelity and it came out as a 110-minute feature. Shearer took on the key role of the wife who has a child by another man (Clark Gable) because there is a streak of insanity on her husband's side. Alexander Kirkland played the husband, May Robson his mother who reveals the family illness and Robert Young was the child grown up into a young man (by which time Gable and Shearer were in unconvincing old-age make-up). Robert Z. Leonard directed. MGM weren't too happy with the result, which was unusually expensive

TEN BEST–CRITICS' CHOICE

The number voting this year was 368, an increase of 28 in the total of critics from newspapers, trade press, other magazines and syndicates contributing their choices of the top 10 films of 1932 to the *Film Daily*'s poll. The winners and votes cast:

1.	*Grand Hotel*	296
2.	*The Champ* [late 1931 release]	214
3.	*Arrowsmith*	192
4.	*The Guardsman*	170
5.	*Smilin' Through*	168
6.	*Dr Jekyll and Mr Hyde*	161
7.	*Emma*	154
8.	*A Bill of Divorcement*	141
9.	*Back Street*	136
10.	*Scarface*	135
	Close Runner Up	
11.	*Shanghai Express*	117

The next nearest (*Broken Lullaby*, known also as *The Man I Killed*) received 92 votes. Apart from *The Guardsman* (the only film that the celebrated stage team of Alfred Lunt and Lynn Fontanne ever made), all the listed pictures clicked at the box-office.

CLOSE RUNNERS UP

17 other films came close to being included among the hits of the year for the month or months indicated: *Blonde Venus* (September), *The Conquerors* (November), *The Dark Horse* (July), *Fireman Save My Child* (March, April), *Girl Crazy* (April), *It's Tough to Be Famous* (April), *Jewel Robbery* (August), *Rain* (October), *Speak Easily* (August), *Symphony of Six Million* (May), *The Tenderfoot* (June), *Too Busy to Work* (November), *Trouble in Paradise* (November), *Unashamed* (July), *Union Depot* (January), *Westward Passage* (June), *You Said a Mouthful* (December).

at $654,000, and gave it a cautious release, begun in October. But Shearer and Gable pulled in the fans, though held by many critics to lack the intensity the parts required, and the picture made a good profit. Gable wore a moustache on screen for the first time in later scenes.

She Done Him Wrong
Cary Grant,
Mae West

In the first few months of the year, conditions reached crisis point. Three of the big circuit-operating companies could no longer keep up with payments due to the mortgage holders for the huge number of movie theatres they had so ravenously acquired a few years earlier. Paramount owed $282.7 million to various creditors. RKO Radio was also in deep trouble, not only losing money on its Orpheum chain but defaulting on payments for its acquisition of Pathé and making losses on film production. Fox was back in profit on its film-making but it had colossal payments due on theatres. Receivers were appointed at Paramount and RKO and for Fox's theatre subsidiary. Many movie houses were taken back by creditors, very often the entrepreneurs who had sold them to the big companies in the first place. Only Warner Bros. bucked this trend. Despite huge operating losses, the company was not under pressure from the banks and in addition to retaining all its theatres it added many more. Loew's (MGM) reported its lowest profit of the decade, $4.3 million (still higher than any profit made in any year of the 1930s by RKO, Columbia, United Artists or Universal).

Although weekly attendances averaged around 60 million as in 1932, there were big fluctuations over the year, and the average price of admission dropped to 23¢ in an attempt to gain more custom. The worst period came in early March when, following a spate of bank moratoria, Franklin D. Roosevelt took office as President and declared a four-day bank holiday nationwide. The lack of access to cash meant that many moviegoers didn't have the wherewithal to enter theatres even if they wanted to, or had more important uses for the cash they still had. Used to taking in some $3 million a day, American theatres suddenly found that one million of this was no longer rolling in. Fortunately, some exceptionally strong attractions – *42nd Street, King Kong, She Done Him Wrong* – helped limit the damage.

In Hollywood, the studio heads wanted to suspend salaries for a period while employees protested that they needed some income to live. The Academy of Motion Picture Arts and Sciences suggested as a compromise a 50 per cent wage cut for everyone, but this was fiercely opposed by the lower-paid workers. The studio heads then decided to impose a 50 per cent pay cut on all employees earning over $50 per week for a period of up to two months (this meant that 75 per cent of working actors were unaffected). The Academy, in association with accountants Price and Waterhouse, were to decide if any of the major companies could afford to end the cut earlier. MGM was the first to restore full salaries. When Harry Warner of Warner Bros. stalled on accepting the Academy's ruling that his company could afford to do the same, his highly-regarded production chief Darryl F. Zanuck resigned on 15 April. Three days later, he made an agreement with Joseph Schenck of United Artists to form a new production company that would have its pictures distributed through UA. The company was called Twentieth Century, and by the end of the year four of its pictures were in release – the first of them, *The Bowery*, proving a considerable hit.

The Academy had lacked powers to enforce its decisions. It had relied on co-operation from the studio heads and it was regarded as a company union. It represented actors and other artists at meetings to establish a Code under the National Recovery Act to govern conditions and pay in the movie industry (this took effect on 8 December). The Code was so favourable

Lilian Harvey, the British-born musical star of German films like *Congress Dances*, was signed up by Fox to work in Hollywood. This scene is from the first and least unpopular of three American films she made, *My Lips Betray*, a mythical kingdom romance in which she was starred opposite John Boles. Like Anna Sten, she did not appeal to American audiences.

to the producers in agreeing to salary limits and the licensing of agents that nearly 1,000 members resigned from the Academy in a week, and over 500 of them joined the newly-created Screen Actors Guild in October with Eddie Cantor as president. The writers had already withdrawn from the Academy in April to form the Screen Writers Guild. (The Screen Directors Guild was formed in 1936.)

Foreign films began to threaten Hollywood's domination of its own home market. Two German productions, *Be Mine Tonight* and *Maedchen in Uniform*, registered huge grosses in the big cities, while the artistic and commercial success of the historical production *The Private Life of Henry VIII* starring Charles Laughton indicated that British films might be learning the knack of appealing to American audiences. Laughton had already worked in Hollywood and was known to American audiences.

Two of these foreign films even appeared in the top 10 chosen by the national critics. Hollywood responded by bringing over big foreign stars like Lilian Harvey and Henri Garat, but they did not have mass appeal. The studios imitated the subject matter of popular foreign films – *Bondage* and *Eight Girls in a Boat* both showed grim conditions in girls' schools like those exposed in *Maedchen in Uniform* but did not impress moviegoers. Gaumont-British even set about establishing its own network of exchanges or sales offices to market its pictures in the United States and launched several of its top attractions at the Roxy and Radio City Music Hall in early 1934.

Mae West, who was the one-woman hope of Paramount in 1933 with her huge-grossing *She Done Him Wrong* and *I'm No Angel*, stirred up the censorship debate with her brazen vulgarity that made even the most innocuous of lines sound saucy. The rising popularity of Jean Harlow also inflamed the puritans. A new book based on four years of studies, *Our Movie-Made Children* by Dr. W. W. Charters and Henry James Forman, suggested that motion pictures had a harmful effect on youth, although it failed to take other influences into account. The Catholic Church became particularly incensed at the failure of the Hays Office to regulate motion picture content, and in November the bishops of America at their annual convention set about organizing the Legion of Decency as a pressure group to campaign for the purification of the cinema.

THE SHOWPLACE OF THE NATION

When John D. Rockefeller leased a large area of mid-town Manhattan in 1928, the original intention was to build a new opera house. Rockefeller then decided to create a commercial centre. He recruited Radio Corporation of America as the principal tenant, causing the project to be known as "Radio City" rather than the more formal Rockefeller Center. RCA owned the NBC radio company and the RKO Radio film studio. Master showman Samuel L. "Roxy" Rothafel was put in charge of the two theatres that were to be included in the $250 million development and severed his connection with the huge Roxy Theater named after him in New York.

Roxy decided that the larger auditorium, seating 5,945, would be a vaudeville theatre called the Radio City Music Hall. The smaller auditorium, seating a still massive 3,509, was to show films and took the name RKO Roxy. The two theatres, like the rest of the development, were ultra-modern in

A stage show in progress at the Radio City Music Hall with the Rockettes lined up along the front of the stage and the orchestra in the pit. Note the curtained openings along each side wall, used to extend the stage for entrances and exits. Director Vincente Minnelli briefly worked on the costume and set designs here during the first year of operation. Later, no fewer than 17 of the films he directed in Hollywood would be shown on the Music Hall screen.

design. The opening night of the Music Hall on 27 December 1932 proved a disaster as the all-star programme ran on for hours into the next morning, and Roxy had to be carried out on a stretcher. He was too ill for the next few months to do any more work. It was decided that the Music Hall would combine films with live stage shows, and this policy commenced on 11 January 1933 with Columbia's *The Bitter Tea of General Yen*, starring Barbara Stanwyck and Nils Asther, as the first movie attraction.

Meanwhile the RKO Roxy at 6th Avenue (now Avenue of the Americas) and 49th Street had opened to the public on 29 December 1932 with RKO's film *The Animal Kingdom*, starring Ann Harding and Leslie Howard, plus a stage show. It became the policy for films that did well in the Music Hall to transfer for a second week to the RKO Roxy, although when *King Kong* was ready it was deemed so big that it opened in both theatres simultaneously. Before the end of 1933, the Music Hall on the corner of 6th Avenue and 50th Street had become a mecca for visitors and lines were a regular sight behind the green velvet ropes. (The entrance on 6th Avenue really came into its own when the El or elevated railway outside was demolished in April 1939.)

During its first year, *Little Women* set a record high when it drew 30,010 paying patrons in a single day and 450,701 during a three-week run. Because of RKO's financial difficulties, the theatre was taken over by the Rockefeller Center in the latter half of 1934 and remained an independently-operated enterprise thereafter.

The RKO Roxy (or Center Theater, as it was re-named at the end of 1933) soon became a venue for stage spectaculars and ice shows, then a television studios, and finally made way for an office building.

For decades, the Music Hall became the most desirable place for distributors to open a film in New York. Every major company – even MGM, with its own huge showcase, the Capitol, on Broadway – was keen to have its best films shown here.

A booking at the Music Hall became a recommendation in itself. The theatre specialized in family entertainment and continued with supporting stage shows featuring its line of chorus girls, the Rockettes, long after such a policy had been dropped elsewhere. Its Christmas and Easter pageants, "The Nativity" and "The Glory of Easter", became annual special attractions. Films would often run a month or more.

Only in the 1970s when it became the practice to open films simultaneously all over New York and when the supply of appealing family fare dried up did the Music Hall fall on difficult times. It was scheduled to close on 12 April 1978 with a typically mediocre film, *Crossed Swords*, accompanying its "Glory of Easter" show. The Music Hall's payboxes ran up the highest box-office total ever recorded for any movie theatre as audiences flocked in for a last look around. It was reprieved and has become almost entirely a venue for live shows after various attempts to re-establish films proved disappointing.

THREE BIG PIGS

A surprise hit of 1933 was Walt Disney's Silly Symphony *Three Little Pigs*, one of his short cartoons based on classic fables. This series used the perfected three-strip Technicolor process and added considerable spice to an otherwise monochrome film show. The Symphonies were sometimes billed ahead of the feature attraction on the marquees. Even so, *Three Little Pigs* had a quite astonishing appeal of its own. It made its debut as part of the supporting programme at Radio City Music Hall in New York City on 25 May 1933 and ran a week. It went on to play two more week-long engagements at the Music Hall; it ran at the Trans-Lux newsreel theatre for eight weeks; it played the giant Roxy four times; it was everywhere on Broadway. It was also a sensation at neighbourhood theatres and across the nation. It kept coming back and back. It became the most popular short subject ever made.

Its optimistic message was just what audiences wanted. Its catchy and defiant musical number "Who's Afraid of the Big Bad Wolf?" was one of the two smash-hit tunes of 1933, constantly heard on the radio, and it replaced "Brother, Can You Spare a Dime?" as the theme tune of the period. Besides the appeal of the song, the cartoon also had much stronger character animation than previous work, and the story demonstrated that commonsense and hard work would solve problems, reinforcing the firm foundation for the future that Roosevelt was seeking to lay. If the Big Bad Wolf represented the

The three little pigs sing "Who's Afraid of the Big Bad Wolf?" in the Walt Disney cartoon. (© The Walt Disney Company).

Depression, the Practical Pig who kept the Wolf away with his house of brick and straw represented a resourceful figure like Roosevelt who helped his weaker brethren (like the other pigs) and was intent on building a stronger America to ward off destructive forces.

The reception accorded *Three Little Pigs* encouraged Disney to embark on his feature-length cartoon *Snow White and the Seven Dwarfs* the following year.

HITS OF THE YEAR

JANUARY

Strange Interlude

The Animal Kingdom Philip Barry's popular Broadway comedy of 1932 had starred Leslie Howard, and for RKO Radio's screen version he re-created his role of the nonconformist publisher who can't decide until the final reel between a respectable, married existence with Myrna Loy and the liberated alternative offered by Ann Harding. Horace Jackson wrote the screenplay and Edward H. Griffith directed. In Britain the film was shown as *The Woman in the House*. RKO sold its rights to Warner Bros., which re-made the subject as *One More Tomorrow* (1946) with Dennis Morgan. For many years RKO's production was thought to have become a lost film, but a print has been located and exhibited as a special attraction.

A Farewell to Arms Director Frank Borzage betrayed the spirit of Ernest Hemingway's novel to create another of his exquisite stories of love conquering all. Gary Cooper was the World War I deserter and Helen Hayes the nurse who loved him and became pregnant. To pacify the Hays Office a form of marriage ceremony was included. To improve its box-office chances, both mother and child were allowed to live and provide a happy ending, although a version in which both died was also made and is the one more often seen today. The Paramount film greatly enhanced Cooper's standing as a serious actor. Adolphe Menjou co-starred, and Benjamin Glazer and Oliver H. P. Garrett were the scenarists. A 1957 re-

make by Selznick starred Rock Hudson and Jennifer Jones.

The Kid from Spain Samuel Goldwyn's annual musical comedy frolic with Eddie Cantor turned him into a suspected bank robber, fleeing to Mexico and being mistaken for a bullfighter. William Anthony McGuire, Bert Kalmar and Harry Ruby wrote the script, with Kalmar and Ruby providing the songs, and Leo McCarey directed. Blonde comedienne Lyda Roberti played Cantor's love interest and performed three of the songs with him; Ruth Hall and Robert Young were the

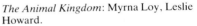

The Animal Kingdom: Myrna Loy, Leslie Howard.

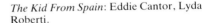

The Kid From Spain: Eddie Cantor, Lyda Roberti.

A Farewell to Arms: Gary Cooper, Helen Hayes.

conventional young lovers; and a genuine American matador called Sidney Franklin participated. Busby Berkeley staged the musical numbers including a water ballet, and among the 76 Goldwyn Girls were Betty Grable (still) and Paulette Goddard. Despite the times, Goldwyn spared no expense and *The Kid from Spain* was reported as costing $1.4 million. It was first opened in New York on 17 November 1932 by United Artists as a special attraction at increased prices but customer resistance forced a conventional play-off that was more successful.

The Sign of the Cross The first costume epic of the sound period, this Cecil B. DeMille picture cast Fredric March as the prefect of ancient Rome whose love for a Christian maid (Elissa Landi) leads him to embrace her faith and face the lions with her in the arena. Charles Laughton (with blocked-in nose) made a plump and pagan Emperor Nero and Claudette Colbert was the Empress Poppaea who fancied the prefect. Its impeccable message of Christian faith and courage permitted DeMille to add spicy and lurid details, including revealing costumes and Poppaea's dip in a 400-gallon pool of asses' milk. Waldemar Young and Sidney Buchman adapted the play by Wilson Barrett. The picture marked DeMille's move to Paramount after an unsuccessful period at MGM. For a 1944 re-issue, a modern prologue written by Dudley Nichols was added.

FEBRUARY

Cavalcade This saga of an upper-crust British couple's experiences over three decades, from New Year's Eve 1899, the dawn of a new century, to the same evening in 1932, was the smash hit of 1933. Noel Coward's lavish pageant had been a London stage success in 1931–2, and Fox bought the rights, assigning Reginald Berkeley to adapt it for the screen. Coward's contract insisted on fidelity to his play, and Fox Movietone News cameramen made a photographic record of the London stage production from various angles to guide the film-makers in Hollywood. Studio chief Winfield Sheehan decided on an all-British cast and worried over whether the subject had wide appeal for American audiences. The studio tried to hold costs down to $1 million but it went over budget by $250,000 as director Frank Lloyd recreated the sweeping story with its huge crowd scenes, such as the departure of the troops by sea for the Boer War. William Cameron Menzies created the vivid montage of World War I. Clive Brook and Diana Wynyard played the couple whose resolve saw them through episodes of tragedy like the death of two sons. Una O'Connor (from the London cast) and Herbert Mundin were the married servants who set up in business on their own, while Frank Lawton and Ursula Jeans were also prominent. *Cavalcade*'s uplifting patriotic flavour and sentimentality proved irresistible to American moviegoers as well as to those in Britain and throughout the British Empire. It became the biggest grosser of the decade until *Mutiny on the Bounty* (by the same director, Frank Lloyd) and was second only to *The Singing Fool* among preceding

The Sign of the Cross: Fredric March, Claudette Colbert.

Cavalcade: Clive Brook, Diana Wynyard.

talking pictures. Its world gross had reached $3.8 million by 1938, nearly three quarters of it from Britain and the Empire.

State Fair Fox was also in the money with this bucolic all-star tale about a farming family's annual trip to the State Fair. Will Rogers was the father keen on the pig contest, Janet Gaynor was the daughter who met Lew Ayres' young reporter, and Sally Eilers was the girl who fell for the son played by Norman Foster. Louise Dresser played the mother who entered the baking contest. Director Henry King showed his deft hand with this kind of

State Fair: Louise Dresser, Will Rogers.

gentle Americana. The film came from a novel by Philip Stong, adapted by Sonya Levien and Paul Green. Fox turned it into musicals in 1944 and 1962.

She Done Him Wrong Studios had puzzled over how to use Mae West in the movies and get her past the Hays Office. Paramount introduced her in a supporting role in *Night After Night* (1932), then made this film version of her 1928 stage sensation *Diamond Lil*. The Hays Office would not allow the title to be used, and the play received no screen acknowledgement as the source of Harvey Thew and John Bright's screenplay, while the character of Diamond Lil had to be re-named Lady Lou and many lurid details toned down. Under Lowell Sherman's capable direction, Mae still made her meanings amply clear as the jewel-studded Bowery saloon-keeper of the Gay Nineties, who describes herself as "one of the finest women who ever walked the streets" and sings songs like "Easy Rider" and "I Like a Man Who Takes His Time". She falls for Cary Grant's handsome Salvation Army officer and offers the now classic invitation, "Why don't you come up sometime, see me?" He turns out to be an undercover detective investigating white slave traffic, but far from immune to her abundant charms. Though there was doubt that younger audiences would be interested in the period setting (long out of favour), that small-town exhibitors would dare show the film and that Mae West would draw outside her stage territory, *She Done Him Wrong* was a huge success, produced for around $200,000 and grossing $2.2 million. It was a life-saver for Paramount, preventing a likely takeover by MGM and the closure of its theatre circuit.

The Sign of the Cross

The Kid from Spain

Hard to Handle A perfect vehicle for the irrepressible talents of James Cagney, this Warner Bros. comedy presented him as a sharp-footed promoter involved in a succession of enterprises from a dance marathon to promoting sales of grapefruit. Mary Brian was the woman who sidestepped him into marriage, and Ruth Donnelly was her resourceful mother. Wilson Mizner and Robert Lord based their script on a story by Houston Branch.

MARCH

42nd Street In a bold return to the backstage musical two years after it had been killed off by audience apathy, Warner Bros. gave Busby Berkeley full rein to exercise his talent for stunning choreography, and the

42nd Street: Ruby Keeler, Warner Baxter, Ginger Rogers. George E. Stone also watching Keeler.

42nd Street: Busby Berkeley's title number with chorus girls moving skyscraper cut-outs.

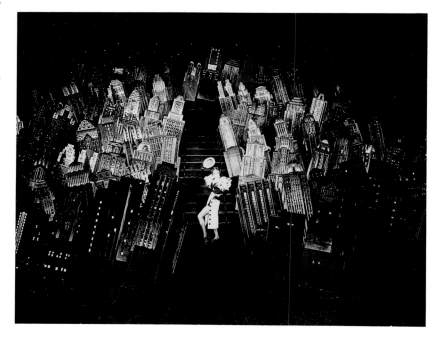

result was sensational. The story was archetypal stuff about putting on a Broadway musical, with Warner Baxter as the producer, Dick Powell as the male star, Bebe Daniels as the troublesome leading lady who is the backer's mistress and Ruby Keeler as the chorus girl who replaces the star on opening night, cueing Baxter's now famous line of encouragement: "You're going out a youngster, but you've got to come back a *star*." It was Keeler's screen debut, and she came out a star, as did Dick Powell in his first major part. Ginger Rogers as the gold-digging "Anytime Annie" had to wait a bit longer for her big break. Also cast were George Brent, Guy Kibbee, Una Merkel, Ned Sparks and Allen Jenkins. The lively script was by

Rian James and James Seymour (from a recent novel by Bradford Ropes), and Lloyd Bacon's direction of the non-musical sequences kept up the pace. But it was Berkeley's mammoth musical set-pieces for the lively songs of Al Dubin and Harry Warren – like the surreal title number and "Shuffle Off to Buffalo", exploding far beyond the confines of a theatre stage – that most delighted audiences, along with the film's message that even in these hard times an ordinary working girl could succeed if she had enough determination and a bit of luck. Warners launched the picture with one of Hollywood's most famous publicity stunts, sending a trainload of stars on a "42nd Street Special" across the country from Los Angeles

Rasputin and the Empress: John, Ethel and Lionel Barrymore with Tad Alexander.

to Washington, with 32 stops in 32 days, to celebrate the inauguration of President Franklin D. Roosevelt, to which studio head Jack L. Warner had been invited. None of the film's stars was on board, but the crowds still turned out – over 200,000 people in Pittsburgh – to meet Tom Mix, Laura LaPlante, Bette Davis, Glenda Farrell, Eleanor Holm, Preston Foster, Lyle Talbot, Claire Dodd, Leo Carrillo and 10 chorus girls. The studio was quick to re-team Powell and Keeler with Berkeley for *The Gold Diggers of 1933*.
She Done Him Wrong
Cavalcade
Rasputin and the Empress MGM tried to get five Barrymores into its historical drama but had to settle for the most famous three – John, Lionel and Ethel (her talkie debut) – when Ethel's son and daughter declined to appear. She was the empress, while Lionel played the mad monk Rasputin who gained influence over her and John was his determined assassin. Others in the cast included Diana Wynyard, Edward Arnold, Ralph Morgan and young Tad Alexander. The film took 104 days to shoot, three times the norm, due to script revisions (the writer was Charles MacArthur), a change of director (to Richard Boleslawski, replacing Charles Brabin), John Barrymore's drinking and other problems. Finally costing over $1 million, its appeal was insufficient to recover such an outlay, and it was one of the studio's bigger loss-makers, especially after the wife of the real killer of Rasputin successfully sued MGM for libel damages in Britain because her

equivalent character in the production was represented as having been Rasputin's lover when she had never met him. MGM deleted the offending passages to continue the film's distribution. The British title was *Rasputin The Mad Monk*.
State Fair

APRIL

King Kong RKO Radio never doubted it had a huge winner on its hands, such was the staggering advance in special effects that it represented thanks to the genius of chief technician Willis O'Brien and his team and to generous funding by the studio. But the creation of the giant ape was more than a technical marvel: he was given a personality of his own to make

audiences care about his fate. (Co-director Merian C. Cooper wrote the "Arabian proverb" which opened the film and described the theme: "And, lo, the beast looked upon the face of beauty. And it stayed its hand from killing. And from that day, it was as one dead.") There was a deliberately slow build-up, delaying Kong's first appearance for 30 minutes and making audiences impatient for something to happen while Max Steiner's music, one of the very first full-fledged film scores, added immeasurably to the excitement when the action got underway. The sound effects developed by Murray Spivack and his team were notable, creating the grunts and roars of King Kong and other prehistoric animals. Fay Wray was to become the "queen of scream" as the object of the ape's tender affections, while Bruce Cabot was a manly hero and Robert Armstrong played the film producer who led the expedition to find Kong and brought him back to display as the eighth wonder of the

King Kong: The eighth wonder of the world. With Fay Wray.

King Kong: The defiant beast.

world in New York. Ernest B. Schoedsack co-directed with Merian C. Cooper. Edgar Wallace worked on the original story with Cooper, while the screenplay was done by James Creelman and Ruth Rose. RKO Radio created a striking exploitation campaign, including radio spot teasers, to whet public interest in seeing the film. On its first release in America, *King Kong* earned nearly three times its negative cost of $672,000, and it was regularly reissued to improve the studio's balance sheet. RKO rushed out a sequel, *Son of Kong*, before the year was over, while the original was re-made in 1976 by producer Dino De Laurentiis.

Cavalcade

42nd Street

The White Sister This was the third filming of the 1909 play by F. Marion Crawford and Walter Hackett about a woman who enters a nunnery believing her lover has been killed in the war and is faced with a difficult choice when he returns. Helen Hayes and Clark Gable starred in Donald Ogden Stewart's adaptation, and Victor Fleming directed for MGM. It was Gable's first film moustached throughout. Lewis Stone, Louise Closser Hale, May Robson and Edward Arnold headed the supporting cast.

A Bedtime Story Maurice Chevalier's breezy charm carried this slight musical comedy, which presented him as a ladies' man who adopts an abandoned baby and is thought to be the father. The Paramount picture made a star out of the six-month-old Baby LeRoy. Helen Twelvetrees played the nursemaid, while Edward Everett Horton and Adrienne Ames

The Working Man: George Arliss, Bette Davis.

were prominently featured. The source of Waldemar Young's screenplay was a novel by Roy Horniman adapted by Benjamin Glazer. The direction was by Norman Taurog.

Gabriel Over the White House Not only is it astonishing to find so politically controversial a film emerging from Hollywood, but it came from the most conservative of studios, MGM. Moreover, it had considerable popularity with audiences and made nearly 100 per cent profit on its meagre production cost. It presented a corrupt American President who is transformed by some kind of divine intervention into a purposeful figure who ends organized crime and obtains full employment, prosperity and world peace. Studio boss Louis B. Mayer saw it as propaganda for Roosevelt and

A Bedtime Story: Baby LeRoy, Helen Twelvetrees, Maurice Chevalier.

deliberately held up its release until Hoover had stepped down from the White House in March, to avoid causing him embarrassment. The film suggested that America needed a kind of benevolent but forceful dictatorship to solve the problems of the Depression. Walter Huston played the key role, with Franchot Tone and Karen Morley in support. The movie was based on a novel (originally written anonymously) by a British Brigadier General, Thomas F. Tweed, and the screenplay was by Carey Wilson and Bertram Bloch. The producer was Walter Wanger (always keen on provocative subjects), the director Gregory La Cava. This was one of many MGM films made under the banner of William Randolph Hearst's Cosmopolitan Productions, which ensured extensive press support in the areas covered by the newspaper magnate's empire. The picture had two endings (both of which survive). In America, the President was seen returning to his old self and dying before he can undo his good work. In Europe, an added five minutes gave an impression of the transformed President as a dangerous figure who is a justifiable subject for euthanasia.

MAY

The Working Man George Arliss starred in a variation on his 1931 hit, *The Millionaire*, as another successful businessman who gives up his own company and takes a rest, this time re-organizing a rival concern and straightening out the profligate lives of two young people (played by Bette Davis and Theodore Newton).

Directed by John Adolfi, the Warner Bros. comedy had a screenplay by Maude T. Howell and Charles Kenyon from an Edgar Franklin story, which later provided the basis for Fox's 1936 *Everybody's Old Man* with Irvin S. Cobb.

Hell Below Walter Huston was the martinet captain of a submarine during World War I, sparring with Robert Montgomery as the disobedient Lieutenant who dies a hero's death. Madge Evans portrayed the captain's daughter who loved the Lieutenant, and Jimmy Durante boxed a kangaroo for light relief. Laird Doyle, Raymond Schrock, John Lee Mahin and John Meehan turned an Edward Ellsberg novel into a screenplay, and Jack Conway directed for MGM.

Picture Snatcher In this bustling Warner Bros. comedy, James Cagney was the ex-convict turned daredevil photographer for a sleazy tabloid who specializes in snapping elusive people. Ralph Bellamy was the editor and former comedienne Alice White, busy making a comeback, was the gal reporter from a rival scandal sheet. Cagney kept up his screen reputation for maltreating the ladies by giving Alice White a rough time as well as snapping the garter on supporting player Renee Whitney. However, Patricia Ellis as his respectable girlfriend gives him a slap across the jaw. Allen Rivkin and P. J. Wolfson scripted from a Danny Ahearn story and Lloyd Bacon called the shots. A limp re-make of 1947 with Richard Travis was called *Escape from Crime*.

JUNE

Gold Diggers of 1933 Warner Bros. wasted no time following up the success of *42nd Street*, returning to Avery Hopwood's 1919 play *The Gold Diggers*, which it had previously filmed as a 1923 silent and as a phenomenally successful 1929 early talkie, for the basis of another backstage musical. The putting-on-a-show theme recurred, with Ned Sparks as the producer in search of backers and wealthy Dick Powell masquerading as a penniless songwriter. Joan Blondell, Ruby Keeler, Aline MacMahon and Ginger Rogers were chorus girls seeking fame or a rich boyfriend, while Warren William and Guy Kibbee were two respectable businessmen who came within grabbing range. Mervyn LeRoy directed the breezy story, scripted by Erwin Gelsey, James Seymour, David Boehm and Ben Markson, but again it was the big musical numbers, staged by Busby Berkeley, that really counted – from the opening "We're in the Money" to the daring "Pettin' in

Picture Snatcher: James Cagney, Ralph Bellamy, Alice White.

the Park" to the brave and mournful "Remember My Forgotten Man", they reflected the moods of the period and delighted with their extravagant sets, camerawork and co-ordinated movement of the numerous performers. The songs were more of the work of Al Dubin and Harry Warren.

Adorable In this Ruritanian romance, Janet Gaynor was the princess who went to a servants' ball disguised as a manicurist and fell in love with a naval lieutenant pretending to be a tradesman. He was played by French actor Henri Garat, the co-star of four European musical films with Lilian Harvey (including the French version of the celebrated *Congress Dances*), making what proved to be his only Hollywood film (on which his first name was spelled Henry). He and Gaynor danced and sang three numbers with lyrics by George Marion Jr and music by Richard A. Whiting. Wilhelm (soon William) Dieterle directed this airy concoction, written by George Marion Jr and Jane Storm,

using the story by Paul Franck and Billy Wilder for a 1931 German film *Ihre Hoheit Befiehlt*.

I Cover the Waterfront This inexpensively-made independent production (by Edward Small's Reliance Pictures, released by United Artists) was a hard-hitting exposé of a smuggling racket, with reporter Ben Lyon befriending Claudette Colbert as the daughter of Ernest Torrence's wily fisherman to uncover her father's method of sneaking Chinese immigrants and opium into the country. (It was Torrence's last film – he had died in May, aged 54.) Jack Jevne and Wells Root scripted from a factual story by Max Miller and the direction was by James Cruze.

JULY

Gold Diggers of 1933

Hold Your Man MGM put Gable and Harlow together again in this comedy drama. He was the con man and she was the hard-boiled dame he betrayed, then returned to when he learned that she was pregnant. Sam Wood directed their lively sparring match, and Anita Loos and Howard Emmett Rogers wrote the script. The rest of the cast included Stuart Erwin, Dorothy Burgess, Muriel Kirkland and Elizabeth Patterson.

The Mayor of Hell James Cagney was the brash young hoodlum who gets a political appointment to run a reformatory and wins the kids over by talking to them on their own level. Madge Evans was the admiring resident nurse and Dudley Digges the tough superintendent he deposed. The boys were led by Frankie Darro and included former Our Gang member Farina. The odd mixture of social drama and melodrama was written by Edward Chodorov from an Islin Auster story. Warner Bros. assigned Archie Mayo to direct. The studio squeezed two later pictures for the Dead End Kids out of more or less the

I COVER THE WATERFRONT

with CLAUDETTE COLBERT BEN LYON ERNEST TORRENCE

Presented by JOSEPH M. SCHENCK
Produced by Edward Small

"I've seen chinamen smuggled into the country in the bellies of sharks — and seen the poor devils thrown overboard — and drowned — ALIVE — to destroy evidence.

"I've seen everything and DONE everything — yes, even loved a dame and shot her father — to get a story — and I got it — and I'm TELLING it!"

From the famous book by Max Miller

UNITED ARTISTS PICTURE

same story: *Crime School* (1938) and *Hell's Kitchen* (1939).

College Humor Paramount gave Bing Crosby a chance to show he had star quality in this musical comedy with a campus background. He was the professor fancied by co-ed Mary Carlisle over Richard Arlen's he-man football star. Jack Oakie contributed to the humour along with George Burns and Gracie Allen. There were four songs by Arthur Johnston and Sam Coslow. Claude Binyon and Frank Butler based the script on a story by Dean Fales. Wesley Ruggles was the director.

When Ladies Meet Ann Harding and Myrna Loy were romantic rivals again, as in *The Animal Kingdom*, this time with Loy as the free thinker and Frank Morgan's publisher the prize they fought over. He is already married to Harding but pursued by Loy's novelist, who is really better suited to Robert Montgomery's newspaperman. Alice Brady, making her first film in 10 years, stole the show as a scatterbrained society hostess. MGM's comedy of manners was based on Rachel Crothers' 1932 stage success. John Meehan and Leon Gordon converted it to a film script for Harry Beaumont to direct. The same studio re-made it in 1941 with Joan Crawford.

AUGUST

Tugboat Annie Re-teamed for the first time since *Min and Bill* in another waterfront piece, Marie Dressler and Wallace Beery bickered and feuded their way through this boisterous

Tugboat Annie: Marie Dressler.

comedy with Robert Young as the son whose naval career was a bone of contention and with Maureen O'Sullivan as the girl he loved. Mervyn LeRoy directed it for MGM

College Humor: Bing Crosby, Lona Andre, Richard Arlen.

from a script by Zelda Sears and Eve Greene based on *Saturday Evening Post* stories by Norman Reilly Raine. The title character returned in *Tugboat Annie Rides Again* (1940), played by Marjorie Rambeau for Warner Bros.

Song of Songs Paramount temporarily broke up the partnership of Marlene Dietrich and director Josef von Sternberg and put their star into this high-flown romantic drama under Rouben Mamoulian's direction. She had to play a virginal peasant girl in 19th-century Germany who is forced into marriage with Lionel Atwill's middle-aged baron when she really loves Brian Aherne's penniless sculptor. Later she performs two songs when she becomes a nightclub artiste. Leon Birinski and Samuel Hoffenstein based their screenplay on a novel by Hermann Sudermann and the 1914 play by Edward Sheldon.

Moonlight and Pretzels Leo Carrillo had achieved some popularity as a gangster in *Hell Bound* (1930). In this penny-pinching putting-on-a-show musical, filmed in New York and released by Universal to cash in on the popularity of *42nd Street* and *Gold Diggers of 1933*, he was the gambler who became a backer and Mary Brian was the *ingénue* who (for a change) declined to step in on the opening night and replace the star (Lillian Miles). The songs were by E. Y. Harburg and Sammy Fain, and others. The director was Monte Brice, who also wrote the picture with Sig Herzig and Arthur Jarrett.

Double Harness More Ann Harding as the ambitious woman who tricks wealthy playboy William Powell into marriage and then has a fight to keep him. In support were Lucile Browne, Henry Stephenson, Reginald Owen, Kay Hammond and others. RKO

Radio's sophisticated comedy came from the play by Edward P. Montgomery, adapted by Jane Murfin and directed by John Cromwell.

Gold Diggers of 1933

SEPTEMBER

Tugboat Annie

Morning Glory Katharine Hepburn consolidated her success in *A Bill of Divorcement* with this theatre drama in which she was the small-town girl determined to be an actress who becomes a star overnight when she replaces a temperamental leading lady. The two men in her life were Adolphe Menjou's suave producer and Douglas Fairbanks Jr's eager playwright. Lowell Sherman directed the RKO Radio picture, which had a screenplay by Howard J. Green from the play by Zoë Akins. The 1957 re-make with Susan Strasberg was called *Stage Struck*.

Captured! A rare prisoner-of-war drama set in a German camp, this

Morning Glory: Adolphe Menjou, Katharine Hepburn.

Warner Bros. production starred Leslie Howard and Douglas Fairbanks Jr as two captive British army officers, old friends from Oxford days (when they also knew the camp commandant, played by Paul Lukas). Margaret Lindsay is the woman they both love. One sacrifices his life helping a mass-escape which enables the other to return to her. A play by Sir Philip Gibbs formed the basis of Edward Chodorov's screenplay. The director was Roy Del Ruth.

The Masquerader Ronald Colman played dual roles, as a dissipated Member of Parliament and as the lookalike cousin, who takes his place at Westminster as well as in his complicated private life, which includes Elissa Landi as an estranged wife and Juliette Compton as a titled mistress. The improbable material had been popular for years, from 1905 when Katherine Cecil Thurston first wrote the novel, becoming a very successful play by John Hunter Booth and a 1922 film. Howard Estabrook handled the latest adaptation, and Richard Wallace directed for Samuel Goldwyn. United Artists distributed the picture, which ended an 18-film association of Colman and Goldwyn on an upbeat note.

Penthouse An MGM crime drama with a light touch, this featured Warner Baxter as the lawyer sleuth, Myrna Loy as the heroine, Mae Clarke as the murderer's victim and Phillips Holmes as the accused. Writers Frances Goodrich and Albert Hackett (working from a story by Arthur Somers Roche) and director W. S. Van Dyke, along with Myrna Loy, would do more of the same with *The Thin Man*. British cinemas showed *Penthouse* as *Crooks in*

Clover. MGM's 1939 re-make with Walter Pidgeon was entitled *Society Lawyer*.

Lady for a Day Heart-warming fantasy: May Robson as Apple Annie

Lady For a Day: Warren William, May Robson.

has been reduced by the Depression to selling apples on Broadway for a living, while pretending to her daughter in Europe that she is well off; when the daughter returns with a posh fiancé, her friends in the gambling and underworld fraternity set her up as a society lady for a day to keep up the pretence. Warren William led the do-gooders. The Damon Runyon story was written by Robert Riskin and proved ideal material for Frank Capra, encouraging him away from drama and on to the series of social comedies for which he is best remembered. The film brought the 75-year-old Miss Robson to her peak of fame and gave Columbia its biggest box-office success of the year as well as providing the mini-major studio

with considerable prestige. Capra re-made it with Bette Davis and Glenn Ford as *Pocketful of Miracles* (1961).

Paddy, The Next Best Thing Janet Gaynor starred as the lovable, well-meaning Irish lass who saves her older sister (Margaret Lindsay) from marrying a wealthy admirer (Warner Baxter) selected by her improvident father (Walter Connolly), only to fall in love with him herself. Gaynor and Baxter charmed audiences as they had in *Daddy Long Legs*, and Harvey Stephens was around as a romantic alternative for the other sister. Harry Lachman was the director and Edwin Burke the scenarist of the Fox picture, based on Gertrude Page's play, previously filmed in England in 1923 with Mae Marsh.

OCTOBER

The Bowery The first Twentieth Century production (released by United Artists) was a roistering comedy set in New York City's Bowery during the Gay Nineties. Built around the rivalry between two saloon keepers played by Wallace Beery and George Raft and culminating in a bet about jumping off the Brooklyn Bridge, the picture had further star appeal with kid actor Jackie Cooper as the newsboy who idolizes Beery much as he did in *The Champ*. Fay Wray and Pert Kelton were also prominent. Howard Estabrook and James Gleason based their screenplay on a novel by Michael Simmons and Bessie Rogow. Raoul Walsh directed.

I'm No Angel Mae West wrote and starred in this further romp as the circus performer who tames lions and men. She had five songs including the title number and gave out with the

The Bowery: Jackie Cooper, Wallace Beery.

now classic lines, "It's not the men in my life but the life in my men" and (to her black maid, played by Gertrude Howard) "Beulah, peel me a grape." Cary Grant was again Mae's choice for leading man. Gregory Ratoff, Edward Arnold and Kent Taylor were also featured. It was slightly milder than *She Done Him Wrong* and even more successful. Lowell Brentano and Harlan Thompson also had a hand in the script, while Wesley Ruggles directed. The picture cost Paramount $225,000 to make and brought the studio 10 times that amount from North America alone, with at least an extra $1 million from abroad.

I'm No Angel: Mae West.

Too Much Harmony Paramount had another success with this Bing Crosby vehicle, a backstage musical comedy written by Harry Ruskin and Joseph L. Mankiewicz, and directed by Edward Sutherland. Bing was the crooner engaged to a gold-digging Lilyan Tashman and loved by the

more decent Judith Allen. Jack Oakie co-starred, and there were songs by Sam Coslow and Arthur Johnston.
Dinner at Eight MGM's all-star follow-up to *Grand Hotel* was cheaper to make and even more profitable. The stars were used as little as possible, working from two to twelve days on the picture, and the cost was kept under $400,000. Based on the 1932 stage comedy-drama by George S. Kaufman and Edna Ferber, it was David O. Selznick's first production on arriving from RKO, and he brought with him George Cukor to direct. Playing the hosts at the dinner were Lionel Barrymore as a shipping magnate with financial and medical problems and Billie Burke as his wife. Guests include Wallace Beery as a vulgar financier with Jean Harlow as his brash and unfaithful young wife; and Marie Dressler as a celebrated actress. John Barrymore was the movie star ruined by the talkies who is involved with the shipping magnate's daughter (Madge Evans). Others featured were Lee Tracy, Edmund Lowe, Jean Hersholt, Karen Morley, Louise Closser Hale, Phillips Holmes and May Robson. The screenplay was by Frances Marion and Herman J. Mankiewicz, with Donald Ogden Stewart contributing the famous concluding lines in which Harlow refers to having read a prophecy that machinery is going to replace women "in every profession" and Dressler eyes her figure up and down and says bitchily, "Oh, my dear, that's something you need never worry about!"
Lady for a Day

NOVEMBER

I'm No Angel
Footlight Parade Warner Bros. scored a hat trick with this rapid musical extravaganza follow-up to *42nd Street* and *Gold Diggers of 1933*. This time James Cagney was an added attraction, playing a producer of live prologues for movie theatres who shuts himself away with his performers to rehearse three big numbers that will out-do his rivals. Ruby Keeler was a hoofer, Dick Powell a singer, and Joan Blondell the producer's tough, devoted secretary. Not only was it a change to see Cagney well-behaved, but he also made his debut in song and dance when he performed the climactic "Shanghai Lil" number (music and lyrics by Harry Warren and Al Dubin), ending up with a tribute to President Roosevelt. This was one of three spectacular sequences devised by Busby Berkeley for the movie, the others being "By a Waterfall" and "Honeymoon Hotel" (with music and lyrics by Sammy Fain and Irving Kahal). Manuel Seff and

James Seymour provided the script and Lloyd Bacon the non-musical direction.
The Kennel Murder Case William Powell returned to the part of the debonair sleuth Philo Vance whom he had previously portrayed in *The Canary Murder Case* (1929) and three other films for Paramount. Warner Bros. made this adaptation of an S. S. Van Dine novel, supporting Powell with Mary Astor, Eugene Pallette, Ralph Morgan, Helen Vinson and Jack LaRue as he proves that a dead man in a locked room did not commit suicide. Director Michael Curtiz zipped through the script by Robert Presnell, Robert N. Lee and Peter Milne with his usual panache.
Hoopla Though *Hoopla* dissatisfied Clara Bow and most critics, it proved again that the former flapper star hadn't lost her appeal to audiences. Nevertheless, she decided to call it quits and retire. In this version of a 1927 John Kenyon Nicholson play, *The Barker*, first filmed under that title as a silent with Dorothy Mackaill in 1928, Clara played the hula dancer in a travelling carnival who, in seducing the son (Richard Cromwell) of the chief barker (Preston Foster) for a bet, finds herself falling for his youthful sincerity. Bow dances at the Chicago World's Fair to help him through his law studies. Also cast were

Herbert Mundin (as a short-changing ticket seller), James Gleason (as Bow's dour manager) and Minna Gombell (another dancer). Frank Lloyd directed at Fox from a screenplay by Bradley King and Joseph Moncure March.

Little Women RKO Radio's lavish film of the Louisa May Alcott novel revealed by its huge success that there was an appetite for gentle stories and period settings. The film also exported well, being noted as the studio's top hit worldwide in 1938. Katharine Hepburn, Joan Bennett, Frances Dee and Jean Parker played the four sisters growing up in difficult times during the Civil War, and Hepburn triumphed as the hoydenish Jo who gains the insight to become a writer. David O. Selznick had instigated the production and assigned the direction to George Cukor before leaving RKO. Sarah Y. Mason and Victor Heerman made the screen adaptation. Paul Lukas, Edna May Oliver, Henry Stephenson, Spring Byington and Douglass Montgomery were also cast. The novel had previously been filmed in 1919 and MGM re-made the RKO version in 1949.

Bombshell Jean Harlow kidded herself as a sexpot movie star who wants to marry and raise a child in this MGM satire. Lee Tracy was the ruthless studio publicist who fixes her up with a phoney lover and makes her glad to get back to work in pictures. Franchot Tone, C. Aubrey Smith and Mary Forbes were the society types she met in Palm Springs, Frank Morgan her inebriated father, Una Merkel her opportunist secretary, and Pat O'Brien offered consolation as the temperamental film director who really loves her. Victor Fleming directed in quick tempo from the screenplay by Jules Furthman and John Lee Mahin based on an unproduced play by Caroline Francke and Mack Crane. The title sounded too much like a war movie for Britain, where it became *Blonde Bombshell*, the title it also often has for American TV showing.

DECEMBER

Little Women
Dancing Lady MGM felt Joan Crawford's appeal was slipping, so delayed production of this new picture until Clark Gable was available to shore her up. She was the lady from burlesque who became a dancing star on Broadway with the help of Gable's hard-boiled director of musicals. Franchot Tone was the millionaire playboy she turned down, Ted Healy and the Three Stooges provided some comedy along with Robert Benchley as a columnist, Nelson Eddy sang a

Dancing Lady: Joan Crawford.

Rodgers and Hart number and Fred Astaire made his screen debut with five minutes of screen time performing a clog number and dancing with Crawford in top hat and tails. The story came from a James Warner Bellah magazine serial adapted for the screen by Allen Rivkin and P. J. Wolfson. The songs included "Everything I Have Is Yours". Robert Z. Leonard was the director.

Only Yesterday: John Boles, Margaret Sullavan.

Alice in Wonderland Paramount's Christmas treat for family audiences was an all-star version of the Lewis Carroll classic tales in which the famous players were hidden behind masks and costumes and recognizable only by their voices. Newcomer Charlotte Henry played Alice, while Richard Arlen (Cheshire Cat), Gary Cooper (White Knight), W. C. Fields (Humpty Dumpty), Cary Grant (Mock Turtle), Edward Everett Horton (Mad Hatter), Jack Oakie (Tweedledum), Edna May Oliver (Red Queen), May Robson (Queen of Hearts) and Charlie Ruggles (March Hare) were among those she met. Joseph L. Mankiewicz collaborated on the screenplay with the art director William Cameron Menzies, while Norman Z. McLeod directed.

Roman Scandals In the fourth Eddie Cantor musical comedy from Samuel Goldwyn, the pop-eyed comic dreamed himself back to ancient Rome to face lions and race chariots. Busby Berkeley's musical numbers, featuring the Goldwyn Girls even more scantily clad than usual (among them, Lucille Ball), included a number with celebrated singer Ruth Etting called "No More Love" and the climactic "Keep Young and Beautiful". Edward Arnold was a cruel emperor and Verree Teasdale a venomous empress. Somehow it took six well-known writers to complete the script (George S. Kaufman, Robert E. Sherwood, William Anthony McGuire, George Oppenheimer,

Arthur Sheekman and Nat Perrin). Goldwyn still believed in spending money to make money and put $1.1 million into *Roman Scandals*, which showed a healthy profit under United Artists release.

Only Yesterday Universal introduced Broadway actress Margaret Sullavan to the screen in this blatant tear-jerker as a woman who has a baby after a one-night affair during World War I, and rises above the stigma of being an unwed mother to succeed in business. She then meets the father (almost inevitably, John Boles), who doesn't even remember her, and she allows him to seduce her all over again. . . . Writers William Hurlbut, Arthur Richman and George O'Neill worked on suggestions from a book by Frederick Lewis Allen, and John M. Stahl directed.

The Invisible Man The special effects were the star attraction of this Universal melodrama in which Claude Rains played the man who finds the secret of invisibility but at tragic cost – the drug he uses slowly drives him mad. Rains had one of the oddest screen debuts – in a starring role but seen for only a few seconds when he becomes visible at the end. John P. Fulton created the technical wizardry, while R. C. Sherriff adapted the H. G. Wells story, which retained its English setting. James Whale's direction emphasized both the eccentric comedy and the pathos of the situation. Supporting players included Gloria Stuart, Henry Travers, William Harrigan, Dudley Digges and Una O'Connor.

THE ACADEMY AWARDS

There were no Academy Awards presented during 1933. The Academy was in a state of crisis and needed time to regain the trust of the community. It was decided to move to a calendar year basis and to achieve this by having the next Awards presented in 1934 for an extended period, covering the whole of 1933 as well as the months of August to December 1932 that had elapsed since the last selection period.

TEN BEST–CRITICS' CHOICE

Slightly fewer – 348 – critics participated in the *Film Daily* poll, producing a 10 best that were decisively headed by *Cavalcade*. The films and votes were:

1.	*Cavalcade*	304
2.	*42nd Street*	209
3.	*The Private Life of Henry VIII* (British)	187
4.	*Lady for a Day*	179
5.	*State Fair*	169
6.	*A Farewell to Arms*	167
7.	*She Done Him Wrong*	158
8.	*I Am a Fugitive from a Chain Gang*	156
9.	*Maedchen in Uniform* (German)	137
10.	*Rasputin and the Empress*	128
	Close Runners Up	
11.	*The Animal Kingdom*	121
12.	*Tugboat Annie*	102

All the films were popular with the public as well.

CLOSE RUNNERS UP

Closest in popularity to the preceding hits of the year were the following: *Christopher Bean* (also known as *His Sweetheart*) (November), *Clear All Wires* (March), *Counsellor-at-Law* (December), *Don't Bet on Love* (August), *Duck Soup* (November), *International House* (June), *The King's Vacation* (February), *Looking Forward* (May), *Mama Loves Papa* (August), *Night Flight* (October), *Out All Night* (May), *The Power and the Glory* (October), *Reunion in Vienna* (June), *They Just Had to Get Married* (January), *Today We Live* (May), *20,000 Years in Sing Sing* (January), *Voltaire* (August).

1934

Flying Down to Rio
Ginger Rogers,
Fred Astaire

In 1934, there was hope. Movie theatre attendances were on the rise, up by some 10 million to an average 70 million a week. The increase was felt least in the downtown areas of the big cities, suggesting resistance to the higher prices charged there. Even so, the studios had more money coming in. Loew's as a whole declared a profit of $7.5 million on the year to September, of which MGM provided $4.7 million, a huge increase over the previous year. Even Universal managed to show a miniscule profit, its first since 1931, while RKO was almost in the black, and only Warner Bros. lost a substantial amount – $2.5 million compared with $6.3 the previous year. The main problem of the year was the campaign by religious and other groups to remove the elements they found offensive in movies – pressure to which Hollywood succumbed, finally making effective the Production Code that had existed since 1930.

Fortunately for Hollywood, a curly-topped, precocious moppet called Shirley Temple proved that there was money to be made from wholesome family entertainment, as did the continuing success of *Little Women* in 1934 and the popularity of other old-fashioned or traditional subjects, *Anne of Green Gables* and *Girl of the Limberlost*. Bing Crosby, too, was fast becoming a favourite. However, Samuel Goldwyn's attempts to launch Anna Sten with *Nana* and *We Live Again* were rebuffed by the public.

THE CLEAN SCREEN

It was undoubtedly Mae West who most outraged church bodies and brought about a new moral crusade to clean up the screen. The campaign, which apparently began in Detroit, gathered power in Philadelphia and Boston thanks to the widespread publicity it gained there. The threat was simply to boycott theatres showing offensive films, and at a time when attendances were still showing the effects of the Depression, it was enough to scare theatre owners and the studios themselves as the idea spread like wildfire. In Washington D.C., for instance, 9,000 Roman Catholic women formed a "Legion of Decency" in May and threatened to start boycotting local theatres showing "offensive" films from two weeks later.

In June, religious leaders gathered in Washington to consider demanding federal censorship. Not only Catholics but other religious and parent-teacher groups and local clubs joined in the campaign. Their targets were films that hurt religion, undermined school education and degraded women. A Catholic survey claimed 107 "major violations" in 133 features released in the first five months of 1934: 26 had plots built on illicit love, there were 13 in which seduction was accomplished, 18 in which characters lived in open adultery, 31 in which murders were committed, 17 in which gangsters enjoyed leading roles, while only 30 were suitable for children or adolescents. There was no conclusive evidence that films had a particular destructive moral influence on children or adults, and the Civil Liberties Union opposed the crusade. But, besides Catholics, there were organizations of Jews, Methodists, Baptists, Lutherans and so forth whose members pledged themselves not to attend films that were designated as offensive.

The Motion Picture Producers and Distributors Association (MPPDA, the Hays Office) rushed to defuse the campaign by putting its house in order. It insisted on strict adherence by its member companies (all the big Hollywood studios) to the Production Code that had been established in 1930, created a new Production Code Administration (PCA) and a new seal to appear on approved films, and instituted fines for studios that infringed the regulations. In future, scripts would be vetted in advance of production to remove offensive elements. No longer would a jury of producers rule on matters of dissension, but appeals would be heard by the board of directors of the MPPDA itself. A Catholic of high repute, Joseph I. Breen, was appointed head of the PCA.

No Hollywood company wanted to be the first to attract publicity for having a film turned down by the PCA or for being fined for breaking the rules by releasing a film not given a seal. And so the studios were forced to re-examine not only their production plans but films already shooting and even some that were being previewed and ready for release.

Paramount had already previewed its new Mae West film, *It Ain't No Sin*, but decided to re-shoot a considerable portion and retitle it *Belle of the Nineties*. Among the losses was footage of 20 cockatoos chirping "It ain't no sin!"; among the additions was a wedding sequence that sanctified a relationship in the film and caused *Variety* to headline "It Ain't – Now". MGM withdrew its completed Jean Harlow film, *Born to Be Kissed*, put it back into production for "laundering" not once but twice, and gave it the anodyne title *The Girl from Missouri* after toying with *It Pays to Be Good*. The company also had to take a close look at its new Garbo picture about infidelity, *The Painted Veil*, as well as *The Green Hat*, its new film from the notorious Michael Arlen novel starring Constance Bennett, which was re-titled *Outcast Lady*. The title of another picture, *Sacred and Profane Love*, was altered to *Chained*. Warner Bros. decided to re-shoot the last two reels of *Madame DuBarry*. The newcomer, Twentieth Century Productions, was forced to re-film large portions of *Born to Be Bad*, leading to its failure at the box-office. As a result of new films being delayed, many theatres were forced to put in reissues like *Min and Bill* to fill the gaps. Distributors had to grant exhibitors the right to drop films they had contracted to show if there was a genuine protest on moral grounds.

The studios also decided that many of their

projects were now too hot to handle. MGM abandoned plans to film James M. Cain's novel *The Postman Always Rings Twice* and Sam Goldwyn postponed *Barbary Coast*, all set to star Gary Cooper and Anna Sten.

Meanwhile, branches of the Legion of Decency started examining films in release and both *The Thin Man* and *The Life of Vergie Winters* were put on the blacklist in some areas. It was noted that the takings of *Vergie Winters* benefited considerably from the attendant publicity when theatres stubbornly continued screening it. In one small town the pastor positioned himself next to the box-office of the only theatre during the run of Mae West's new film and greeted a surprising number of his parishioners taking a stroll past the theatre. On a more apocryphal note, a woman clutching a dog was refused entry to a theatre showing DeMille's bathtub epic *Cleopatra* and retorted, "How absurd! What possible harm can *Cleopatra* do to my pet?"

Hollywood was disturbed to note that many magazines were also taking up the idea of rating films as a way of telling their readers what to see. Despite Hollywood's efforts to put its house in order, the churches still went ahead and had pledges printed for widespread distribution, planning a start date of nationally organized resistance to morally objectionable films. The problem was that by then there weren't any. In *The Painted Veil*, for instance, Garbo was still an unfaithful wife but the Catholics approved of her adultery because it was shown as "a cruel, unlovely, bitter and shameful thing". Nevertheless, over seven million Catholics are believed to have signed the pledges.

The Production Code was abolished in 1967.

For Better Motion Pictures

DECLARATION OF PURPOSE

(sign and give to your pastor or organization)*

I wish to join with other Protestants, cooperating with Catholics and Jews, in condemning vile and unwholesome moving pictures. I unite with all who protest against them as a grave menace to youth, to home life, to country, and to religion.

I condemn absolutely those salacious motion pictures which, with other degrading agencies, are corrupting public morals and promoting a sex mania in our land.

I shall do all that I can to arouse public opinion against the portrayal of vice as a normal condition of affairs, and against depicting criminals of any class as heroes and heroines, presenting their filthy philosophy of life as something acceptable to decent men and women.

I unite with all who condemn the display of suggestive advertisements on bill-boards, at theatre entrances, and the favorable notices given to immoral motion pictures.

Considering these evils, I declare my purpose to remain away from all motion pictures which offend decency and Christian morality. I will try to induce others to do the same.

I make this protest in a spirit of self-respect, and with the conviction that the American public does not demand filthy pictures, but clean entertainment and educational features.

Name..

Address ....

That there may be a united front, the pledge of the Legion of Decency has been used with only slight changes. Organizations and individuals are free to formulate their own pledges. The important thing is not the form of a pledge but to keep its purpose.

(Issued by the Federal Council of Churches, 105 East 22nd Street, New York.)

*A duplicate copy of this Declaration to be retained by the signer.

A pledge written for circulation to Protestants in 1934.

HITS OF THE YEAR

JANUARY

Dinner at Eight (On wider release at normal prices.)

Flying Down to Rio Two stars were born when Fred Astaire and Ginger Rogers performed "The Carioca" and danced away with this RKO Radio musical, one of the few films of the 1930s to be set in Latin America. Ginger also led the aerial ballet set on the wings of airplanes over Rio. Gene Raymond (as an orchestra leader), Dolores Del Rio (as a Brazilian bombshell) and Raul Roulien (as her fiancé) were billed ahead of Astaire and Rogers, but they were left behind as Fred and Ginger registered their powerful chemistry together. Thornton Freeland directed, Dave Gould staged the dances, Vincent Youmans wrote the music, Gus Kahn and Edward Elischu provided the lyrics, and Cyril Hume, H. W. Hanneman and Erwin Gelsey based their script on an Anne Caldwell play.

Design for Living Ernst Lubitsch made this screen version of Noel Coward's hit play in which the author had co-starred with Alfred Lunt and Lynn Fontanne on Broadway. For the screen, Gary Cooper and Fredric March were the artistic types who shared the affections of Miriam Hopkins when she couldn't decide between them, while Edward Everett Horton was the husband she left behind. Cooper and March gave it a slower pace and replaced the more brittle sophistication of the play with an eccentric sense of humour, but it was still outrageously immoral for the period. Ben Hecht did the screen adaptation for Paramount, boasting that he had retained only one of Coward's lines.

Roman Scandals

By Candlelight This romantic comedy in a European setting had Paul Lukas as a butler and Elissa Landi as a personal maid who meet on a train and mistake each other for a prince and a *grande dame*. Four writers (Hans Kraly, F. Hugh Herbert, Karen de Wolf and Ruth Cummings) fashioned a shooting script out of a play by Siegried Geyer for Universal, and it took a change of director (James Whale stepping in after production had started) to realize the delicate charm of the material. Nils Asther co-starred as the real prince whose amorous reputation has been assumed by his manservant.

Dancing Lady

Little Women

Son of Kong RKO Radio put out this tame follow-up to *King Kong* while

Flying Down to Rio: Gene Raymond, Fred Astaire, Ginger Rogers.

the interest was still hot, and made Kong's furry offspring into a cuddly, playful character who was amusing rather than fearful. The film clearly had none of the power of its predecessor but lower-cost sequels were as sure a way of making money in the 1930s as later. Special effects genius Willis O'Brien and his team worked on it, and Ernest B. Schoedsack directed from a screenplay by his wife Ruth Rose. Robert Armstrong carried over his role from the earlier film, while Helen Mack was the suffering heroine.

Sons of the Desert This feature-length Laurel and Hardy comedy is the one in which they sneak off to the annual convention of the social fraternity known as the Sons of the Desert in Chicago, while pretending to their wives (Mae Busch and Dorothy Christie) that they are going to Honolulu for the sake of Ollie's health. Frank Craven and Byron Morgan developed the story and William A. Seiter directed Hal Roach's production for MGM release. In Britain, it was retitled as *Fraternally Yours*, since the US title suggested an African adventure.

FEBRUARY

Carolina Fox returned to some of the elements that had made *State Fair* so popular in this gentle story of Janet Gaynor as the daughter of a Yankee tenant farmer falling in love with the owner of a Southern plantation (Robert Young) soon after the Civil War. Henry King directed Reginald Berkeley's adaptation of a 1931 Paul Green play. Lionel Barrymore and Henrietta Crosman played the girl's parents and Shirley Temple had a small bit in her first appearance in a Fox film. Parts were shot on location in the South and there were songs included.

Queen Christina Garbo's first film in more than a year presented her as the 17th-century Swedish sovereign, faced with an arranged marriage, who dresses in male costume to travel around undetected. Forced to share accommodation at an inn with John Gilbert's newly arrived Spanish ambassador, she is soon caught up in a rapturous love affair. The scene in which she carefully memorizes the

Sons of the Desert: Oliver Hardy, Mae Busch, Stan Laurel.

room they've shared and the concluding shot in which she stands expressionless at the bows of a ship taking her lover's body home to Spain have become classic sequences, a tribute to director Rouben Mamoulian's masterful direction. Garbo insisted on John Gilbert co-starring wih her although production had started with Laurence Olivier in the ambassador's role, and it was Gilbert's best opportunity in sound films. S. N. Behrman, H. M. Harwood, Salka Viertel and Margaret F. Levin were responsible for the story and screenplay of MGM's film, produced by Walter Wanger, with a supporting cast that included Ian Keith, Lewis Stone, C. Aubrey Smith and Reginald Owen.

Moulin Rouge Constance Bennett took on a dual role in this Twentieth Century production: the blonde wife of songwriter Franchot Tone, she masquerades as her brunette sister to rekindle her marriage and singing career. The Harry Warren–Al Dubin score included "Boulevard of Broken Dreams" (sung by Constance Bennett) and "Coffee in the Morning" (sung by Russ Columbo). The script by Nunnally Johnson and Henry Lehrman was based on a play by Lyon de Bri but seemed to be an uncredited re-working of a 1925 Constance Talmadge comedy, *Her Sister from Paris*, which also had close similarities to the 1931 MGM film *The Guardsman*. Sidney Lanfield's direction helped to establish Constance Bennett as a comedienne. It was a United Artists release.

MARCH

It Happened One Night Here was a slight piece about a runaway heiress (Claudette Colbert) and a brash reporter (Clark Gable) who have fun together travelling on the cheap across the country. The film that director Frank Capra and writer Robert Riskin created from Samuel Hopkins Adams' short story proved a thorough delight for audiences and became one of the year's biggest hits. With no suitable stars of its own, Columbia had to borrow Colbert from Paramount and Gable from MGM, with neither star too enthusiastic about the assignment and both revealing new depths as ingratiating comedians. Among its highlights were the hitchhiking episode in which Colbert demonstrates the power of a shapely leg to attract a lift, and the "Wall of

It Happened One Night: Clark Gable, Claudette Colbert.

Jericho" scene in which a blanket is hung down the middle of a cabin to give Colbert some protection from Gable when they are forced to share a tourist cabin overnight. Gable reputedly dealt a body blow to the underwear industry when he revealed that he didn't wear an undershirt. Walter Connolly was the spoiled brat's irascible father. The 1956 musical remake was called *You Can't Run Away from It*.

Death Takes a Holiday Death assumes human guise in the form of Fredric March to discover why he is so feared

Queen Christina: Greta Garbo, John Gilbert.

Death Takes a Holiday: Evelyn Venable, Fredric March.

on earth. He finds a young girl, played by Evelyn Venable, who loves him even on learning his true identity. Maxwell Anderson had adapted a play by Alberto Casella into a Broadway success of 1929–30. He worked on

THE ACADEMY AWARDS

This year's awards were presented on 16 March at the Ambassador Hotel, and eligible pictures were those shown from August 1932 to the end of 1933. *Cavalcade* won the award for Best Picture, Best Director and Best Interior Decoration (William S. Darling). Charles Laughton won as Best Actor for *The Private Life of Henry VIII*, a big honour for a British-made film. Katharine Hepburn was Best Actress for *Morning Glory*. Writing awards went to *Little Women* (Best Adaptation – Victor Heerman and Sarah Y. Mason) and *One Way Passage* (Best Original Story – by Robert Lord). *A Farewell to Arms* won for Best Cinematography (Charles B. Lang Jr) and Best Sound Recording (Harold C. Lewis). Walt Disney's *Three Little Pigs* gave the producer his second win in the Best Cartoon category. In his acceptance speech he referred to the Award as an "Oscar", the first use of its nickname in public. It seems most likely that a member of the Academy's staff, Margaret Herrick, originated the nickname when she said that the statuette was reminiscent of her uncle Oscar, although Bette Davis and columnist Sidney Skolsky have also laid claim to providing the sobriquet.

again on show in this First National (Warner Bros.) musical drama set in a Paris nightspot with various intermingled stories. Al Jolson recovered some of his old popularity playing the club's owner and singing once again in blackface a jaunty minstrel-style number (now considered racially offensive), "Going to Heaven on a Mule" (one of six pieces by Warren and Dubin); Dolores Del Rio was the Montmartre club's singer; Dick Powell was the bandleader who vied with Jolson for her affections; Ricardo Cortez was the dancer she loved; Kay Francis was the bored wife of a banker; and Guy Kibbee and Hugh Herbert were providers of comic relief. Berkeley's most celebrated number featured some eight dancers endlessly multiplied by mirrors so that they seemed to number hundreds. Lloyd Bacon directed. Earl Baldwin's script came from a German play by Geza Herczeg, Karl Farkas and Robert Katscher.

Paramount's screen version with Gladys Lehman. Thanks to intelligent handling by March, director Mitchell Leisen and photographer Charles Lang, the fantasy had considerable poetic force and atmosphere. Sir Guy Standing and Gail Patrick were among the supporting players. Paramount feared the title might be off-putting, tested the film with alternatives and found it wasn't.
Queen Christina

APRIL

Riptide Norma Shearer had lost none of her popularity after 18 months away from the screen when she reappeared

in this marital drama, playing the American wife of Herbert Marshall's British aristocrat. Their marriage is strained by her renewed friendship with an old flame, Robert Montgomery's man about town. Mrs Patrick Campbell made her second screen appearance as the husband's aunt and it was Lilyan Tashman's last, as Shearer's fun-loving sister (she died of cancer on 21 March in her mid-thirties). MGM's picture was a screen original written and directed by Edmund Goulding.
Wonder Bar Busby Berkeley's dazzling choreographic skills were

Riptide: Norma Shearer, Robert Montgomery, Herbert Marshall.

The House of Rothschild George Arliss starred in this biopic about the rise of the Rothschild banking empire. From difficult material that eulogized bankers in a time of Depression, and that covered anti-Semitism, came the top box-office attraction of the year, and a huge boost for the standing of Darryl Zanuck's Twentieth Century Productions. Arliss played not only Nathan Rothschild but also his father, Mayer, while Mrs George Arliss played Nathan's devoted wife, Hannah. Boris Karloff was the bigoted German heavy (who prompted comparison with the treatment of Jews in modern Germany), C. Aubrey Smith cameoed as the Duke of Wellington, Robert

Young and Loretta Young carried the love interest, and the film broke out into breath-taking perfected Technicolor for the final reel. Nunnally Johnson delivered the screenplay and Alfred Werker directed the United Artists release.

The House of Rothschild: Boris Karloff, Reginald Owen, George Arliss, Murray Kinnell.

Melody in Spring Paramount's breezy comedy starred the Charlie Ruggles–Mary Boland team. He was the dog-biscuit and puppy-pretzel tycoon who collects antique bedpost-knobs for a hobby, while Lanny Ross was the popular radio crooner who tries to collect his daughter's hand in marriage and get on the radio show he sponsors. Mary Boland was Ruggles' silly, fluttering wife and Ann Sothern their daughter. Benn W. Levy and Jane Storm concocted the script from a Frank Leon Smith story, and Norman Z. McLeod directed.

It Happened One Night

MAY

The House of Rothschild
Viva Villa! It was David O. Selznick's idea to star Wallace Beery as the bandit hero Pancho Villa, and he won the co-operation of the Mexican government to film in that country, using army soldiers and local peasants. There was much controversy while shooting proceeded under the direction of Howard Hawks, capped by an incident in which a drunken Lee Tracy (who played an American newspaperman in the film) urinated on some Mexican cadets from his hotel balcony and had to be rushed out of the country. He was sacked by MGM, which then had to scrap most of the Mexican footage. Production was re-started on Californian locations with Stuart Erwin replacing Tracy and Jack Conway taking over the direction from Hawks, while a second-unit under Richard Rosson did more filming in Mexico. Fay Wray had

another suffering role (horsewhipped by Villa as an aristocrat's wife) and Leo Carrillo, Joseph Schildkraut and Katherine De Mille also appeared. The Ben Hecht screenplay was based on a book by Edgcumb Pinchon and O. B. Stade. The production cost over

$1 million and did well enough to squeeze out a small profit.
Stand Up and Cheer And cheers there were for five-year-old Shirley Temple who became an overnight sensation for the way she performed the song and dance number "Baby Take a Bow", her first conspicuous part in pictures, in which she was partnered by James Dunn and Patricia White. Will Rogers devised with Philip Klein the story for the Fox revue in which a new Secretary of Amusement is appointed by the Federal Government to lift the country's mood by arranging a big revue. Warner Baxter repeated his harassed producer act of *42nd Street* while others in the cast were Madge Evans, Nigel Bruce, Stepin Fetchit, Lila Lee, Ralph Morgan, John Boles and George K. Arthur. Lew Brown and Jay Gorney provided the songs, Ralph Spence did the screenplay, and Hamilton McFadden was the director.
Twentieth Century John Barrymore clearly relished this opportunity to play a ham Broadway producer, and he stimulated Carole Lombard to prove herself a blazing comedienne in the role of the star that Barrymore desperately needs for his next Broadway play. The principal setting was the crack train, the Twentieth Century Limited, *en route* from Chicago to New York. The scintillating dialogue of Ben Hecht and Charles MacArthur and skilful direction by Howard Hawks set a pace that almost left the train behind. Columbia's picture had meaty supporting roles for Walter Connolly, Roscoe Karns and, as a harmless nutcase, Etienne Girardot.
We're Not Dressing Carole Lombard was also seen, to much slighter effect, as one of the idle rich in this Paramount musical comedy inspired

by James Barrie's *The Admirable Crichton*. Of greatest appeal were Bing Crosby (as the deck hand on a private yacht who takes charge of the wealthy survivors after a shipwreck) and George Burns and Gracie Allen (as daffy botanists on the tropical island). Crosby crooned "Love Thy Neighbor" and other songs by Mack Gordon and Harry Revel. Ethel Merman and Leon Errol co-starred. Horace Jackson, George Marion Jr and Francis Martin scripted from Benjamin Glazer's screen story, while Norman Taurog directed.

JUNE

Many Happy Returns Paramount's musical comedy toplined George Burns and Gracie Allen indulging in their crazy crosstalk: she was the daughter of a department store owner (George Barbier) who decided in his absence to tear it down for a bird sanctuary, and he was the radio announcer persuaded to marry her for a travelling allowance of $10 a mile. Ray Milland had a small part. Guy Lombardo and His Royal Canadians supplied some musical fizz to the proceedings, which were scripted by J. P. McEvoy, Claude Binyon, Keene Thompson and Ray Harris from a play by Lady Mary Cameron and directed by Norman Z. McLeod.
Little Miss Marker Paramount benefited from the wave of interest in Shirley Temple, having signed her before the success of *Stand Up and Cheer* to play in this adaptation of a Damon Runyon yarn (the author being in vogue after the success of *Lady for a Day*). She was the tot who is reluctantly taken as a "marker" or security for a gambling debt by Adolphe Menjou's mean-spirited racetrack bookie. Charles Bickford was the big shot who persuaded the mob to pose as storybook knights out of King Arthur to please the little girl, and Dorothy Dell, tragically killed in a car crash during this month, played his soft-hearted girlfriend and cabaret singer. Miss Temple took fourth billing after Menjou, Bickford and Dell, but had top pictorial emphasis in the advertising. Alexander Hall directed and the screenwriters were William R. Lipman, Sam Hellman and Gladys Lehman. There were three songs by Ralph Rainger and Leo Robin. The British release title was *The Girl in Pawn*. The story was re-made with Bob Hope (*Sorrowful Jones*, 1949) and Walter Matthau (1980).
The Thin Man Shot in only 16 days by director W. S. "Woody" Van Dyke II with William Powell and Myrna Loy, this film version of Dashiell Hammett's detective story was

rapturously welcomed by critics for its intelligent humour. It proved so appealing that it spawned a whole series of *Thin Man* adventures (even though the actual thin man was murdered in this first picture). Powell and Loy's affectionate wisecracking and delight in good living as husband and wife Nick and Nora Charles pointed the way to "screwball comedy", while their wirehair terrier, Asta, became the most famous dog since Lassie. Frances Goodrich and Albert Hackett penned the screenplay.

JULY

Baby Take a Bow Fox signed Shirley Temple to a seven-year contract after seeing *Stand Up and Cheer*, and this was her first starring vehicle. Critics and audiences were enchanted by her performance as the daughter of an ex-convict (James Dunn) who saves him from false accusations of theft. The pair performed a song, "On Accounta I Love You". Claire Trevor appeared as her mother. Harry Lachman directed, and Philip Klein and E. E. Paramore Jr wrote the script from a successful 1926 play by James P. Judge.

The Life of Vergie Winters: Ann Harding.

The Life of Vergie Winters This gained something of a scandalous reputation after being banned by churches in Los Angeles and elsewhere, benefiting considerably from the attendant publicity. Ann Harding's Vergie Winters was the small-town girl who has an illegitimate daughter and keeps on seeing the father (John Boles, typecast again) for 20 years. When he finally decides to marry her, his enraged wife (Helen Vinson) shoots

The Thin Man: William Powell, Myrna Loy, Asta.

him dead. Vergie goes on trial for murder to protect his political reputation. Alfred Santell directed RKO Radio's tear-jerker, scripted from a Louis Bromfield novel by Jane Murfin.

Of Human Bondage: Bette Davis, Leslie Howard.

Of Human Bondage In the role of the tawdry, vicious Cockney waitress Mildred Rogers, Bette Davis showed what she could do with a really meaty part, and her performance electrified critics and moviegoers alike. Leslie Howard played opposite her as the sensitive, club-footed medical student who falls hopelessly in love with her. Other victims of her wiles were played by Reginald Denny and Alan Hale, while Frances Dee was the decent girl who showed up her shortcomings. W. Somerset Maugham's novel was adapted for the screen by Lester Cole and directed by John Cromwell at RKO Radio. The story was re-made by Warner Bros. in 1946 with Eleanor Parker, and by Seven Arts in 1964 with Kim Novak.

The Thin Man

AUGUST

Treasure Island MGM re-teamed Wallace Beery as the rascally old buccaneer Long John Silver (with peg leg and parrot) and Jackie Cooper as the courageous young Jim Hawkins in a lavish and spirited version of the Robert Louis Stevenson classic, directed by Victor Fleming and scripted by John Lee Mahin. Also cast were Lionel Barrymore, Lewis Stone, Nigel Bruce, Otto Kruger and Charles "Chic" Sale. Walt Disney was next to film the story in 1950 with Robert Newton.

Handy Andy In this typical Will Rogers comedy, he was the small-town druggist persuaded to sell out to a big chain by his wife who has ideas above her station. His attempts to amuse himself amused audiences, especially his dancing in a Tarzan costume at the Mardi Gras. Peggy Wood was his snobbish wife, Mary Carlisle his likable daughter and Robert Taylor (in his film debut, on loan-out from MGM) played the pleasant young man who won her hand in marriage. The writers were William Conselman, Henry Johnson and Kubec Glasmon, working from a short-lived 1929 Broadway play *Merry Andrew* by Lewis Beach, and the director of the Fox picture was David Butler.

She Loves Me Not Bing Crosby had a stronger plot than usual in this Paramount musical comedy based on a 1933 hit play by Howard Lindsay (itself from a novel by Edward Hope). Bing was the college student who sheltered a murder witness, Miriam Hopkins' nightclub dancer, and then helped her masquerade as a man. Among the film's songs was "Love in Bloom" by Ralph Rainger and Leo Robin. Singer Kitty Carlisle was

HE SAVED
THE LIFE OF
THE MUG
WHO STOLE
HIS GAL--
so he could poke
him in the eye
again! . . .

See these wise-crackin', heart-breakin', chin-bustin' champs of the screen . . . as two fightin' gobs whose private war almost sank the navy! Plow the briny ocean with Uncle Sam's fighting fleet — soar through the clouds with the giant battleships of the air—hit a new high in breathless drama with—

GREATEST THRILL EVER FILMED!
The rescue from the runaway dirigible—heroically restaged from actual records of the naval department!

"HERE COMES THE NAVY"

Warner Bros. Triumph with
JAMES CAGNEY
PAT O'BRIEN
GLORIA STUART
FRANK McHUGH
DOROTHY TREE

town. Mae's poses in front of a giant spider and as the Statue of Liberty in the "My American Beauty" number were memorable, as were her appearances with Duke Ellington and his Orchestra singing "Memphis Blues" and "Troubled Waters". Mae wrote the movie and Leo McCarey directed. The songs were by Arthur Johnston and Sam Coslow.

Dames Busby Berkeley came up with some more of his dazzling precision numbers for another Warner backstage musical. They included the title number with girls seemingly thrown into the downward-looking camera from far below, and the fantasy "I Only Have Eyes for You" with its multiple images of Ruby Keeler. The plot seemed the same as before, with Dick Powell as the songwriter, Ruby Keeler the devoted girlfriend, Joan Blondell a gold-digging chorus girl and a show that needed a backer. However, Delmer Daves's script made gentle fun of the puritan backlash with Hugh Herbert as the president of a Foundation for the Elevation of American Morals who learns that showbiz isn't as wicked as he thought. Al Dubin and Harry Warren provided some of the

songs, including the title one with its pithy encapsulation of the film's appeal ("What do you go for, Go see a show for? Tell the truth, you go to see those beautiful dames"). Ray Enright directed the non-musical sequences.
Chained MGM's latest romantic vehicle for Gable and Crawford had them falling in love on a long voyage,

Dames: Ruby Keeler, Dick Powell.

Dames: Overhead camera view of Busby Berkeley number with chorus girls' legs in black.

Bing's girlfriend. Edward Nugent and Henry Stephenson were in support. Benjamin Glazer did the screenplay, and Elliott Nugent directed. The same story was the basis of two later films, *True to the Army* (1942) and *How To Be Very, Very Popular* (1955).
Here Comes the Navy James Cagney and Pat O'Brien were teamed for the first of eight times in this comedy-drama of the ocean waves, with the pugnacious Cagney learning to accept the discipline of service life. Gloria Stuart provided the love interest, while Dorothy Tree was a treacherous blonde spared Cagney's usual rough stuff by the official new restraints on screen behaviour. The writers were Ben Markson and Earl Baldwin, while Lloyd Bacon handled the direction of the Warner Bros. picture.

SEPTEMBER

Belle of the Nineties Stripped of its best innuendoes and generally sanitized to meet new standards of screen "decency", Mae West's new film for Paramount still had her hordes of admirers standing in line to see her. She was the nightclub entertainer in the Gay Nineties, fought over by Roger Pryor's prizefighter, John Miljan's nightclub operator and Johnny Mack Brown's man about

leaving her with the problem of breaking the news to her kindly benefactor (Otto Kruger) who has arranged a divorce to marry her. Edgar Selwyn's story was scripted by John Lee Mahin and directed by Clarence Brown. The movie was originally to be entitled *Sacred and Profane Love*, but this was too provocative for the times.

Hide-Out Robert Montgomery was the injured gentleman racketeer who takes refuge with a farming family in Connecticut, falls for the daughter (Maureen O'Sullivan) and turns over a new leaf. Frances Goodrich and Albert Hackett wrote the MGM movie from a story by Mauri Grashin, and W. S. Van Dyke II directed. Edward Arnold, Elizabeth Patterson and Mickey Rooney headed the supporting cast.

One Night of Love Columbia was well rewarded for its gamble on the appeal of opera star Grace Moore, whose two previous film appearances for MGM in 1930 had been in costly failures. It was the unexpected popularity of Polish tenor Jan Kiepura in Universal's British import of 1933, *Be Mine Tonight*, that had alerted studios to the new potential of opera stories. For *One Night of Love*, it took five writers (Dorothy Speare, Charles Beahan, Edmund North, James Gow and S. K. Lauren) to fashion the story of Grace Moore as an aspiring opera star making her New York Metropolitan Opera debut with Tullio Carminati as the exacting tutor with whom she falls in love. A popular highlight was the sequence in which Moore sings on a balcony at a conservatory and the other students stop rehearsing with their instruments to accompany her. Mona Barrie and Lyle Talbot introduced romantic complications; Jessie Ralph and Luis Alberni supplied character support. The director was Victor Schertzinger (a former conductor of classical music), and various operatic excerpts were worked into the narrative. The picture's huge success touched off a flood of Hollywood pictures with opera stars including Paramount's *Give Us This Night* with Kiepura and Met soprano Gladys Swarthout, but there were no more really massive hits.

Girl of the Limberlost Monogram made this straightforward adaptation of the late Gene Stratton Porter's 1909 novel, then reckoned as the fourth best-selling book of all time (excluding the Bible) with a total sale of 1.7 million copies (the same author's *Freckles* was the second biggest seller). Porter himself had made a silent version of his heart-warming story in 1924. This new film did well in big city bookings but it found its major audience in small

One Night of Love: Tullio Carminati (left), Grace Moore.

towns, where its lack of sophistication and "clean" storyline were appreciated as it played off over the winter months. Marian Marsh starred as the girl of the Indiana marshlands whose worthless father was drowned long ago. She has to contend with the

Girl of the Limberlost: Louise Dresser, Marian Marsh.

dislike her mother (Louise Dresser) feels towards her, but is helped by a kind neighbour (Ralph Morgan), who takes a paternal interest in her welfare. Adele Comandini wrote the adaptation and Christy Cabanne directed. Columbia was next to film the story in 1945.

OCTOBER

The Barretts of Wimpole Street MGM made a lengthy (110 minutes) and faithful screen version of the Rudolph Besier play, which had starred Katharine Cornell on Broadway in

1931. The role of the invalid poetess Elizabeth Barrett in the London of the mid-19th century was a coveted one, given to his talented wife Norma Shearer by producer Irving Thalberg. Charles Laughton played the tyrannical father obsessed with holding her, while Fredric March was the poet Robert Browning whose love helped her break free. Claudine West, Ernest Vajda and Donald Ogden Stewart wrote the screen version, and Sidney Franklin directed. It was re-made by Franklin in 1957 with Jennifer Jones, and this earlier version is sometimes presented on TV as *Forbidden Alliance*.

Judge Priest This was the second of three Fox films in which Will Rogers starred under the direction of John Ford (the first had been *Doctor Bull* in 1933). Based on stories by Irvin S. Cobb, it presented Rogers as the wise Judge Billy Priest who brings his influence to bear in a Kentucky town still upset by the Civil War and who talks over events to his dead wife at her tombstone. This was a more profound part for Rogers than usual, although he re-worked the lines to suit his style, for it substituted feeling for the customary wisecracks. Dudley Nichols and Lamar Trotti provided the screenplay. Henry B. Walthall, Tom Brown, Anita Louise, Rochelle Hudson, Berton Churchill, David Landau and black comic actor Stepin Fetchit were also cast. Ford re-made the subject with his 1953 production, *The Sun Shines Bright*, starring Charles Winninger.

The Gay Divorcee RKO gave Fred Astaire and Ginger Rogers their first starring vehicle and the pair proved as superbly suited to each other as *Flying Down to Rio* had suggested. Here their big production number was "The Continental". They also duetted in

The Barretts of Wimpole Street: Fredric
March, Norma Shearer, Charles Laughton.

(Elissa Landi). Director Rowland V.
Lee collaborated on the screenplay
with Philip Dunne and Dan Totheroh.
The next screen rendition of the story
came from France in 1942.
One Night of Love
Girl of the Limberlost

NOVEMBER

The Merry Widow Maurice Chevalier
and Jeanette MacDonald teamed
again in Ernst Lubitsch's version of
the Franz Lehár operetta, the two
stars and director having left
Paramount for MGM. In this Irving
Thalberg production, she was the
immensely wealthy widow whose
departure from the kingdom of
Marshovia threatens its financial
stability. He was the randy captain
sent to Paris to woo her back. . . .
Edward Everett Horton and Una
Merkel provided strong support.
Chevalier and MacDonald had
separate songs except for "The Merry
Widow Waltz". Richard Rodgers
provided new music, and Lorenz Hart
and Gus Kahn new lyrics. Samson
Raphaelson and Ernest Vajda
handled the script adaptation. The
two leads made a French language
version as well. Some of the sequences
involving royalty had to be deleted for
British and Belgian consumption. The
production was so exceptionally
expensive that its success was
insufficient to recoup its total cost of
$1.6 million. (Grace Moore, who had
wanted to star in this film, had the
satisfaction of seeing her *One Night of
Love* show much greater box-office
stamina.) Already somewhat inhibited
by the censorship problem, *The Merry
Widow* subsequently lost a further
seven minutes of suggestive details
from its 110-minute running time to
clean it up for TV use when it gained
the title *The Lady Dances* to
distinguish it from MGM's 1952

"Night and Day", the only number
retained from Cole Porter's Broadway
musical *The Gay Divorce* in which
Astaire had starred. Four new songs
were added and the film version had to
be slightly retitled for the screen to
please the bluenoses who would not
allow a divorce to be cheerful. (In
Britain the title *The Gay Divorce* was
preserved.) Rogers played the wife
seeking to end her marriage and
Astaire was the man she mistook for

screen musical with George Marion
Jr, Dorothy Yost and Edward
Kaufman penning the film's script and
Mark Sandrich directing.
The Count of Monte Cristo Brought
over from England, Robert Donat
made a striking American debut
playing Alexandre Dumas' classic
hero, Edmond Dantes, in this version
by Edward Small's Reliance Pictures,
released by United Artists, that
proved a pleasant surprise, doing far
better business than had ever been
envisaged. In what proved to be his
only made-in-Hollywood movie,
Donat was the wrongly imprisoned
Count who escapes from a grim gaol
to exact revenge from the three men
(Louis Calhern, Sidney Blackmer,
Raymond Walburn) whose false
evidence led to his conviction. His
protruding stomach won Ferdinand
Munier the part of Louis XVIII. This
adaptation allowed a happy ending,
reuniting Donat with his love

The Gay Divorcee: Fred Astaire, Ginger
Rogers.

the professional co-respondent hired
to help her obtain a divorce. Edward
Everett Horton and Alice Brady were
in comic support. Dwight Taylor's
novel was the source of the stage and

The Merry Widow: Jeanette MacDonald,
Maurice Chevalier, Minna Gombell.

version with Lana Turner. (The studio had also made a notable silent version with Mae Murray in 1925.)

One Night of Love

The Gay Divorcee

Kid Millions Samuel Goldwyn's annual Eddie Cantor musical comedy had a slight plot about Eddie, as the heir to a fortune extracted from ancient tombs, visiting Egypt and nearly being boiled in oil by an angry sheik. Ethel Merman gave him strong competition in the musical numbers. George Murphy and Ann Sothern were the love interest and also had a number of their own. The 1934 Goldwyn Girls included Lucille Ball (and Doris Davenport until she was taken out of the chorus line and given a featured role). Cantor had his usual blackface number, and the film was topped off by a Technicolor musical sequence (costing $200,000) about the opening of an ice cream factory in New York. Seymour Felix staged the numbers (Busby Berkeley was now tied to Warners), and the songs were by Walter Donaldson and Gus Kahn, Burton Lane and Harold Adamson, and Irving Berlin. Arthur Sheekman, Nat Perrin and Nunnally Johnson wrote the script, and Roy Del Ruth directed. United Artists released.

Kentucky Kernels The soon eminent George Stevens was cutting his directorial teeth on RKO Radio films like this Wheeler and Woolsey comedy, putting to good practice his earlier experience as a photographer of Laurel and Hardy shorts. The script of this one, by Bert Kalmar, Harry Ruby and Fred Guiol, had the comic duo escorting little Spanky McFarland (from the *Our Gang* shorts) to claim an inheritance down South. They become involved in a bristling family feud and the antics of a drunken horse. Marx Brothers' foil Margaret Dumont was in it somewhere. *Triple Trouble* was its title for British consumption.

Girl of the Limberlost

DECEMBER

Flirtation Walk Dedicated to the West Point Academy, this flag-waving First National (Warner Bros.) musical romance starred Dick Powell as the cadet who wooed and won Ruby Keeler, the commanding officer's daughter. It was their fifth pairing. The script was by Delmer Daves (he devised the story with Lou Edelman) while Frank Borzage directed. The score was by Mort Dixon and Allie Wrubel and the dance direction by Bobby Connolly. Pat O'Brien (as a friendly sergeant) and Ross Alexander were prominently in support, while Tyrone Power was a uniformed extra.

Bright Eyes Shirley Temple was the orphaned girl protected by her late

father's best friend (James Dunn) from attempts by an evil family that included a sadistic young Jane Withers to gain custody of her. Shirley sang the celebrated "On the Good Ship Lollipop" by Sidney Clare and Richard Whiting. Director David Butler collaborated with Edwin Burke on the story, which was scripted for Fox by William Conselman.

Babes in Toyland This screen version of Victor Herbert's comic operetta, a Hal Roach production released by MGM, worked in Laurel and Hardy as bungling toymakers who build giant wooden soldiers in Toyland, with Charlotte Henry and Felix Knight as young lovers and Harry Kleinbach (later known as Henry Brandon) as the villainous leader of invading Bogeymen. Gus Meins and Charles Rogers handled the direction, while Nick Grinde and Frank Butler shared the writing credit. Victor Herbert's collaborator on the book and lyrics was Glen MacDonough, while the hit number "Who's Afraid of the Big Bad Wolf?" from *Three Little Pigs* was added. It is now more often known by its reissue title, *March of the Wooden Soldiers*, to distinguish it from Disney's 1961 version of the operetta.

College Rhythm Paramount's musical comedy presented Jack Oakie as the bombastic star of a department store's

Anne of Green Gables: Anne Shirley, O. P. Heggie.

football team and Lanny Ross as the timid son of the store's owner who plays piccolo in the college band and croons pleasantly. Popular radio comic Joe Penner made his feature film debut after several shorts. Mary Brian, Lyda Roberti and Helen Mack had the principal female roles. Norman Taurog directed from a script by Walter DeLeon, John McDermott and Francis Martin (story by George Marion Jr). The songs were by Mack Gordon and Harry Ravel and included "Stay As Sweet As You Are".

Anne of Green Gables RKO Radio shrewdly followed up the success of *Little Women* with a film of Lucy Maud Montgomery's 1904 novel, another great favourite with girls. Actress Dawn O'Day celebrated her success in obtaining the leading role of Anne Shirley by changing her name to that of the character (which was a good publicity break for her and the film). She appeared as the sweet and charming orphan girl who went to live with an elderly farmer (O. P. Heggie) and his sister (Helen Westley). Tom Brown was her sweetheart. George Nicholls Jr directed from Sam Mintz's screenplay. Mary Miles Minter had starred in a 1919 version. RKO would make a sequel, *Anne of Windy Poplars*, in 1940.

The Painted Veil Preceding the tide of light family holiday fare there was MGM's release from W. Somerset Maugham's novel, which had to

The Painted Veil: Greta Garbo, Herbert Marshall.

squeeze its way past the censors to tell its story of an unfaithful wife (Greta Garbo) living in China who betrayed her doctor husband (Herbert Marshall) by having an affair with a diplomat (George Brent). Through emphasis on her ultimate repentance (helping hubbie fight a cholera epidemic), her sins became permissible screen fare. Warner Oland and Jean Hersholt lent support. Richard Boleslawski directed from a script by John Meehan, Salka Viertel and Edith Fitzgerald. W. S. Van Dyke II directed the extensive re-takes. Garbo's cameraman was, as usual, William Daniels. The 1957 re-make with Eleanor Parker was called *The Seventh Sin*.

Imitation of Life Opening late November/early December, Universal's melodramatic tear-jerker from the Fannie Hurst novel cast Claudette Colbert as the woman who makes a business fortune thanks to the pancake recipe of her loyal and self-effacing black housekeeper (Louise Beavers). A tragic sub-plot involved the latter's daughter who passes for white and disowns her mother – a part played by black actress Fredi Washington, whose later refusal to play mocking racial stereotypes ended her Hollywood career. Warren William, Ned Sparks and Rochelle Hudson were also prominent. William Hurlbut did the screenplay, and John Stahl directed. The film's length (110 minutes) was a handicap to fitting in as many showings as first-run exhibitors would have liked to meet the demand for seats. It also proved to have exceptional strength on later showings and was booked more than once by many subsequent-run theatres, making it Universal's biggest grosser in the first half of 1935. The studio made a new version in 1959 with Lana Turner.

TEN BEST - CRITICS' CHOICE

The annual *Film Daily* poll improved its catch of critics by raising the number to 425 and collecting for the first time the vote of the critic of *The New York Times* (André Sennwald). Films and votes were:

1.	*The Barretts of Wimpole Street*	348
2.	*The House of Rothschild*	338
3.	*It Happened One Night*	281
4.	*One Night of Love*	265
5.	*Little Women* [late 1933 release]	264
6.	*The Thin Man*	249
7.	*Viva Villa!*	188
8.	*Dinner at Eight* [late 1933 release]	172
9.	*The Count of Monte Cristo*	145
10.	*Berkeley Square*	119

Principal Runners Up

11.	*The Gay Divorcee*	117
12.	*Judge Priest*	101

Only *Berkeley Square* lacked the same degree of appeal with the public.

CLOSE RUNNERS UP

20 other films attracted much more than average support: *The Cat and the Fiddle* (February), *The Cat's Paw* (September), *Cleopatra* (August), *David Harum* (March), *Fashions of 1934* (February), *George White's Scandals* (April), *The Girl from Missouri* (August), *Lady by Choice* (November), *Little Man, What Now?* (June), *Manhattan Melodrama* (May), *Men in White* (April), *The Mighty Barnum* (December, also January 1935), *Now and Forever* (September), *One More River* (August), *Operator 13* (June), *Palooka* (March), *Sadie McKee* (April), *Spitfire* (March), *The White Parade* (November), *Wild Cargo* (April).

1935

Shirley Temple
who received a special Oscar

Things were looking up. Hollywood could begin to see the silver lining. People were coming back to the theatres, encouraged in part by "bank nites" with prizes awarded to winners by seat numbers, bingo (or "screeno"), "dish nites" of free crockery and gifts of cosmetics and silverware. But it had its price: some theatres were giving away plates it cost them 8 or 9¢ each to buy to patrons paying 15 or 20¢ for a ticket. Once every theatre in an area was offering the same incentives, the competitive advantage was lost. The same applied to the value-for-money policy of double features plus shorts that had spread to half the nation's theatres, which hit box-office takings because it allowed only one evening show.

By May the movie business was estimated to be up 12 per cent on the same time a year ago and the book-keepers hoped they might rake in as much money from the 1935–6 season as they had back in the fondly remembered boom year of 1929. As it turned out, for the year as a whole movie attendances averaged out at 80 million per week, 10 million up on 1934 and the highest figure since 1930.

Profits were being made almost everywhere – even RKO Radio was in the black, for the first time since 1930. But Universal made a small loss, after being in profit the previous year, and its future was again a subject of debate. Paramount was operating profitably again, and a merger with RKO Radio was foreseen but never took place. However, United Artists ran into a major setback when it lost one of its principal suppliers, Twentieth Century Productions, which, after discussions with several studios, merged with Fox to form 20th Century-Fox. However, David O. Selznick contracted to release the output of his new independent company, Selznick International, through United Artists.

A new studio started up in April: Republic, an amalgamation of Monogram, Mascot and Consolidated Film Laboratories headed by Herbert J. Yates. Its first release was a B western starring John Wayne, *Westward Ho*, filmed at a cost of only $37,000.

This was the year that the first complete feature in perfected Technicolor was made, *Becky Sharp*, but the results did not indicate a huge public enthusiasm for colour. Musicals in black-and-white were back in favour as the team of Fred Astaire and Ginger Rogers was named among the top box-office stars of the year. Nelson Eddy and Jeanette MacDonald also made a hit teamed together for the first time.

Hollywood was confident enough to risk the occasional prestige picture, to show that obviously artistic films weren't only the province of foreign film-makers. Warner Bros. made *A Midsummer Night's Dream* at considerable expense and actually did well financially with it. RKO Radio allowed John Ford to make *The Informer* in just eight days at a negative cost of only $243,000 to minimize the financial risk. The company was rewarded with critical raves, its best showing yet in the Academy Awards and even a modest profit on its investment (the biggest problem was persuading leading theatres to show *The Informer*: those that took the chance were often pleasantly surprised at the appeal it had).

Two of Warner Bros.' top stars appeared in its Shakespearian comedy *A Midsummer Night's Dream*: Joe E. Brown as Flute, James Cagney as Bottom.

British pictures continued to enjoy some success in the United States, especially *Escape Me Never* with Elisabeth Bergner and *The Scarlet Pimpernel* with Leslie Howard, but, as they were distributed by major American companies, this did not pose the same threat as that by British concerns. Gaumont-British brought over such films as Hitchcock's *The Man Who Knew Too Much* and *The 39 Steps* with some success and the other British major company, British International Pictures (part of John Maxwell's ABC empire), also launched a new attack on the American market.

TWENTIETH CENTURY AND FOX

In 1933, Darryl Zanuck resigned as production head of Warner Bros. He had been brilliantly successful with cycles of gangster films (such as *Little Caesar*), biographical pictures (*Disraeli*), topical stories (*I Am A Fugitive from a Chain Gang*) and musicals (*42nd Street*), although the company had been losing money heavily in the Depression. In 1933, when pay cuts were introduced to help the studios survive, Harry Warner stalled on ending them at the agreed time, and Zanuck resigned on 15 April as a matter of principle, to be replaced by Hal B. Wallis.

Other studios had courted Zanuck before, and he was sure to be in demand. He may have already held discussions about going into independent production. Joseph Schenck, president of United Artists, made the most attractive proposal, of starting a new company with him to make films for distribution by United Artists. The company was called Twentieth Century and was part financed by Louis B. Mayer of MGM. More important, MGM's stars were loaned to the new company to supplement the players (like George Arliss and Loretta Young) who had followed him from Warners. Why were MGM so helpful to a budding rival? Joe Schenck's brother, Nicholas, was president of MGM, and Louis B. Mayer wanted his son-in-law, William Goetz, to have a key post in the new company. In fact, Goetz invested in it and became a vice president while he and Raymond Griffith (the former comedian whose throat ailment prevented him from talking on screen) worked as associate producers and Zanuck's right-hand men.

Twentieth Century's first film, *The Bowery*, was a big hit and starred Wallace Beery, George Raft and Jackie Cooper, all on loan from MGM. Its first film with George Arliss, *The House of Rothschild*, was the biggest attraction of 1934. It released four pictures in 1933 and nine in 1934. Almost all of its productions were successful, and they were of high quality and delivered on time. When the existing partners in United Artists refused to give Twentieth Century a stock interest in the company in recognition of its huge contribution to UA's activities, Joe Schenck resigned. Sidney Kent, head of Fox, had earlier approached Zanuck about a merger, and this was quickly arranged and announced on 29 May 1935.

The merger was very attractive to Fox, because it involved no duplication of studio facilities, distribution networks or theatre interests. Twentieth Century was essentially the efficient production

Darryl Francis Zanuck: he knew what he wanted.

team run by Zanuck. Fox itself was successfully making films but was overly reliant on Will Rogers and Shirley Temple. It had about the same earnings as Twentieth Century despite the disparity in size and assets. It needed fresh blood and the main casualty of the merger was Fox's head of production, Winfield R. Sheehan, who promptly resigned, making way for Zanuck to run the combined companies.

Sidney Kent was anxious to drop the Fox name because William Fox no longer had any connection with the company, although he was still making headlines over a legal wrangle concerning sound patents, and because it was the best way of burying the company's recent, well-publicized financial difficulties. The Fox name was attached to Twentieth Century but the original idea was to drop it off after a year or so.

Zanuck moved into Fox in August 1935, Joe Schenck became chairman, and Kent was president. Two new stages were erected at Westwood to accommodate the increased production programme of the new company. Despite the early blow of Will Rogers' accidental death, the merger worked as planned and the old Fox company became highly prosperous as 20th Century-Fox.

For a short while, films continued to be billed as either "A Fox Picture – Darryl F. Zanuck in charge of production" or "A Darryl F. Zanuck Twentieth Century Production" according to which half of the company they emanated from, but production was soon fully merged.

IN PERFECT TECHNICOLOR

"It is probably the most significant event of the 1935 cinema," said André Sennwald, critic of the *New York Times*, in his review of *Becky Sharp*, the first feature-length motion picture in Technicolor's new three-colour process. "This is not the coloration of natural life," the critic added, "but a vividly pigmented dream world of artistic imagination."

The film was made by Pioneer Pictures, formed by producer Merian C. Cooper and financier C. V. Whitney to produce motion pictures in the perfected Technicolor. It had been used before *Becky Sharp* in Disney cartoons, in a comedy short *La Cucaracha* (the initial production of Pioneer) and in short climactic sequences in three 1934 features, *The Cat and the Fiddle*, *The House of Rothschild* and *Kid Millions*, and earlier in 1935 in *The Little Colonel*. But its impact as an integral part of an entire feature was an unknown quantity. Was another revolution on hand, like the coming of sound? Would all pictures be made in colour before long?

Although the period setting, the costumes and uniforms, were ideally suited to demonstrate what the new Technicolor could do, and director Rouben Mamoulian thoughtfully employed it to dramatic ends, *Becky Sharp* was not the best vehicle for the system as the story was found to be tedious and the cast was weak in drawing power. Cinemagoers curious about colour flocked to see it but it did not attract the same numbers as it might have done with Clark Gable or Joan Crawford.

To many eyes, Technicolor seemed lurid and over-ripe, especially as far as the players' complexions were concerned, and some leading actresses refused to be photographed in it. With its use of three negatives individually sensitive to red, blue and green, it was also, of course, very expensive and time-consuming. There was no great rush to adopt the new system. Four features used it in 1936. Paramount filmed the popular *The Trail of the Lonesome Pine* in the process (but, observers asked, wouldn't it have been a success without colour?), and Pioneer Pictures made a musical called *The Dancing Pirate*, which was a failure and led to the company's dissolution. Whitney joined David O. Selznick, and they filmed *The Garden of Allah* with Marlene Dietrich in Technicolor and 20th Century-Fox made *Ramona* with Loretta Young in the system.

Only slowly over the years did the number of Technicolor productions creep upwards (there were 28 Hollywood features using it in 1945), until the time came when more economical, visually satisfactory colour processes were offered, especially Eastmancolor in the early 1950s. The three-color Technicolor system was used for the last time on a Hollywood feature with Jane Russell called *Foxfire* (1955).

STRONGER SHORTS:

The March of Time and *Crime Does Not Pay*

It was in February 1935 that Time Inc. launched the monthly screen magazine *The March of Time* which investigated current affairs and soon became highly influential. Under producer Louis de Rochemont, the series was crusading and often controversial, unconcerned with documentary exactness and balance, and staccato-paced to hold the audience's attention. It explored issues, more concerned with the ideas behind events than the events themselves. It took sides emotively and in the absence of suitable newsreel footage it often reconstructed situations with actors to make its points as dramatically as possible. This was "fakery in allegiance to the truth," as Time Inc.'s head Henry Luce put it.

Among its first subjects were the rise of fascism under Hitler in Germany and the career of demagogue and presidential candidate Huey Long in Louisiana. Several topics were covered in each 20-minute issue (the Huey Long story was deleted in New Orleans) until 1938, when single subjects began to be covered. *The March of Time* was issued abroad, and in 1937 was being shown in 10,000 theatres around the world (while still showing a slight financial loss as far as Time Inc. was concerned).

A British unit under Edgar Anstey was established in 1936. One of its stories was on malnutrition in Britain, which was pointed out as weakening Britain's ability to resist its enemies abroad. One anti-Nazi story was banned in Britain for fear of upsetting Germany.

It made a considerable contribution to the war effort and continued successfully until its role was replaced by television reporting and the last episode was issued in 1951. It obviously expressed an American attitude to events and this stimulated a British equivalent, *This Modern Age*, to project a different point of view, which ran from 1946 to 1949.

MGM's *Crime Does Not Pay* series dramatized various kinds of crime in a semi-documentary fashion. The two-reelers ran for approximately 20 minutes and were essentially mini-features. They were a change from the escapist cartoons, comedies and travelogues that dominated the short entertainment field. While some of the subjects covered by the series from 1935 to 1945 (with one addition in 1947) concerned big-time crimes like extortion, and others were war-time propaganda warning against spies and saboteurs, episodes more often tackled unorthodox rackets, exposing quack doctors and fake spiritualists, or focused on such anti-social activities as drunken driving and evading customs duty. For the studio, the series was a useful way of breaking in new talent: Robert Taylor starred in the very first of the shorts, *Buried Loot* (1935), but it was particularly a training ground for directors – Fred Zinnemann, Jacques Tourneur and Joseph Losey were among those who demonstrated their abilities and progressed to features.

HITS OF THE YEAR

JANUARY

Forsaking All Others MGM's three-star romantic comedy of the smart set presented Joan Crawford as the woman jilted at the altar by Robert Montgomery's selfish hedonist. He soon regrets not marrying her and woos her again. But she realizes that sturdy Clark Gable, who has quietly loved her all along, is the man for her, and this time she abandons Montgomery at the wedding ceremony. There was verbal and slapstick humour in Joseph L. Mankiewicz's adaptation of a play by Edward Barry Roberts and Frank Morgan Cavett that had starred Tallulah Bankhead on Broadway in 1933. W. S. Van Dyke II directed, and a top-notch supporting cast included Charles Butterworth, Frances Drake and Rosalind Russell.

The Little Minister Katharine Hepburn starred in RKO Radio's lengthy (110 minutes) adaptation of J. M. Barrie's novel and play. She was the gypsy lass whose friendship with John Beal's young minister causes a scandal. Five writers (Jane Murfin, Sarah Y. Mason, Victor Heerman, Mortimer Offner and Jack Wagner) were credited with whipping the emotional drama into shape for Richard Wallace to direct, and Alan Hale, Donald Crisp and Frank Conroy had other roles. With its studio-created Scottish settings, *The Little Minister* was particularly expensive to make, but only just failed to recoup its $648,000 production cost on release. There had been two competing earlier screen versions of the story made in 1921.

Broadway Bill Frank Capra and writer Robert Riskin got together again at Columbia for this comedy drama from a Mark Hellinger story. Warner Baxter portrayed the man who throws up a business career to do what he likes doing best – racing horses. In the process he loses his stuffy, blue-blooded wife (Helen Vinson) and marries her easy-going sister (Myrna Loy). Walter Connolly was the blustery father-in-law; Raymond Walburn, Lynne Overman and Margaret Hamilton also appeared. The British release title was *Strictly Confidential*. Capra re-made it with Bing Crosby as *Riding High* (1950).

The Lives of a Bengal Lancer Gary Cooper, Franchot Tone and Richard Cromwell were the three officers who quelled an uprising on the north-west frontier of India in Paramount's highly acclaimed adaptation of Major Francis Yeats-Brown's 1930 novel. The story (adapted by Waldemar Young, John L. Balderston, Achmed Abdullah, Grover Jones and William Slavens McNutt) was a bit more realistic than most adventures, encompassing torture and the death of two of the principals, but it was also stirring stuff, almost a western except that it glorified the British Empire. Cooper adopted a Gable-like moustache and revitalized his career, while Henry Hathaway's robust direction made him a top director and a lasting favourite of the star. Charles Lang's cinematography helped enormously to create an Indian atmosphere. British stalwarts in the supporting cast included Sir Guy Standing and C. Aubrey Smith.

Bright Eyes

The County Chairman Will Rogers (in a straighter than usual role) played the sly small-town lawyer in late-19th-century Wyoming who puts up his young partner (Kent Taylor) to run for office against the ageing hypocrite (Berton Churchill) standing for re-election. Evelyn Venable was cast as the old man's daughter who is in love with his opponent. Mickey Rooney appeared as a kid called Freckles. Louise Dresser was Will Rogers' wife, as often before. John Blystone handled the Fox picture, written by Sam Hellman and Gladys Lehman from George Ade's stage hit of 1903. (The film's appearance stimulated a Broadway revival with Charles Coburn in 1936.)

FEBRUARY

David Copperfield A typically lavish David O. Selznick production from the Charles Dickens classic, it was rapturously received by critics and a smash hit with the public – further proof, after *Little Women* and *The Count of Monte Cristo*, that there was a vast audience for literary classics. The complex storyline was simplified in the screenplay by Hugh Walpole and Howard Estabrook, but it was

David Copperfield: W. C. Fields as Mr Micawber, Freddie Bartholomew as young David.

faithful to the spirit of Dickens' tale, and MGM's picture still ran 132 minutes, very long for 1935. It lacked star names, apart from W. C. Fields as a splendid Mr Micawber (a hurried

The Lives of a Bengal Lancer: In enemy hands: Gary Cooper, Richard Cromwell (rear), Franchot Tone.

THE ACADEMY AWARDS

The Awards presented on 27 February 1935 at the Biltmore Hotel and covering films shown in 1934 went largely to *It Happened One Night* – winner for Best Picture, Best Actor (Clark Gable), Best Actress (Claudette Colbert), Best Director (Frank Capra) and Best Adaptation (Robert Riskin). Arthur Caesar won the Best Original Story award for *Manhattan Melodrama*, Victor Milner took the Best Cinematography award for *Cleopatra* and Cedric Gibbons and Frederic Hope received the award for Best Interior Decoration for *The Merry Widow*. Walt Disney again won in the cartoon category for *The Tortoise and the Hare*, while in the comedy field *La Cucaracha* in the new three-strip Technicolor process was honoured. Music was introduced as a category and the first Oscars went to *The Gay Divorcee* for Best Song ("The Continental" by Herb Magidson and Con Conrad) and to Louis Silvers for Best Score (*One Night of Love*). (Silvers was merely the music director for Columbia – the score was actually the work of Victor Schertzinger and Gus Kahn!) The first recipient of a new Oscar for Film Editing was Conrad Nervig for *Eskimo*. Shirley Temple won a special award – a miniature statuette – for entertaining the nation so well during 1934.

Carl Erickson and Warren B. Duff, and Alfred E. Green provided the direction except for the musical sequences, which were handled by Bobby Connolly.

The Good Fairy In her third picture, Margaret Sullavan displayed a way with comedy in this Preston Sturges script from a Ferenc Molnar play (performed on Broadway in 1931 by Helen Hayes). She was a girl called Luisa Ginglebusher from an orphanage who wants to do good in the world while enjoying the luxuries of life. She uses her influence with Frank Morgan's amorous businessman to help the career of a stuffy, impecunious lawyer (Herbert Marshall). Director William Wyler had trouble with his leading lady, then resolved it by marrying her in mid-production. It was a Universal picture, re-made by the studio as *I'll Be Yours* in 1947 with Deanna Durbin.

MARCH

Roberta Irene Dunne starred in RKO Radio's musical as a Russian princess in Paris, and she sang "Smoke Gets in Your Eyes" and "Lovely to Look At". Randolph Scott was her romantic partner as the heir to the dressmaking establishment where she works. The setting prompts a long fashion parade at the end (with Lucille Ball as one of the models). Despite their success on their own as stars of *The Gay Divorcee*, Fred Astaire and Ginger Rogers were brought in as co-stars with distinctly supporting roles as a stranded orchestra leader and phoney Polish countess respectively. They were there to help ensure that RKO recovered its hefty outlay in purchasing the rights of the 1933 Broadway musical smash by Jerome Kern and Otto Harbach on which the film was based. The pair had three

replacement for Charles Laughton, who withdrew during production). But it was superbly cast with newcomer Freddie Bartholomew as the young David and Frank Lawton as the grown-up one, Edna May Oliver as eccentric Aunt Betsey, Lionel Barrymore as Dan Peggotty, Roland Young as the unctuous Uriah Heep, Basil Rathbone as cruel Mr Murdstone, plus Maureen O'Sullivan and Madge Evans as the women in the adult David's life. Director George Cukor masterfully handled the huge cast, while the art direction (Cedric Gibbons, Merrill Pye) and set decoration (Edwin B. Willis) brought the English period settings vividly to life.

The Lives of a Bengal Lancer
The Woman in Red Barbara Stanwyck's last movie under a long Warner Bros./First National contract was this society drama. She was the professional horsewoman who marries a blue blood (Gene Raymond) and has to endure the contempt and suspicion of his family when she rallies to the side of a friend (John Eldredge) falsely accused of murder. Genevieve Tobin, Phillip Reed and Dorothy Tree were in support, and Robert Florey directed from Peter Milne and Mary McCall Jr's screen adaptation of a Wallace Irwin novel. The First National picture was one of the studio's more concise productions, running only 68 minutes, and Stanwyck's spirited denunciation of upper-crust snobbery delighted ordinary audiences.

Sweet Music A new experiment with the drawing power of radio crooner Rudy Vallee as a lead in a musical (he had done *The Vagabond Lover* for RKO in 1929), this Warner Bros. picture was a slight but longish (100 minutes) affair with Vallee as the orchestra leader and Ann Dvorak as the singer (dubbed in her songs), whose on-off romance with him filled the time between the various musical numbers. Helen Morgan was also featured with her own magnificent voice. The script was by Jerry Wald,

The Good Fairy: Frank Morgan, Reginald Owen, Margaret Sullavan, Herbert Marshall.

dance routines together (Astaire, who devised the dances, had a fourth on his own), and they stole the picture. It proved to be the third highest-grossing release of the year, and Astaire and Rogers were quickly propelled into another starring vehicle of their own, *Top Hat*. William A. Seiter directed *Roberta* and Jane Murfin and Sam Mintz wrote the script with an assist from Glenn Tryon and Allan Scott. MGM re-made it as *Lovely to Look At* (1951).

Roberta: Ginger Rogers, Fred Astaire. "I'll Be Hard to Handle" number.

Ruggles of Red Gap In this third filming of Harry Leon Wilson's famous story, Charles Laughton played the grave English valet transported to the American West where he achieves his own independence. Charles Ruggles and Mary Boland were teamed yet again as his proud owners after Roland Young as his old employer loses him in a card game in Paris, while ZaSu Pitts was the woman who helped him set up in the restaurant business. Laughton's admirably restrained performance (especially his hesitant recitation of the Gettysburg Address in an American saloon) added genuine sentiment to the Paramount comedy (an aspect abandoned when the studio pressed the material into service as a vehicle for Bob Hope, retitled *Fancy Pants*, in 1950). Walter DeLeon, Harlan Thompson and Humphrey Pearson handled the screen adaptation, while director Leo McCarey enhanced his reputation for comedy.
The Little Colonel Confident of Shirley Temple's appeal, Fox lavished money on a major starring vehicle for the

Ruggles of Red Gap: Charlie Ruggles, Charles Laughton, Mary Boland.

young miss, who was six years old when she made this post-Civil War story. She singlehandedly patched up a family feud, played cupid to her sister, foiled some rascally landgrabbers and softened up her crotchety grandfather (Lionel Barrymore). Her achievements were celebrated in a Technicolored party finale. She didn't sing, but she danced up and down a staircase with Bill "Bojangles" Robinson, the famous black vaudeville star making his second film and the first of five with the precocious moppet. Evelyn Venable and John Lodge played the parents. William Conselman's screenplay was derived from the novel by Annie Fellows Johnston, and David Butler directed.

Folies Bergere de Paris Maurice Chevalier starred in this musical comedy, which proved to be his last Hollywood film for 20 years. He played dual roles as a banker and as the Folies Bergere comic who impersonates him during a financial crisis. Merle Oberon was the banker's wife and Ann Sothern the comic's stage partner. An involved plot, taken from a play by Rudolph Lothar and Hans Adler, had the performer patching up the tattered marriage of the banker. Bess Meredyth and Hal Long wrote the screenplay and Roy Del Ruth directed. Chevalier sang several songs, joined in two of them by Ann Sothern, and Dave Gould created some spectacular dance numbers in the Busby Berkeley

The Little Colonel: Bill "Bojangles" Robinson, Shirley Temple.

manner for the Twentieth Century production released by United Artists. A more risqué French-language version was made simultaneously, Chevalier performing with a French cast and the chorus girls appearing bare-chested. In Britain, it was retitled *The Man from the Folies Bergere*. The same plot was re-used in *That Night in Rio* (1941) and *On the Riviera* (1952).

APRIL

Roberta
Naughty Marietta The film that first paired Jeanette MacDonald and

Naughty Marietta: Nelson Eddy, Jeanette Macdonald.

Nelson Eddy was based on a 1910 operetta by Victor Herbert. She appeared as the French princess who sails to colonial New Orleans, is captured by pirates, and rescued by Nelson Eddy's captain and his soldiers whose marching song is "Tramp, Tramp, Tramp Along the Highway". The two leads sang "Ah, Sweet Mystery of Life" among others, and proved there was an audience for filmed operettas, at least when they were performing them. Frank Morgan and Elsa Lanchester added comedy touches, and Douglass Dumbrille was also in support. W. S. Van Dyke II directed from a screenplay by John Lee Mahin, Frances Goodrich and Albert Hackett that discarded the operetta's original book.
Mississippi This Paramount musical comedy cast Bing Crosby as the showboat singer who accidentally gains a reputation as a killer and upsets girlfriend Joan Bennett. The Rodgers and Hart score provided Bing with "Down by the River", "Soon" and "Easy to Remember". W. C. Fields co-starred as the riverboat's captain with a classic sequence playing a crooked game of poker. Edward A. Sutherland was the director, and Jack Cunningham and Francis Martin wrote the script from a Booth Tarkington novel and play, which had been filmed before as *The Fighting*

Coward (1924) and *River of Romance* (1929).
Life Begins at 40 Like *The County Chairman*, this was a Will Rogers vehicle that embroiled him in small-town politics. He puts up a no-good loafer (Slim Summerville) to run for office against the local banker and newspaper proprietor (George Barbier) whose son (Thomas Beck) is ultimately revealed as a crook. For the customary juvenile romance, there was Richard Cromwell as the wrongly-convicted bank thief and Rochelle Hudson as Rogers' niece. The film had farcical interludes involving a duel and a stampede by pigs. Taking little more than its title from a book by Walter B. Pitkin, the Fox movie was written by Lamar Trotti and Robert Quillen and directed by George Marshall.
Gold Diggers of 1935 No longer confined to the production numbers, Busby Berkeley directed this First National (Warner Bros.) musical comedy in its entirety. The plot had Alice Brady as a miserly millionairess who stages an annual show for charity at a summer hotel, with Dick Powell as the hotel clerk who falls in love with her pretty daughter, played by Gloria Stuart, and Adolphe Menjou as a Russian impresario. Comedy stalwarts on hand were Hugh Herbert, Glenda Farrell and Frank McHugh. Manuel Seff, Peter Milne and Robert Lord wrote it. Best of the musical sequences was undoubtedly the extended "Lullaby of Broadway" number featuring Winifred Shaw with its startling, nightmarish conclusion. Berkeley also created a spectacular piece with 50 pianos waltzing to "The Words Are in My Heart", but critics

Gold Diggers of 1935: The Busby Berkeley number, "The Words Are in My Heart".

and audiences were no longer so impressed by such elaborate numbers, and it attracted little comment. The music and lyrics were again by Al Dubin and Harry Warren.
The Bride of Frankenstein This belated sequel to *Frankenstein* was first scripted by William Hurlbut and then angled for outrageous black humour by director James Whale and writer John L. Balderston. Rather than simply turn Frankenstein's monster loose again, the film developed the character (played again by Boris Karloff) into someone who has learned to speak, smoke cigars and drink wine. Ernest Thesiger joined Colin Clive's Henry Frankenstein as the mad Doctor Pretorius, creator of bottled homunculi and of the artificial woman (Elsa Lanchester) intended to be the creature's mate. Moodily photographed by John Mescall and scored by Franz Waxman, with Kenneth Strickfaden's electrical apparatus hissing and spluttering away once more, the film was macabre enough to hold audience interest despite its sophistication. Its success gave Universal head Carl Laemmle valuable breathing space to consider the company's future – losses had brought him to the point of selling. Running 75 minutes at its full length, *The Bride of Frankenstein* has a prologue with Elsa Lanchester as authoress Mary Shelley, which has sometimes been deleted. Universal returned to the subject in 1939's *Son of Frankenstein*.

MAY

G-Men Making amends for its past glamourization of gangsters, Hollywood set about glorifying the

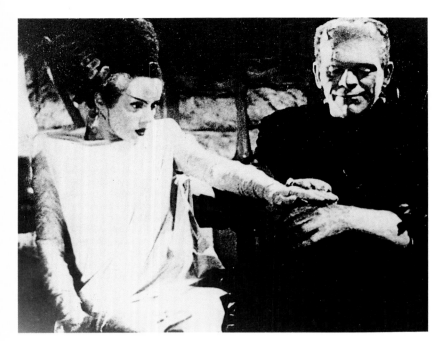

The Bride of Frankenstein: Elsa Lanchester, Boris Karloff.

forces of law and order, especially the crime-busting activities of the Department of Justice in Washington and its Federal Bureau of Investigation. And who better forcefully to rout the villains than the same actors who had so colourfully portrayed them earlier? Warner Bros.' *G-Men* was first on the scene. "Hollywood's Most Famous Bad Man Joins the 'G-Men' and Halts the March of Crime!" trumpeted the advertising. Edward G. Robinson had been first choice to play the government racket buster, but he declined. James Cagney was the next obvious choice, and he turned his customary pugnacious vitality to good effect as the federal agent who finds himself in conflict with the racketeer who befriended him in the slums of his youth. It was just as violent as previous crime pictures and made a huge profit on its modest $300,000 production cost, helped by newspaper headlines about a current real-life kidnapping case. William Keighley directed from Seton I. Miller's script based on a Gregory Rogers story. Ann Dvorak, Margaret Lindsay, Robert Armstrong, Barton MacLane and Lloyd Nolan supported.

Goin' to Town Mae West wrote herself another plum part as the western saloon entertainer who becomes an oil heiress and marries into society. She was the only Hollywood performer of the decade to write her own screenplays (although W. C. Fields created storylines and Will Rogers coloured his roles to suit his established style). Mae had several songs and was particularly notable satirizing opera by singing the part of Delilah from *Samson and Delilah* ("There's one lady barber that made good"). Mae's rather limp choice of

lovers – Paul Cavanagh, Monroe Owsley, Fred Kohler – ensured that she remained the centre of attraction. Marion Morgan and George B. Dowell provided the original story, and Alexander Hall directed the Paramount picture.

Naughty Marietta

Les Miserables Twentieth Century Productions made this lavish and intelligent adaptation of the Victor Hugo classic, with Fredric March as the convict whose later attempts to become a pillar of the community are threatened by Charles Laughton's unforgiving police officer, Javert. Cedric Hardwicke was a kindly

G-Men: Edward Pawley, James Cagney.

bishop, and March's actress wife Florence Eldridge played a social outcast. Others cast were Rochelle Hudson, Frances Drake, John Beal and Jessie Ralph. W. P. Lipscomb wrote the screenplay and Richard Boleslawski directed. Gregg Toland's cinematography was a major asset to the United Artists release. The oft-filmed story was next re-made in Hollywood in 1952 by 20th Century-Fox.

Bride of Frankenstein

Our Little Girl Shirley Temple again helped by a clever canine. Joel McCrea was her struggling doctor father who devotes himself to research, Rosemary Ames was her neglected mother whose attention is wandering towards the wealthy playboy portrayed by Lyle Talbot – but then Shirley steps in and stops her parents splitting up. The sentimental Fox drama drew women and children in droves. It was taken from a story, "Heaven's Gate", by Florence Leighton Pfalzgraf, and scripted by Stephen Avery and Allen Rivkin. John Robertson directed.

JUNE

No More Ladies Joan Crawford was the wife who marries Robert Montgomery's philanderer and eventually reforms him by clever means. Also on the scene were Franchot Tone (the devoted other man in the film, to be Crawford's husband in real life from October), and Edna May Oliver (playing a racy grandmother). MGM's production of A. E. Thomas's sophisticated comedy (a Broadway success in 1934 with Melvyn Douglas) was scripted by Donald Ogden Stewart and Horace Jackson and directed by Edward H. Griffith.

Oil for the Lamps of China The film version of a best-seller by Alice Tisdale Hobart, this showed Pat O'Brien as the loyal employee posted to China by an oil company and shabbily treated. Josephine Hutchinson was his long-suffering wife. The First National picture had a contrived happy ending, but there was no mistaking its denunciation of American business practices. Laird Doyle wrote the screenplay, and Mervyn LeRoy directed. The film was one of four completed that year under the Cosmopolitan banner. It was loosely remade as *Law of the Tropics* (1941).

Doubting Thomas Will Rogers again – this time he has to contend with his wife's determination to make a fool of herself in a local amateur play production. Billie Burke played the stage-struck spouse, and Alison Skipworth was the pompous producer. Rogers himself dressed up at one point, becoming barely recognizable as a crooner with slicked-back hair. Sterling Holloway, Gail Patrick and Helen Flint were among the supporting players. The Fox picture was derived from George Kelly's 1922 stage satire *The Torch Bearers* and revised for the screen by William Conselman. The director was David Butler. At the time of Will Rogers' death in an air crash on 15 August it was ending its run in lesser theatres, and there was a considerable upsurge in attendances.

Les Miserables

Becky Sharp This screen adaptation of Thackeray's classic *Vanity Fair* followed on quickly from a minor 1932 version with Myrna Loy. Its trump card was being the first feature in three-colour Technicolor throughout, although the renewed interest in period stories also boded well. Director Rouben Mamoulian (replacing Lowell Sherman, who had died after starting the film last December) worked with production designer Robert Edmond Jones and cinematographer Ray Rennahan to make intelligent use of colour for dramatic purposes, especially in the scene where the sound of war intrudes on the dancing in the ballroom and the red cloaks of the military fill the picture, but the film seemed dully confined to its drawing-room sets. The colour was praised but the treatment of the story pronounced dull. The absence of a sympathetic central character and of a handsome male lead was no help, although Miriam Hopkins was well cast as the ambitious, self-centred Becky who attempts to conquer Regency society. Alan Mowbray, Cedric Hardwicke and Nigel Bruce were some of the men in her life, while Frances Dee was the woman whose sweet manner contrasted with Becky's ruthlessness. The Francis Edwards Faragoh screenplay was based on the Landon Mitchell stage adaptation as much as on Thackeray's original text. Costing $950,000 before the manufacture of colour release prints, the Pioneer production was well attended but not the smash hit predicted. Its distributor, RKO Radio, had been reluctant to release it during the slack summer period, but it started off well in a dozen or more key cities this month, playing in New York at the Radio City Music Hall. In later years, it was reissued in Cinecolor (a primitive, two-colour process), and then put on American television in black-and-white, cut to 67 minutes from its original 83-minute running time. However, it was restored to its full Technicolor glory in 1984 and had a special presentation at the New York Film Festival, playing in 1985 at the London Film Festival.

JULY

Love Me Forever For its second Grace Moore film, Columbia followed *One Night of Love* with this story of a society girl reduced to singing in a café. She is groomed for opera stardom by a tough, music-loving nightclub owner (Leo Carrillo) and she gratefully settles his gambling losses after she has become a star at the Met and he has turned to drink. There were generous excerpts from *Rigoletto* and *La Bohème* (among others) in which Moore was partnered by Michael Bartlett. Though RKO was competing in the opera stakes with Lily Pons in *I Dream Too Much* and Paramount with Gladys Swarthout in *Rose of the Rancho*, they couldn't match Grace Moore's popularity. Victor Schertzinger directed from a script by Jo Swerling and Sidney Buchman. Robert Allen and Spring Byington headed the supporting cast. The original British release title was *On Wings of Song*.

Becky Sharp

Curly Top Fox's third new Shirley Temple feature of the year was loosely based on the Jean Webster novel *Daddy Long Legs*, which the studio had last filmed in 1931. She played the orphan who captivates wealthy playboy John Boles, sorts out his business problems and fixes him up with her older sister (Rochelle Hudson). Shirley danced and sang the songs "Animal Crackers in My Soup" and "When I Grow Up" (both by Ted Koehler, Irving Caesar and Ray Henderson). Jane Darwell, Arthur Treacher and Rafaela Ottiano were also cast. Irving Cummings directed from a screenplay by Patterson McNutt and Arthur Beckhard.

Front Page Woman Bette Davis and George Brent were rival news-hounds in love in this snappy Warner Bros. comedy, directed by Michael Curtiz. She was determined to show that women could make just as good reporters as men and solved a murder case to prove it. Roscoe Karns was a wisecracking photographer and Winifred Shaw a vital witness. The script, from a story by Richard Macaulay, was by Roy Chanslor, Lillie Hayward and Laird Doyle.

The Raven Universal maintained its reputation for horror with this crisp 61-minute tale supposedly inspired by Edgar Allan Poe's poem. It reunited the two horror kings, Bela Lugosi and Boris Karloff, previously teamed in 1934's *The Black Cat*. Lugosi was the mad doctor, obsessed by the works of Poe, who constructs a torture chamber in his dungeon and seeks revenge on the girl (Irene Ware) who spurned his love, on her obstructive father (Samuel S. Hinds), and on the man she really loves (Lester Matthews). Karloff was the wanted criminal with mutilated features who reluctantly assists Lugosi. The film was mutilated by censors in New York, Ohio, Pennsylvania, Virginia and elsewhere who objected to the torture and shooting scenes. David Boehm wrote the picture, which Louis Friedlander (later known as Lew Landers) directed.

No More Ladies

Broadway Gondolier Dick Powell was the New York taxi driver who wants to be a radio singer. He goes to Venice and hits the jackpot after becoming a singing gondolier. Joan Blondell was Powell's girlfriend in the film; it was the fifth time they'd worked together and they married in real life later in the year. (Blondell remained friendly with her previous husband, cinematographer George Barnes, who photographed this and others of her pictures.) The script came from Sig Herzig, Warren Duff, Jerry Wald, Julius J. Epstein, Hans Kraly and E. Y. Harburg, and made fun of commercial radio. The seven songs were by Harry Warren and Al Dubin and included "Lulu's Back in Town", which became a standard, and "The Rose in Her Hair". The Mills Brothers and Ted Fiorita and his Orchestra supported Powell. The director was Lloyd Bacon and the other key players in the Warner Bros.' musical were Adolphe Menjou, Louise Fazenda and Grant Mitchell.

AUGUST

Curly Top

China Seas Irving Thalberg put three top stars together – Clark Gable, Jean Harlow and Wallace Beery – and spared no expense on this gusty and sometimes brutal adventure yarn,

China Seas: Wallace Beery, Clark Gable, Ivan Lebedeff. Torture in a Chinese foot rack.

written by Jules Furthman and James Kevin McGuinness, from the novel by Crosbie Garstin, and directed by Tay Garnett. Gable was the ship's captain who carries a gold shipment safely across the China Seas despite the efforts of an old flame called China Doll (Harlow) and a crooked trader (Beery) to help pirates prise it from him. Lewis Stone, Rosalind Russell (as an aristocratic Britisher), Dudley Digges, C. Aubrey Smith and Robert Benchley provided strong support. Unusually, for a top MGM attraction, this film required almost no work after previews and the number of re-takes was a record low.
Broadway Gondolier
Alice Adams Katharine Hepburn had the title role in RKO Radio's adaptation of the Booth Tarkington novel (previously filmed in 1923). Her small-town girl, ashamed of her modest background, wants to climb the social tree. Fred MacMurray was the nice young man who comes to dinner with her family – when all her special arrangements to appear posh go disastrously wrong in a scene of exquisite embarrassment. Hepburn and her young director, George Stevens, retained sympathy for the ambitious Alice. Ann Shoemaker and Fred Stone played the parents, Frank Albertson the brash brother. Jane Murfin, Dorothy Yost and Mortimer Offner were the scenarists.

SEPTEMBER

Top Hat Fred Astaire and Ginger Rogers proved triumphantly that they could carry a picture on their own as *Top Hat* became the biggest hit of the year so far. There was an amiable plot, copied pretty much from *The Gay Divorcee* – a romance hindered by mistakes of identity, starting in London, moving to a gorgeously

fantasized Venice – and there was deft comedy from Edward Everett Horton and Eric Blore, along with Helen Broderick. But the song and dance numbers made the big impact: Fred in his solo "Top Hat, White Tie and Tails"; the pair singing, then dancing "Cheek to Cheek"; and their speciality dance "The Piccolino", etc. Irving Berlin wrote his first complete film musical since 1930, while Dwight Taylor and Allan Scott provided the screenplay for the RKO Radio picture, directed by Mark Sandrich.
Steamboat Round the Bend Will Rogers had died before this accomplished comedy, his third with director John Ford, came out. It was rushed into release although some

Top Hat: Ginger Rogers, Fred Astaire. "Isn't This a Lovely Day?" number.

Alice Adams: Ann Shoemaker, Fred MacMurray, Hattie McDaniel, Katharine Hepburn, Fred Stone. Putting on airs: the calamitous dinner.

exhibitors delayed playing it, fearful that they would seem to be cashing in on his death. Rogers played the patent medicine salesman who becomes captain of a Mississippi stern-wheeler with a waxworks show on board. There was a near hanging of his nephew, found guilty of murder, and a steamboat race to the rescue. Anne Shirley, Eugene Pallette, John McGuire, Berton Churchill and Irvin S. Cobb appeared, while Stepin Fetchit contributed some imbecilic humour, which has now become a source of embarrassment. Dudley Nichols and Lamar Trotti wrote the script from a story by Ben Lucian Burman. The Fox production was one of the first to be released by the merged 20th Century-Fox.
Anna Karenina Garbo was applauded by the critics for her portrayal of Tolstoy's tragic heroine who loses everything for love. Basil Rathbone was the husband she deserts, Fredric March the army officer she chooses instead and Freddie Bartholomew followed *David Copperfield* by playing the son she reluctantly leaves behind. Also cast in David O. Selznick's MGM production were Maureen O'Sullivan, May Robson, Reginald Owen and Reginald Denny. Clemence Dane, Salka Viertel and S. N. Behrman wrote the screenplay, and Clarence Brown directed. Garbo had previously made a silent version of the story, *Love* (1927).
China Seas
Diamond Jim Bulky character actor Edward Arnold portrayed Diamond Jim Brady in this screen biography by Preston Sturges from a book by Parker Morrell. An incurable romantic continually disappointed in love, the clumsy, well-intentioned Jim indulges his other great passion for food and finally feasts to death when he has nothing left to live for. Jean

Steamboat Round the Bend: Anne Shirley, Will Rogers.

Arthur had a dual role as two of the women who didn't love him, while Binnie Barnes played the singer Lillian Russell who also turned him down. Edward A. Sutherland directed the Universal picture. Edward Arnold played Brady again in the 1940 musical, *Lillian Russell*.

OCTOBER

Broadway Melody of 1936 The second of four MGM *Broadway Melody* pictures (the first had been a smash hit of 1929), this gave Eleanor Powell her big break and established her as the studio's new dancing draw and closest

Diamond Jim: Edward Arnold, Jean Arthur.

thing to a female Fred Astaire. She played the old childhood sweetheart of a stage producer (Robert Taylor, too young for the part but getting his best chance yet), and she masquerades as a fictitious Parisian star to win the lead in his new production. Jack Benny was top-billed as the obnoxious Broadway columnist feuding with the producer, while June Knight appeared as an untalented leading lady. Frances Langford sang "Broadway Rhythm" and other songs by Arthur Freed and Nacio Herb Brown. Moss Hart provided the original story, developed into a screenplay by Sid Silvers (who also appeared) and Jack McGowan. Roy Del Ruth was the director.

Barbary Coast This story of San Francisco during the turbulent gold rush days was the picture that Samuel Goldwyn had been forced to postpone earlier. Miriam Hopkins made her

first for the producer as the gambling hostess in a San Francisco saloon and mistress of its proprietor (Edward G. Robinson). He proves reluctant to give her up when she falls for an idealistic young prospector (Joel McCrea). Playing Robinson's tough henchman was Brian Donlevy, while Walter Brennan became a character actor to note as the toothless old-timer known as "Old Atrocity". A vital role was that of the crusading newspaper editor played by Frank Craven, as his perspective on the district's immorality made the subject acceptable to the Hays Office for filming after 15 months of hassle. David Niven had probably his first role, a bit as a Cockney sailor with a drooping moustache. The script was by Ben Hecht and Charles MacArthur, and the direction was by Howard Hawks. As usual for a Goldwyn picture, United Artists distributed. There was a close imitation from Warner Bros., *The Frisco Kid* with James Cagney, while the Barbary Coast was soon to be the setting for MGM's *San Francisco*.

She Married Her Boss Claudette Colbert starred as the secretary who marries her wealthy boss (Melvyn Douglas) and liberates him and his family from their stuffy, affected ways. Edith Fellows played his brattish daughter and Katharine Alexander his hoity-toity sister, while Raymond Walburn was the knowing butler. Gregory La Cava directed the Columbia comedy from a screenplay by Sidney Buchman based on a story by Thyra Samter Winslow.

NOVEMBER

Mutiny on the Bounty Irving Thalberg's MGM production overtook *Top Hat* to become the box-office champion of the year, enabling its director Frank Lloyd to match his success with *Cavalcade*. The studio spent $1,905,000 to bring the seafaring adventure story by Charles Nordhoff and James Hall to the screen, making it the costliest talkie to date. Clark Gable was initially dubious about being seen in the knicker outfit of leading mutineer Fletcher Christian (he also shed his moustache for the role), but Charles Laughton relished the opportunity to play the sadistic Captain Bligh, and Gable had to watch him steal the picture. Franchot Tone was cast as a midshipman who befriends Christian, and Movita and Momo played Tahitian girls with whom they fell in love. Scenes were shot at Catalina Island off the Californian coast over a four-month period, using a full-scale *H.M.S. Bounty*, and in the studio tank, while special background footage was shot in Tahiti for the sequences set there. Talbots Jennings, Jules Furthman and Carey Wilson wrote the screenplay. The picture made a handsome profit, approaching $1 million, and was disastrously re-made in 1962 by the studio.

A Night at the Opera The Marx Brothers resumed their screen career (minus straight man Zeppo) under Irving Thalberg's aegis at MGM, accepting his assessment that their anarchic humour needed to be softened to widen their appeal. The script, devised by the team's old writers, George S. Kaufman and Morrie Ryskind, from a story by James Kevin McGuinness, was specially tested for laughs on a West coast tour of vaudeville theatres to get it into the best possible shape. Many of its sequences have become classics – Chico and Groucho's contract scene, the jam-packed stateroom episode, the climactic wrecking of the opera performance – but the Marxes were subtly diminished in stature to gain some sympathy. They also had to stand aside for a trite romance and some good songs from Kitty Carlisle and Allan Jones. Margaret Dumont was again a magnificent foil for Groucho, and Siegfried Rumann as the pompous director of the opera house was an ideal subject for Marxian deflation. Sam Wood directed.

Thanks a Million Dick Powell was borrowed from Warner Bros. to star as a band singer in 20th Century-Fox's political satire. He replaces Raymond Walburn's inept politician and runs for governor as a stunt to gain more attention as a performer. Fred Allen made his screen debut as Powell's shrewd manager while Ann Dvorak was the girl. Paul Whiteman and his Orchestra were featured. The script was by Nunnally Johnson from a story by production head Darryl F. Zanuck (using his Melville Crossman pseudonym). Roy Del Ruth directed,

Mutiny on the Bounty: Charles Laughton, Clark Gable.

and there were songs by Gus Kahn, Arthur Johnston, Bert Kalmar and Harry Ruby.

A Midsummer Night's Dream For 30 years the German producer Max Reinhardt had been staging *A Midsummer Night's Dream* in all kinds of settings, and his presentation of Shakespeare's comedy in the Hollywood Bowl had taken the town by storm, playing to over 100,000 spectators in a seven-night run and taking over a quarter of a million dollars. When Warner Bros. invited Reinhardt to make a film version, the studio's stars fell over themselves to be in it. Mickey Rooney, who had played Puck so successfully at the Bowl, was borrowed from MGM to

repeat the part in the film, and Olivia de Havilland, the understudy who had played Hermia on opening night, was signed by Warner Bros. at Max Reinhardt's request. From the Warner ranks came James Cagney (Bottom), Dick Powell (Lysander), Joe E. Brown (Flute), Ian Hunter (the only British player, as Theseus), Frank McHugh (Quince), Hugh Herbert (Snout), Ross Alexander (Demetrius) and others. The film was lavishly made with William Dieterle as co-director (to help Reinhardt with cinematic technicalities), Hal Mohr as cameraman, and Erich Wolfgang Korngold adapting and conducting the music of Felix Mendlessohn (and starting his career at Warner Bros. where he became a staff composer). Charles Kenyon and Mary McCall Jr wrote the screen adaptation. The very

A Night at the Opera: Harpo Marx, Chico Marx and Allan Jones (all behind whiskers), Groucho Marx, Robert Emmett O'Connor (to Groucho's left).

expensive picture (costing around $1.3 million) was carefully exploited and attracted a mixture of the stars' fans and the carriage trade. It was reported to have reached a very impressive $1,543,447 in rental by mid-June 1936, and brought (in the words of production chief Hal B. Wallis) "unlimited prestige" to Warner Bros. The company announced (but never made) films of four other Shakespearean comedies while MGM was encouraged to tackle *Romeo and Juliet*.

DECEMBER

Mutiny on the Bounty
A Night at the Opera
In Old Kentucky In his last film, the late Will Rogers was seen in a typical rustic comedy as a veteran horse-trainer caught up in a feud that is resolved by a big race. Dorothy Wilson and Russell Hardie provided the romantic interest, Bill Robinson added some of his lightning tap-dancing, and Etienne Girardot had a scene-stealing part as rainmaker Pluvius J. Aspinwall, called in to produce a muddy track to benefit the steed that Will Rogers is training. Charles T. Dazey's source play had been filmed twice previously in 1909 and 1927 – this time round it was adapted by Sam Hellman and Gladys Johnson, directed by George Marshall and released by 20th Century-Fox.

Annie Oakley Not a western but a romantic drama, this gave a golden opportunity to Barbara Stanwyck, playing the sharpshooter from the Ohio backwoods who becomes a performer in the Wild West show of Moroni Olsen's Buffalo Bill. Preston Foster co-starred as the marksman she outmatched, and the film was really the story of a woman's triumph in a man's world. Melvyn Douglas appeared as the show's manager, and Chief Thundercloud was Sitting Bull. The RKO Radio picture was directed by George Stevens and scripted by Joel Sayre and John Twist from a story by Joseph A. Fields and Ewart Adamson.

Thanks a Million
Frisco Kid James Cagney asserted himself in San Francisco's notorious waterfront area in the Gay Nineties in

this Warner Bros. imitation of the recent Goldwyn picture, *Barbary Coast*. Margaret Lindsay was the crusading newspaper editor, Barton MacLane a burly villain and Fred Kohler was the hook-armed heavy

with whom Cagney brawled. Warren Duff and Seton I. Miller wrote the script, Lloyd Bacon directed. This was one of the films that Cagney complained about in his contract dispute.

TEN BEST-CRITICS' CHOICE

In the *Film Daily* annual poll, in which 451 critics, reviewers and entertainment editors participated, the voting for the year's best pictures was as follows:

1.	*David Copperfield*	339
2.	*The Lives of a Bengal Lancer*	278
3.	*The Informer*	256
4.	*Naughty Marietta*	250
5.	*Les Miserables*	235
6.	*Ruggles of Red Gap*	222
7.	*Top Hat*	174
8.	*Broadway Melody of 1936*	166
9.	*Roberta*	155
10.	*Anna Karenina*	129
	Close Runners Up	
11.	*Alice Adams*	115
12.	*The Dark Angel*	96
13.	*Imitation of Life* [late 1934 release]	89

Popular taste differed markedly from that of the professional commentators only in respect of John Ford's drama of the Irish troubles, *The Informer*, which still attracted enough of an audience to cover its very low budget and brought its makers, RKO Radio, considerable prestige.

CLOSE RUNNERS UP

21 more films also gained considerable support from big city moviegoers and came close to being included among the hits of the year: *Accent on Youth* (August), *The Big Broadcast of 1936* (September), *Call of the Wild* (August, September), *The Crusades* (November), *The Dark Angel* (September), *Devil Dogs of the Air* (February), *The Gilded Lily* (February), *The Irish In Us* (August), *I Live My Life* (October), *Let 'Em Have It* (June), *Metropolitan* (November), *The Mighty Barnum* (January, also December 1934), *Public Hero Number One* (June), *Reckless* (April), *Sequoia* (March), *Shipmates Forever* (October), *So Red the Rose* (December), *Star of Midnight* (April), *West Point of the Air* (March), *The Whole Town's Talking* (March), *Wings in the Dark* (February).

1936

Magnificent Obsession
Robert Taylor,
Irene Dunne

Prosperity was in the air as attendances at American movie theatres climbed to a weekly average of 88 million from 80 million the year before. New theatres were again being built and opened, although without the enormous seating capacities of before. There was some fall-back in the use of gimmicks like gift stamps and bingo to haul the customers in, but they continued for the rest of the decade (some of the prize games became a regular source of profit to theatre operators). Vaudeville support became less popular as big circuits like Loew's and RKO dropped it from many theatres in favour of double-bill programmes.

The major film companies were in a healthier state. Loew's (MGM) was the profit leader as usual with $10.6 million. MGM's production of *San Francisco* was the year's best single item of good news as it became the first really huge domestic money-maker of the decade. MGM also had the big new star of the year, Robert Taylor, as well as Jeanette MacDonald, who became a top draw in America for the first time, thanks to *San Francisco* and her teaming with Nelson Eddy.

Paramount was well in the black, too, and film men took back control from the bankers. 20th Century-Fox was making big money, proving the wisdom of merging Fox and Twentieth Century. RKO Radio was making profits but remained in the hands of trustees because of an inability to reach a settlement on a claim for $9.1 million by the Rockefeller interests.

Only Universal was operating in the red, and founder Carl Laemmle sold his stock and retired from the company with his son, production head Carl Laemmle Jr. Universal had been the last of the big companies still being operated by its founder. Control passed to the Standard Capital Corporation, which was in part backed by a British group headed by C. M. Woolf, whose General Film Distributors gained distribution rights to Universal pictures in Britain.

New legislation removed certain tax advantages in maintaining subsidiaries. One effect was that Warner Bros. dissolved First National and the last films were copyrighted in its name in 1936. However, Warners still kept the name in use and there were "First National pictures" for many years to come. (In Britain, First National continued as a separate entity with a different London address, a different managing director from Warner Bros. – although with other directors in common – and with its own branch offices until late August 1939, releasing the films from Hollywood carrying its trade name.)

Here two new young stars have made an impression in cement for display in the forecourt of Grauman's Chinese Theater on Hollywood Boulevard. Footprints, handprints, signature and message were customary and continue to be added, with paving stones of now-forgotten stars reputedly removed into storage to make way for the new. Designed by Meyer and Holler for showman Sid Grauman and opened in 1927, the Chinese was often the setting for spectacular premieres, both real and as re-created in movies about Hollywood. The one in progress above is for *Morocco* on 25 November 1930. The fantasy forecourt in the style of an Oriental garden leads into an auditorium behind (searchlights mounted on the roof), which continues the Chinese motif and originally seated 2,258 on a single floor. In 1987, the theatre continues in business as Mann's Chinese, seating 1,492, with two additional auditoria (added in 1979).

British films continued to make an impact on the American box-office, especially the Alexander Korda London Films productions *The Ghost Goes West* and *Things to Come* and the Gaumont-British productions *It's Love Again* and *Mr Hobo* (the American title for *The Guvnor*). These films generally had British stars familiar to American moviegoers and American players in co-starring roles (like Robert Young opposite British musical star Jessie Matthews in *It's Love Again*). These films also relied considerably on American talent behind the scenes – writers, art directors, cinematographers – to help make them more acceptable to American audiences.

There was more and more pressure from the craft guilds in Hollywood representing actors, directors and writers to give them full recognition and negotiating rights with the big studios. Largely funded by the big studios whose bosses had founded it, the Academy of Motion Picture Arts and Sciences continued to come under attack as a company tool, and its survival seemed threatened. Many stars boycotted the Academy Awards, and new president Frank Capra took rapid steps to ensure AMPAS's future independence and to regain the support of the industry's rank and file.

STAR WARS

In 1936 the stars began to fight the bosses. It was Warner Bros. that stirred up the most trouble.

In the previous year, the company had gone to court in England to try and make Robert Donat star in *Captain Blood* and *Anthony Adverse*, but the judge found that there was no proper and binding agreement, and Warner Bros. lost its appeal against the decision.

Now James Cagney went to court seeking to have his contract terminated because of violations. He maintained that he had an oral agreement with Jack L. Warner that he would have to make no more than four pictures a year, yet he had been making five. He referred to *Devil Dogs of the Air* (1935) and others as films that were so bad that they were harming his career. Cagney won the case, more on a technicality than anything else, and was free to work where he wanted. Despite his immense popularity, no major studio would break ranks and sign him. He eventually went to work with the newly-formed Grand National Pictures, making two films – *Great Guy* (1936) and *Something to Sing About* (1937) – that were nowhere near as popular as his Warner films.

He made peace with Warners, which gave him all the conditions he wanted, and resumed his career there with *Boy Meets Girl* (1938).

Others, like Bette Davis, watched. She was dismayed that after appearing in such worthwhile films as *Of Human Bondage* and *The Petrified Forest*, she was being put in feeble pictures like *The Golden Arrow* and *Satan Met a Lady*. She went on suspension and decided to break her contract by making two films in England for producer Ludovic Toeplitz. Warners went to court and won an injunction to prevent her working there. On advice from George Arliss, she decided against an appeal and returned to Hollywood. Warner Bros. recognized that she was serious about her career, and welcomed her back with better parts.

Elsewhere, stars like Marlene Dietrich, Mae West and Grace Moore were also in dispute with the bosses. But it would be another Warner star, Olivia de Havilland, who rebelled against the conditions of her contract in the early 1940s and won a major victory after a three-year fight.

HITS OF THE YEAR

JANUARY

Magnificent Obsession Universal's weepie romance top-starred Irene Dunne as a blinded widow, but it was Robert Taylor (borrowed from MGM) who stole the attention. He was the drunken playboy who, to redeem himself after causing her accident, becomes a leading eye surgeon and eventually restores her sight. Dunne had gone much the same dramatic route in *Symphony of Six Million*.) Charles Butterworth, Betty Furness and Ralph Morgan were also featured. George O'Neill, Sarah Y. Mason and Victor Heerman handled the adaptation of Lloyd C. Douglas's best seller and John M. Stahl directed. The 1954 re-make made a major new star out of Rock Hudson.

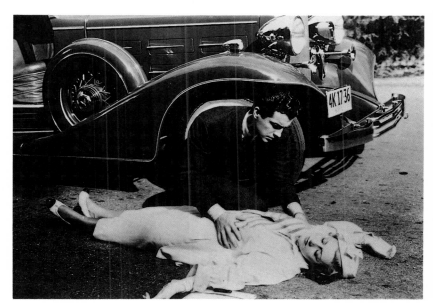

Magnificent Obsession: Robert Taylor, Irene Dunne.

A Tale of Two Cities David O. Selznick followed *David Copperfield* with another adaptation of Charles Dickens, his last picture for MGM before becoming a leading independent producer. Shed of his

A Tale of Two Cities: Ronald Colman, Donald Woods.

moustache, Ronald Colman was the dissolute Sydney Carton who did the far, far better thing by going to the guillotine during the French Revolution in place of Donald Woods' French aristocrat. Elizabeth Allan was the woman who prompted his sacrifice, Isabel Jewell the one he comforted in the tumbril. Basil Rathbone, Edna May Oliver and Blanche Yurka had notable supporting roles. Jack Conway directed from a screenplay by W. P. Lipscomb and S. N. Behrman. The Revolution sequence was directed by Val Lewton and Jacques Tourneur.

The Littlest Rebel This time Shirley Temple saved her Confederate officer father (John Boles) from being shot by having a quiet word with President Lincoln (Frank McGlynn Sr). She also sang "Polly Woodle Doodle" and danced again with Bill Robinson as the family butler. Jack Holt was a kind-hearted Union officer. Edward Peple's 1911 stage play (previously filmed in 1914) was adapted by Edwin Burke and directed for 20th Century-Fox by David Butler.

King of Burlesque Warner Baxter was the former burlesque producer whose career in the legitimate theatre is in trouble. Alice Faye (in her first big opportunity) was the singer who loves him and rallies to his side. She had the hit song "I'm Shootin' High" as well as "Lovely Lady" and "I've Got My Fingers Crossed". Jack Oakie delivered the comedy, Fats Waller performed briefly. The 20th Century-Fox musical had distinct echoes of *42nd Street*. Gene Markey and Harry Tugend were the scriptwriters, working from a story by Vina Delmar, and Sidney Lanfield directed.

Captain Blood Cashing in on the predictable enthusiasm for nautical subjects after *Mutiny on the Bounty*, Warner Bros. revived the sea-faring swashbuckler with this stirring new film version of Rafael Sabatini's 1922 novel (first filmed in 1923). Errol Flynn was a virtually unknown contract artist with a few Hollywood supporting roles behind him when he

Captain Blood: Olivia de Havilland, Errol Flynn.

was cast as the young physician who escapes from prison in Jamaica and becomes a pirate. The film made him a star. Playing a plantation owner's daughter, Olivia de Havilland was another recent newcomer to films, and she clinched her position as a leading lady, as well as becoming the ideal co-star for Errol. In support, Basil Rathbone was a French pirate who duelled with Flynn on a Caribbean shore (actually Laguna Beach), while Lionel Atwill, Ross Alexander, Guy Kibbee and Henry Stephenson appeared in other roles. Casey Robinson did the screenplay, Michael Curtiz directed with panache, and Erich Wolfgang Korngold contributed his first original film score. This was a First National (Warner Bros.) picture through Cosmopolitan Productions.

The Bride Comes Home Will Claudette Colbert's impoverished socialite remain true to her class and marry wealthy magazine publisher Robert Young or will she succumb to the advances of his burly bodyguard Fred MacMurray? Edgar Kennedy's justice of the peace slow-burned while Colbert dithered, much as she had done in another romantic comedy, *The Gilded Lily*, for the same studio (Paramount), director (Wesley Ruggles) and writer (Claude Binyon, using an Elizabeth Sanxay Holding story). Even one of her co-stars (MacMurray) was the same.

FEBRUARY

Rose Marie Nelson Eddy and Jeanette MacDonald confirmed their drawing power in screen operetta in MGM's follow-up to *Naughty Marietta*, stimulated by the 1924 work of Otto Harbach and Oscar Hammerstein II (book and lyrics) and Rudolf Friml (music). She was the Canadian opera star, he was the Mountie and newcomer James Stewart was her killer brother they both sought in the wilds for different reasons. Another newcomer, David Niven, was seen as one of MacDonald's suitors. She and Eddy sang "Indian Love Call", "Song of the Mounties" and "Rose Marie, I Love You" among others. W. S. Van

Rose Marie: Nelson Eddy, Jeanette MacDonald. Singing "Indian Love Call".

Dyke II handled the direction, while the script was delivered by Frances Goodrich, Albert Hackett and Alice Duer Miller. *Indian Love Call* became its television title to distinguish it from the 1954 *Rose Marie* with Ann Blyth and Howard Keel. MGM had also made a silent version with Joan Crawford in 1927.

Modern Times In his first film since 1931's *City Lights*, Charles Chaplin wrote, produced, directed, scored and starred in his comic vision of the modern machine age. Yet again Chaplin resisted speech, relying on a musical accompaniment and sound effects (although his voice could be heard singing a jumble of meaningless phrases at the end). *Modern Times* marked the last appearance of the Gentleman Tramp, who here is unable to adapt to the times and prefers life in jail until his love for a waif (Paulette Goddard) gives him new hope for the

future. Chaplin's painstaking methods meant that his film cost $1.5 million to produce, too much to recover from the American market. The Nazi government in Germany banned it, but otherwise Charlie's worldwide popularity (enhanced by the film's lack of dialogue) ensured a profit for United Artists.

Follow the Fleet In the new Astaire and Rogers musical, sailor Fred and buddy Randolph Scott romanced dance-hall sisters Ginger and Harriet Hilliard (a popular radio songstress). Irving Berlin gave it seven new songs including "Let's Face the Music and Dance", to the music of which Fred and Ginger did indeed dance in the casino finale. The film dispensed with the droll supporting humour of its predecessors, and the subsidiary romance between Scott and Hilliard was a heavy-going substitute. Mark Sandrich and Dwight Taylor again

Modern Times: Charlie Chaplin.

handled directing and writing respectively, the source material being a play by Herbert Osborne that had inspired an earlier RKO musical, *Hit the Deck* (1930). Lucille Ball and Betty Grable had bits.

A Tale of Two Cities

The Story of Louis Pasteur Warner Bros. returned to biographical portraits of history's great men for the first time since *Voltaire* in 1933, with Paul Muni taking the place of George Arliss. The First National (Warner Bros.) production went in straightforward fashion from Pasteur's early years of struggle, when his ideas for fighting disease were derided, through to the ultimate accolade of his profession. With its brief scientific

The Story of Louis Pasteur: Donald
Woods, Paul Muni.

explanations, it counted as an
educational aid, attracting special
screenings for schools. Muni
nominated the film, with Josephine
Hutchinson and Anita Louise as his
wife and daughter and Donald
Woods, Fritz Leiber, Henry O'Neill,
Porter Hall and others as members of
the medical profession. Sheridan
Gibney and Pierre Collings provided
the screenplay and William Dieterle
directed.

Ceiling Zero Cagney's last film for
Warner Bros. before his breakaway
cast him as an aerial daredevil who
makes amends for his irresponsibility
by testing a new de-icing device in
dangerous conditions. Pat O'Brien
was an airline manager and Stuart
Erwin a flying pal, while June Travis
was the aviatrix with whom Cagney
dallied when he should have been up
in the sky. Frank Wead wrote it from
his stage play, and Howard Hawks
directed. It was billed as a
Cosmopolitan production and later
adapted for *International Squadron*
(1941).

MARCH

Follow the Fleet
The Country Doctor 20th Century-Fox
found an even younger attraction than
Shirley Temple – the famous Dionne
Quintuplets, born two years before.
The infants – Yvonne, Cecile, Marie,
Annette and Emelie – were the
highlight of this drama concerning an
unappreciated, hard-working doctor
(Jean Hersholt) in a small Canadian
community whose pleas for a proper
hospital are heard only after he
becomes a national hero delivering
quintuplets and making medical

history. Henry King directed from
Sonya Levien's script. June Lang,
Slim Summerville, Michael Whalen,
Dorothy Peterson and John Qualen
were also cast, while the real country
doctor, Allan Roy Dafoe, acted as
consultant. Following the success of

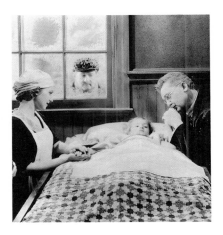

The Country Doctor: June Lang, one of the
Dionnes, Jean Hersholt.

this film's mass launch into 322
theatres simultaneously from 6 March,
the Dionnes were rushed into a
sequel, *Reunion*, released later this
year, and also did *Five of a Kind*
(1938), again for 20th Century-Fox.
(RKO Radio moved in on their fifth
anniversary, putting them in a two-
reeler, *Five Times Five*, with
Alexander Woollcott.)

Wife vs. Secretary The title told all:
Myrna Loy's spouse fought Jean
Harlow's office girl with Clark Gable's
magazine publisher as the prize.
When, as required by the moral
climate of the times, the sanctity of
marriage was upheld, Harlow's old
boyfriend (James Stewart, still in the
supporting ranks) was on hand to
console her. MGM's comedy was
written by Norman Krasna, Alice
Duer Miller and John Lee Mahin from
a Faith Baldwin story, while Clarence
Brown directed. May Robson and
George Barbier also acted in it.

Modern Times
The Story of Louis Pasteur
The Trail of the Lonesome Pine The
use of the three-strip Technicolor
process for location filming in the
great outdoors impressed audiences
much more than the artificial settings
of *Becky Sharp*, because it was less
distracting and more natural in its
application. But then the Walter
Wanger/Paramount production also
had the help of a strong if familiar
storyline (twice filmed before) and
attractive players. Fred MacMurray
was the engineer who walks into the
middle of a long-running feud
between two mountain clans. Sylvia
Sidney was the girl who wants revenge
when her young brother (Spanky
McFarland) is killed, and Henry
Fonda (in his fourth film) was an
idealistic member of the family who
dies in the quest for revenge (his
performance was reputedly the
inspiration for Al Capp to create L'il

The Trail of the Lonesome Pine: Beulah
Bondi, Fred Stone, Henry Fonda.

Abner). Beulah Bondi appeared as the mother who craves peace. Harvey Thew, Horace McCoy and Grover Jones adapted John Fox Jr's novel to the screen and, as in *The Lives of a Bengal Lancer*, Henry Hathaway demonstrated his proficiency as an action director. W. Howard Greene was the Technicolor cinematographer.

Klondike Annie Mae West was in trouble again, but the mass audience still liked her. She went way over schedule as usual and pushed the cost of the picture (originally budgeted at $750,000) towards $1.5 million (sacking her original cameraman and running up huge extra costs – in dressmaking, particularly, as she fussed over looking her best). Then the film was classified "objectionable in part" by the Legion of Decency and fiercely attacked by the Hearst press, which in Baltimore refused even to carry advertising for the picture. The main objection was to Mae's masquerade as a Salvation Army missionary to avoid the police, although she is shown becoming sincerely interested in revitalizing the weekly meetings and lifting the mission hall's debts. Among her songs was "Occidental Woman" ("I'm an Occidental Woman in an Oriental Mood for Love"). The men in her life were ship's captain Victor McLaglen and Mountie Philip Reed. Once again Mae wrote her own script for the film, which Raoul Walsh directed for Paramount.

Colleen The first big Warner Bros. musical for nearly a year opened with a splash at 200 theatres. It would be the last time that Dick Powell romanced Ruby Keeler. She sang and danced "You Gotta Know How to Dance" with Paul Draper, while Powell sang "An Evening with You". In another of Harry Warren and Al Dubin's four songs, Joan Blondell joined Jack Oakie in the comical "A Boulevardier from the Bronx". Hugh Herbert was around as an eccentric millionaire who likes gold-diggers. Bobby Connolly staged the dances, while Alfred E. Green was the director. Peter Milne and F. Hugh Herbert (a different Herbert from the character actor) scripted from a Robert Lord story.

APRIL

Mr Deeds Goes to Town Frank Capra's Depression fable enchanted critics and public alike. Gary Cooper's naïve greetings-card poet who inherits $20 million and wants to give it away to the deserving poor was an immensely sympathetic character, and Robert Riskin's script (from a story by Clarence Budington Kelland) skilfully stacked up the odds against him,

THE ACADEMY AWARDS

The Academy's standing was at a low ebb. Membership had dwindled to a few hundred. The Screen Actors Guild and the Writers Guild were in open warfare with the Academy over their demand for recognition from producers and acceptance of their standard form of contract. They advised their members to boycott the Academy Awards. The studios gave seats away to secretaries, but even so there were some empty places at the banquet on 5 March at the Biltmore Hotel. To counter what looked like being a disastrous evening, Academy President Frank Capra arranged for D. W. Griffith to be given a special statuette in recognition of all his achievements. This brought the director back to the town where he was no longer able to work for his first trip in some years. In an attempt to be more democratic, the Academy also allowed write-in votes in all categories except art direction, though this resulted in Jack Warner exhorting his employees to show their loyalty and write in top talent at the studio. The nominations in particular fields were by those Academy members who practised in that area – thus Academy members who were directors nominated the best directors, although the whole membership voted to choose the actual winner and could write in their own choice. In many categories voters did write in names that came second to the winner, while Warner's initiative actually succeeded when the Best Cinematography Award went to Hal Mohr for *A Midsummer Night's Dream*, even though he hadn't been officially nominated.

Some of the evening's winners were deliberately absent, but the Academy could be thankful that the winners for Best Actor and Best Actress were there. D. W. Griffith presented Oscars to Victor McLaglen for *The Informer* and Bette Davis for *Dangerous*. The latter was a big surprise, and it was generally felt to be in belated recognition of her work in *Of Human Bondage* the year before (for which she hadn't been nominated). *The Informer* also won the Award for Best Director and Best Screenplay, but neither John Ford nor Dudley Nichols was present, and Nichols subsequently refused to accept his Oscar because of the writers' dispute with the Academy and regretted that he had allowed himself to be nominated. (Two years later, Nichols collected the Award when the Academy had reformed itself.)

The Informer was one of 12 films nominated as Best Picture, and it looked odd when it didn't win after picking up three other key Awards. It came second to *Mutiny on the Bounty*. Other winners were Ben Hecht and Charles MacArthur for Best Story (*The Scoundrel*); Richard Day for Best Interior Decoration (*The Dark Angel*); Max Steiner for Best Score (*The Informer* again); Ralph Dawson for Best Editing (*A Midsummer Night's Dream*); Harry Warren and Al Dubin for Best Song ("Lullaby of Broadway" from *Gold Diggers of 1935*); and Walt Disney for Best Cartoon (*Three Orphan Kittens*).

making his ultimate victory at an insanity hearing all the most satisfying. Jean Arthur became an important star playing the sophisticated newspaper woman who ridicules him, then comes to appreciate his innate honesty. Capra gave the film heart and moments of delightful eccentric humour. In support were Raymond Walburn, Lionel Stander, Walter Catlett, George Bancroft, Douglass Dumbrille and H. B. Warner, not forgetting Margaret Seddon and Margaret McWade as the two experts on being "pixilated". It was another great prestige-raising and money-making triumph for Columbia.

The Great Ziegfeld This was very much an MGM special, running one minute under three hours in length and designed as an "event", although oddly enough it was Universal that had originated the idea, set the title, commissioned the script by William Anthony McGuire and cast William Powell in the leading role, before selling the whole package. MGM opened the film this month at 23 theatres as a reserved-seat show with higher prices. Well over $2 million were lavished on this biopic of Broadway impresario Florenz Ziegfeld (1867–1932), famous for his musical Follies, making it the studio's most expensive film of the decade so far. Opposite William Powell were Luise Rainer and Myrna Loy as Ziegfeld's performer wives Anna Held and Billie Burke. Fanny (*Funny Girl*) Brice, Ray Bolger and Leon Errol played themselves; Frank Morgan was Ziggy's right-hand man; and Reginald Owen, Virginia Bruce, Nat Pendleton, Ernest Cossart and Raymond Walburn also appeared. The colossal dance numbers, staged

The Great Ziegfeld: Virginia Bruce aloft during the number "A Pretty Girl Is Like a Melody".

Mr Deeds Goes to Town: Gary Cooper, Jean Arthur. Urging him to defend himself at the insanity hearing.

The Great Ziegfeld: William Powell, Luise Rainer.

by Seymour Felix on sets designed by John Harkrider, included the famous "A Pretty Girl Is Like a Melody". Robert Z. Leonard was the director and Hunt Stromberg the producer. Playing for months, the film generated substantial profits, and William Powell returned to the role in the studio's *Ziegfeld Follies* (1946).

Captain January Shirley Temple was the little girl rescued from a shipwreck that drowns her parents and adopted by Guy Kibbee's kind-hearted lighthouse keeper until officialdom decrees that she would be better off at a boarding school. Buddy Ebsen made a strong impression dancing the "At the Codfish Ball" number with Temple (choreographed by Jack Donahue). Drawn from a Laura E. Richards novel (screenplay by Sam Hellman, Gladys Lehman and Harry Tugend), the 20th Century-Fox picture was directed by David Butler.

Wife vs. Secretary

These Three Samuel Goldwyn owned the film rights to Lillian Hellman's sensational Broadway hit of 1934, *The Children's Hour*, which raised the subject of lesbianism. He had to change the title and eliminate the lesbian aspect before the Hays Office would allow him to make the film, and he was not permitted to publicize its connection with the play, although, of course, the press did that for him. Lillian Hellman was recruited to write the screenplay, and skilfully re-worked the material while making it just as effective a demonstration of her key point about the power of malicious lies to destroy lives and reputations. Miriam Hopkins and Merle Oberon were the heads of a private school, one of whom is accused of having an affair with the other's fiancé (Joel McCrea's doctor) by a venomous 12-year-old pupil (a much applauded performance by young Bonita Granville, which was to win her an Oscar nomination). William Wyler directed his first Goldwyn picture (released, as usual, by United Artists). In 1962, Wyler directed a faithful version of the play, using its title, with Audrey Hepburn and Shirley MacLaine.

MAY

Under Two Flags Ouida's classic story of the Foreign Legion (last filmed in 1922) was dusted off by 20th Century-Fox and revised for the screen by W. P. Lipscomb and Walter Ferris, with direction assigned to Frank Lloyd. The lavish adventure movie, which recalled *Beau Geste* and *Morocco*, starred Ronald Colman as the aristocratic Englishman who joins the Legion after taking the blame for a crime he didn't commit and distinguishes himself in action. The studio's new French discovery, Simone Simon, was set to co-star but was belatedly replaced by the too mature Claudette Colbert as the French-Arab girl called Cigarette, a "mascot" of the Legion who falls for Colman. Victor McLaglen was the commanding officer who tries to get Colman killed in action in the hope

that she will love him instead. Rosalind Russell was the society lady whose dignity and reserve makes the standard contrast with the tomboyish Cigarette. Gregory Ratoff and Nigel Bruce were among the other players.

Show Boat: Irene Dunne, Allan Jones.

Show Boat Universal owned the rights to the huge stage success of 1927, written by Jerome Kern and Oscar Hammerstein II, after having made a part-talking version in 1928. The story of life on a Mississippi showboat (based on Edna Ferber's dramatic novel) was scripted by Hammerstein and directed by Englishman James Whale, who brought great pictorial style to the film, working with his favourite cameraman, John Mescall. Irene Dunne starred as the daughter of showboat captain Charles Winninger; Allan Jones was the river

These Three: Alma Kruger, Bonita Granville, Merle Oberon (behind), Miriam Hopkins, Joel McCrea. Getting at the truth.

gambler she marries; Helen Morgan and Donald Cook were the lovers in the strong miscegenation sub-plot; and Paul Robeson and Hattie McDaniel were others on board. Robeson sang "Ol' Man River" to great effect, Helen Morgan had the memorable torch song "My Bill", Irene Dunne scored with "Can't Help Lovin' Dat Man" and teamed up with Allan Jones in the well-remembered "Make Believe". Other leading performers were Helen Westley and Sunnie O'Dea. It was the last major film completed during Carl Laemmle's reign at Universal. As in the case of *The Great Ziegfeld*, Universal sold the rights to MGM (but this time after filming the material). MGM acquired them in July 1938 but it was not until 1951 that its re-make with Kathryn Grayson appeared.

The Great Ziegfeld

Mr Deeds Goes to Town

JUNE

Bullets or Ballots Edward G. Robinson now had the chance to play the gangbuster that he'd spurned with *G-Men*. In this First National (Warner Bros.) opus, he was the cop who goes undercover to infiltrate the criminal organization run by Humphrey Bogart (following up his spectacular appearance as a public enemy in *The Petrified Forest* earlier in the year). Robinson dies along with Bogart following a shoot-out on a staircase, indicating the high price of combating crime. Joan Blondell was a gangster's moll who changes sides and Barton MacLane the gang boss that Bogart supplants. Seton I. Miller wrote it from a story he devised with Martin Mooney, and William Keighley directed.

The King Steps Out Grace Moore's third Columbia picture was a historical musical romance set in Austria and adapted from the operetta *Cissy* by Fritz Kreisler with new lyrics by Dorothy Fields. As the daughter of Walter Connolly's Austrian duke, she falls in love with Franchot Tone, the future Emperor Franz Josef, while he is engaged, sight unseen, to her sister, played by Nana Bryant. The director was the autocratic Josef von Sternberg, who continually clashed with Moore. She complained bitterly to the press about working with him, in particular having to milk a cow while singing (a scene not in the released film). For his part, Sternberg felt defeated by subject and star and disowned the film. Sidney Buchman was the screenwriter. Supporting players included Raymond Walburn, Herman Bing, Victor Jory and Elizabeth Risdon.

Show Boat

The Great Ziegfeld

Private Number 20th Century-Fox re-made the 1930 hit *Common Clay* with the hot new name Robert Taylor (borrowed from MGM) playing (as in the concurrent *Small Town Girl*) a rich scion of society who has to make amends to the opposite sex. Here he secretly marries family servant girl Loretta Young who bears him a child while he is away at college. His parents conspire with the unpleasant family butler (Basil Rathbone) to keep them apart and obtain a divorce. The Cleves Kinkead play was considerably toned down by writers Gene Markey and William Conselman to meet the puritanipal restrictions on screen content. Roy Del Ruth directed a cast that also included Patsy Kelly, Marjorie Gateson, Paul Harvey and Jane Darwell.

Poppy This film version of the play that had been one of W. C. Fields' great stage successes 20 years ago brought him back to the screen, after nearly a year's absence through illness, to recreate his role of Professor Eustace McGargle, patent medicine man in a travelling carnival. He had also played it in a 1924 screen version, *Sally of the Sawdust*. It had quintessential moments of Fieldsian humour, notably his sale of a talking dog to a hard-bitten bartender. Rochelle Hudson played the daughter, Richard Cromwell the mayor's son who falls for her and Catherine Doucet was the phoney Countess Maggie Tubbs DePuizzi who makes eyes at Fields, while Lynne Overman was a drinking companion and attorney. The late Tammany Young made his final appearance as one of Field's favourite foils. Waldemar Young and Virginia Van Upp adapted Dorothy Donnelly's work to the screen, and Paramount

Bullets or Ballots: Humphrey Bogart, Edward G. Robinson.

turned the direction over to A. Edward Sutherland.

The Princess Comes Across This ocean-going mystery comedy starred Carole Lombard as the showgirl from Brooklyn who hopes to become a movie star by posing as a Swedish princess and sailing into New York. Fred MacMurray co-starred as the bandleader who helps solve the murder of a man trying to blackmail her. Alison Skipworth, William Frawley, Douglass Dumbrille, Sig Rumann and Mischa Auer had roles in Paramount's relaxed movie, scripted by Walter De Leon, Francis Martin, Frank Butler and Don Hartman from a story by Philip MacDonald and a

novel by Louis Lucien Rogger. William K. Howard directed.

JULY

San Francisco MGM had an unbeatable combination: three big stars, songs and a spectacular earthquake. The story began as another in the cycle of rowdy Barbary Coast sagas with Clark Gable as the tough café proprietor, Jeanette MacDonald as the fiery singer with operatic ambitions who performs in his establishment and Spencer Tracy as the two-fisted chaplain of a mission in the heart of the wicked district. Jeanette MacDonald had ample

San Francisco: Clark Gable, Jack Holt, Spencer Tracy, Jeanette MacDonald.

opportunities to sing, especially at the end when she rallies the survivors of the 'quake by leading them in the defiant title song (by Gus Kahn, Bronislau Kaper and Walter Jurmann). The 10-minute-long, skilfully developed sequence depicting the destruction of the city early on 18 April 1906 (seemingly a punishment for the wickedness of the Barbary Coast) was the most impressive piece of special effects since *King Kong*, the work of many artists including James Basevi (uncredited), A. Arnold Gillespie and editor John Hoffman, and it was carried out with no serious injuries to the more than 400 extras involved. Anita Loos wrote the screenplay from a story by Robert Hopkins, and W. S. Van Dyke II directed. Jack Holt and Jessie Ralph also had substantial roles. Made for $1.3 million (no more than the cost of other big Metro pictures at the time such as *A Tale of Two Cities* and *Camille*), it was the company's biggest profit-maker of the decade ($2,237,000 in its first five years of release worldwide).

Poor Little Rich Girl The third of the year's Shirley Temple vehicles presented her as the lost daughter of a widowed soap manufacturer (Michael Whalen). She is adopted by a song and dance team (Alice Faye, Jack Haley) and put into the act, which becomes a radio sensation. Shirley sang "You Gotta Each Your Spinach, Baby" and other songs by Mack Gordon and Harry Revel. From stories by Eleanor Gates and Ralph Spence, it was scripted by Sam Hellman, Gladys Lehman and Harry Tugend. Irving Cummings directed for 20th Century-Fox. Part of the story material had served for a Mary Pickford film in 1917.

The Green Pastures This film with its simple, charming Negro children's view of an all-black Heaven was a bold undertaking by Warner Bros. Rex Ingram played "De Lawd" in the series of Old Testament stories, with Eddie "Rochester" Anderson as Noah, Oscar Polk as Gabriel and Frank Wilson as Moses. The last all-black Hollywood films – *Hearts in Dixie* and *Hallelujah* (both 1929) – had encountered considerable resistance from exhibitors and lost money. But the studio was encouraged by the response to *A Midsummer Night's Dream* and wanted to make more noteworthy films. Besides, this had the potential to be popular, coming from the Pulitzer Prize winning play by Marc Connelly, which had run for 640 performances on Broadway at the start of the decade (it, in turn, was inspired by stories in Roark Bradford's *Ol' Man Adam an' His Chillun*). Connelly was recruited to revise it for the screen with the help of Sheridan Gibney and to co-direct it with William Keighley who provided the cinematic expertise that Dieterle had given Reinhardt on *A Midsummer Night's Dream* the year before. Two more of the Shakespeare film's key creative team – cinematographer Hal Mohr and composer Erich Wolfgang Korngold – were also assigned to this work to ensure the same high standards. However, costs were kept down to $600,000 and Warners gained both prestige and profits. *Green Pastures* was warmly welcomed by most black commentators at the time, though it has inevitably become regarded by many later observers as condescending and crassly caricatured.

The Great Ziegfeld
Poppy

AUGUST

His Brother's Wife MGM exploited interest in the real-life romance of Barbara Stanwyck and Robert Taylor by starring them in this poor romantic drama. The love scenes seemed to have unusual conviction if nothing else did. He as a scientist and she as a model shared a 10-day love affair before he ran off to South America to find a cure for spotted fever and she married his pompous brother (John Eldredge) in revenge. Jean Hersholt, Joseph Calleia and Samuel S. Hinds had other roles in the film, written by Leon Gordon and John Meehan from a story by George Auerbach and directed by W. S. Van Dyke II.

Mary of Scotland RKO Radio's Academy Award winners John Ford and Dudley Nichols followed *The Informer* with another sombre, poetic study for the studio, a film version of Maxwell Anderson's 1933 stage success with Helen Hayes. Katharine Hepburn played the doomed Queen of Scots with Fredric March as her lover and March's real-life wife Florence Eldridge as Queen Elizabeth. It offered little scope for Ford's interests but it was visually striking thanks to Joseph H. August's cinematography (he, of course, also came from *The Informer*) and the sets by Van Nest Polglase and Carroll Clark. Considering its high cost, the box-office result was on the disappointing side.

The Green Pastures
San Francisco
To Mary – With Love Warner Baxter was still a box-office draw (and one of the highest-paid stars of 1936). Here he was partnered with Myrna Loy as a couple who survive the thick and thin of marriage with a helping hand from

Poor Little Rich Girl: Jack Haley, Shirley Temple, Alice Faye.

The Green Pastures: Oscar Polk as the Angel Gabriel, Rex Ingram as De Lawd.

Ian Hunter as their best friend who represses his own love for the wife. Claire Trevor and Jean Dixon were also involved. This was the picture with Myrna Loy's famous line, "Some people think the movies should be more like life. I don't. I think life should be more like the movies." The 20th Century-Fox picture came from a Richard Sherman novel, which he adapted with Howard Ellis Smith for John Cromwell to direct.

Suzy Jean Harlow was an American showgirl whose first husband, an Irish inventor (Franchot Tone), turns up from the dead after she marries a celebrated French flyer (Cary Grant). Grant was in a supporting role and tidied things up being bumped off by a German spy (Benita Hume). The comedy drama was written by Dorothy Parker and Alan Campbell, Horace Jackson and Lenore Coffee, working from a novel by Herbert Gorman. George Fitzmaurice directed for MGM.

Rhythm on the Range Paramount's musical comedy had Bing Crosby and sidekick Bob Burns (the popular radio comic) running a dude ranch and romancing Frances Farmer and Martha Raye respectively. Raye made a powerful debut with her raucous comedy, while Bing crooned sweetly to the runaway rich girl played by Farmer. At least seven writers who made significant contributions to the slight script went uncredited, with John C. Moffitt, Sidney Salkow, Walter De Leon and Francis Martin actually being named on screen along with Mervin J. Houser for his story. Norman Taurog directed.

SEPTEMBER

Swing Time Fred Astaire and Ginger Rogers came up with the goods again for RKO Radio. There was Fred tap-dancing to three silhouettes of himself in the athletic "Bojangles of Harlem", and Ginger singing "A Fine Romance", and the pair gliding through "Waltz in Swing Time" and "The Way You Look Tonight", as well as a joke sequence of Ginger

Swing Time: Fred Astaire, Ginger Rogers.

giving dancing lessons to Fred. Jerome Kern and Dorothy Fields supplied the songs, George Stevens took the directorial reins and Howard Lindsay and Allan Scott wrote the screenplay from a story by Erwin Gelsey, providing meaty supporting roles for Eric Blore, Georges Metaxa, Victor Moore and Helen Broderick.

Anthony Adverse Hervey Allen's massive best seller of 1933 (1,200 pages) turned into a sprawling Warner Bros. picture (its biggest of the year, budgeted at a little over $1 million, and its longest of the decade at 140 minutes). Fredric March was too old for the part of the long-suffering Anthony in this saga of life in the Napoleonic era. Episodes depicted his trading trips to Cuba and Africa and then his return to Paris to find that his one true love (Olivia de Havilland) has borne him a son and become Napoleon's mistress. Edmund Gwenn was the kindly benefactor of the young Anthony (played as a child by Billy Mauch), while Claude Rains and Gale Sondergaard conspired to deprive him of his inheritance. Others featured were Anita Louise, Louis Hayward, Steffi Duna and Donald Woods. Sheridan Gibney adapted the novel and Mervyn LeRoy directed. Erich Wolfgang Korngold wrote the score, and Anton Grot supplied the art direction. Both critics and audiences were impressed by its lavishness and detail.

Romeo and Juliet Producer Irving Thalberg forced a reluctant MGM to make this film with his wife Norma Shearer as Juliet. He wanted it to be her crowning achievement. The studio had happily allowed her to burlesque the play's balcony scene with John Gilbert in *The Hollywood Revue of*

Anthony Adverse: Fredric March, Steffi Duna.

1929 but a serious production was another matter. Once committed to it, though, the studio spared no expense to make it a faithful and lavish production. After apparently being offered to Clark Gable, the role of Romeo went to Leslie Howard. Though both he and Shearer were far too old for the roles and had too much reserve to convey the passion required, they did their best under George Cukor's painstaking direction, but John Barrymore fared better in the colourful role of Mercutio. Edna May Oliver was the Nurse, Shakespeare veteran Basil Rathbone played Tybalt, C. Aubrey Smith appeared as Lord Capulet and Ralph Forbes was Paris. Leading Shakespearean expert Professor William Strunk Jr of Cornell was engaged to advise screenwriter Talbot Jennings on the adaptation. Oliver Messel was brought over from England to work with Cedric Gibbons and Frederic Hope on the sets and with Adrian on the costumes as well as to be a further overall artistic consultant. It was the last film that Thalberg completed; he died a few weeks after its opening. MGM put the final cost of the picture at $2,066,000 and recorded a loss of $922,000 on its first release.

The Great Ziegfeld (Now showing at popular prices.)

The Gorgeous Hussy MGM had intended Jean Harlow to star in this period costume affair about the innkeeper's daughter whose friendship with President Andrew Jackson caused a scandal. Instead it went, less fittingly, to Joan Crawford

Romeo and Juliet: Henry Kolker, Leslie Howard, Norma Shearer.

whose male admirers in the film, besides Lionel Barrymore's Jackson, numbered Robert Taylor, Melvyn Douglas, Franchot Tone and James Stewart. In other roles were Louis Calhern, Alison Skipworth and Beulah Bondi. The writers were Ainsworth Morgan and Stephen Morehouse Avery (working from Samuel Hopkins Adams' novel) and the direction was by Clarence Brown.

My Man Godfrey Universal's comedy about the eccentric ways of the idle rich starred William Powell as a "forgotten man" of the Depression, collected in a scavenger hunt by Carole Lombard's scatty socialite and retained to become the family butler. Alice Brady was the even scattier mother who kept Mischa Auer around the house as a pet, Gail Patrick the snooty sister, and Eugene Pallette the exasperated head of the household. It was a delightful tonic under Gregory

La Cava's free-flowing direction, adapted by author Eric Hatch from his novel in association with Morrie Ryskind. A re-make with David Niven came out in 1957.

OCTOBER

The Big Broadcast of 1937 For the latest of these star round-ups, Paramount cast Jack Benny as the radio station manager with George Burns and Gracie Allen as his sponsors. Bob Burns and Martha Raye also featured. Leopold Stokowski and His Symphony Orchestra playing "Impregnable Fortress" were a scoop as guest artists; there were also Benny Goodman and his Orchestra, Larry Adler and others. Shirley Ross and Ray Milland

provided a touch of romance. The script was assembled by Erwin Gelsey, Arthur Kober, Barry Trivers, Walter De Leon and Francis Martin, while Mitchell Leisen was the director.

Dodsworth Samuel Goldwyn took a chance in making this drama of a retired businessman reassessing his life and belatedly seeking happiness. It had been a 1929 novel by Sinclair Lewis, turned into a hit play of 1933 by Sidney Howard with Walter Huston starring. But its subject matter seemed unlikely to attract younger moviegoers, and Goldwyn's choice of Huston to star in the film version was risky as the actor was not a strong box-office draw. Cast as the silly wife, Ruth Chatterton was well past her peak, too. However, the producer had some useful publicity when, during production, the actress playing the "other woman", Mary Astor, hit the headlines during a court battle for custody of her child: her former husband produced her diary with alleged descriptions of extra-marital love affairs which appeared in the press, precipitating a meeting of Hollywood's top echelon (including Goldwyn) to try and contain the damage to Hollywood's reputation that the huge scandal was causing. Others in *Dodsworth* were Paul Lukas, David Niven and Gregory Gaye, while making their screen debuts were Maria Ouspenskaya (the veteran Russian-born actress, from the stage production) and John Payne. William Wyler directed the picture, which was warmly received by critics. It was released by United Artists.

Anthony Adverse

Libeled Lady MGM's star-packed comedy had Jean Harlow marrying

Dodsworth: Ruth Chatterton, Walter Huston, Mary Astor.

My Man Godfrey: Carole Lombard, Franklin Pangborn (rear), William Powell.

William Powell solely so that he could encourage Myrna Loy to fall for him and demonstrate that she was a husband stealer. It was a scheme devised by Spencer Tracy's newspaper editor to counter a libel suit from Loy. Walter Connolly was the libelled lady's father. The brash and lively picture was directed by Jack Conway and written by Maurine Watkins, Howard Emmett Rogers and George Oppenheimer from a story by Wallace Sullivan.

The Big Game This was one of the winners in a flurry of football pictures that also included Paramount's *Rose Bowl* and Fox's *Pigskin Parade*. It showed a notorious gambler bribing members of a team and kidnapping a star player just before a crucial game. Philip Huston, James Gleason, June Travis, Bruce Cabot and Andy Devine appeared, supported by eight prominent professional players of the time. George Nicholls Jr directed the RKO Radio picture. The screenplay, from a novel by Francis Wallace, was the work of Irwin Shaw, who had recently made a notable Broadway debut with *Bury the Dead* but who had nothing distinctive to add to this drama.

My Man Godfrey

NOVEMBER

Libeled Lady

Pigskin Parade This musical comedy from 20th Century-Fox starred Stuart Erwin as the hillbilly farmer who becomes a college football hero under the tuition of coach Jack Haley. Its main claim to fame is that it contains the feature debut of a somewhat plump 14-year-old Judy Garland, on loan-out from MGM. She sang "It's Love I'm After", "The Texas Tornado" and "The Balboa" and demonstrated her potential to MGM. Tony (then Anthony) Martin and Betty Grable were other future stars in the film, which was written by Harry Tugend, Jack Yellen and William Conselman from a story by Yellen, Arthur Sheekman and Mark Kelly. David Butler directed. In Britain it took the title *Harmony Parade*.

Come and Get It Edward Arnold basically repeated his part in *Diamond Jim* as another man who finds that wealth – a fortune in timber – can't buy happiness. This time it was Frances Farmer who played a dual role as the two women who entrance him. Here he fought with his own son (Joel McCrea) before realizing the foolishness of wanting the daughter of the woman he should have married long ago. Walter Brennan had his biggest opportunity to date as a Swedish lumberjack, while Andrea

Leeds, Frank Shields, Mady Christians and Mary Nash were also cast. The Samuel Goldwyn production for United Artists release was based on Edna Ferber's novel, written for the screen by Jules Furthman and Jane Murfin. Howard Hawks directed the picture (the second unit under Richard Rosson contributed the impressive location footage of timber felling and logging). Goldwyn wanted extensive re-takes of the last half which Hawks refused to do (he had another picture to start in any case), William Wyler was contractually obliged to do the work under protest and received co-director credit.

The Big Broadcast of 1937

The Charge of the Light Brigade Errol Flynn followed *Captain Blood* with this fictitious account of the famous charge, made at a cost of $1.2 million. The first part of the film was set in India and imitated *The Lives of a Bengal Lancer*. Flynn was the major in the British Lancers who survives the massacre of a British garrison by an Indian potentate (C. Henry Gordon). Later in the Crimea, he changes orders to lead 700 men in the famous charge against the potentate and his Russian allies. Olivia de Havilland was Flynn's fiancée, Patric Knowles his brother, David Niven a fellow officer and Donald Crisp the Colonel, while Nigel Bruce and Henry Stephenson were knighted diplomats. Moving over from RKO, Max Steiner contributed his first score to a Warner Bros. picture. The writers were Michel Jacoby and Rowland Leigh. Michael Curtiz directed and collaborated with action specialist B.

Born to Dance: Eleanor Powell. Art directors: Cedric Gibbons, Joseph Wright.

Reeves Eason on the climactic charge into the Valley of Death. This took several weeks to shoot with up to 700 players at Californian locations, causing numerous injuries among the riders and killing a great many horses. There were protests from the SPCA, and token fines were imposed on three unit members.

DECEMBER

Born to Dance MGM's musical was designed to showcase the tapping talent of Eleanor Powell after her impact in *Broadway Melody of 1936*. Jack McGowan and Sid Silvers wrote the story with B. G. DeSylva – it was familiar backstage stuff with Powell as the understudy who gets her big chance, becomes an overnight sensation and wins her sailor boyfriend (James Stewart) for keeps. Cole Porter provided the score, his first original work in Hollywood, which included "I've Got You Under My Skin" and "Easy to Love", the latter crooned by Stewart to Powell as a once-only indication of his musical abilities. The battleship finale with Powell dancing over the decks, backed by hundreds of singing sailors, bandsmen and chorus girls culminating in a six-gun flag-popping salute, was deliriously extravagant and had audiences cheering. Virginia Bruce, Una Merkel, Sid Silvers (who also helped to write it), Frances Langford, Raymond Walburn and Buddy Ebsen appeared under Roy Del Ruth's direction.

After the Thin Man Observing William Powell's continuing appeal in imitations of *The Thin Man* at RKO, MGM came up with a polished sequel

which reunited him with Myrna Loy as Nick and Nora Charles, not forgetting Asta. There was no longer any Thin Man (he'd been disposed of in the first picture), but Frances Goodrich and Albert Hackett wrote an absorbing murder mystery from material by Dashiell Hammett, had Asta chew up a few of the clues and worked up a nice bunch of suspicious characters including James Stewart, Elissa Landi, Joseph Calleia, Jessie Ralph, Alan Marshall and George Zucco. Sam Levene was the cop on the case. W. S. Van Dyke II directed.

College Holiday Paramount producer Harlan Thompson came up with another thin pretext to bundle together a strong line up of musical comedy talent. Mary Boland wants to turn a bankrupt holiday hotel into a centre for experiments in eugenics. She persuades bandleader Jack Benny to gather some perfect specimens of boys and girls from the college crowd to stage a minstrel show and raise some money. Benny went through his routine of trying to play the violin; Gracie Allen, as the daughter of an eccentric professor (Etienne Girardot), clowned with George Burns; Martha Raye was a student called Daisy Schloggenheimer looking for love; and Marsha Hunt and Leif Erickson handled the songs and romance. The script was concocted by J. P. McEvoy, Harlan Ware, Jay Gorney and Henry Myers, while Frank Tuttle directed.

Theodora Goes Wild Columbia launched Irene Dunne on a whole new career as a spirited comedienne, playing the prim-seeming small-town Sunday school teacher who writes a shocking best-seller under a pseudonym and tries to keep it a secret. However, once she has fallen for the book's visiting illustrator (Melvyn Douglas) and committed the sin of fishing with him on a Sunday, she heads for New York and goes wild posing as "the other woman" to help him end his broken marriage. Mary McCarthy wrote the original story on which Sidney Buchman based the screenplay that Richard Boleslawski directed. Others caught up in the antic complications of this screwball comedy were Thomas Mitchell as a newspaper editor, Leona Maricle as the discarded wife, Elizabeth Risdon and Margaret McWade as two maiden aunts and Thurston Hall as a publisher.

Rainbow on the River Independent producer Sol Lesser had some success in promoting young radio performer Bobby Breen as a singing star of the movies. Aged eight when he made it, this was his second starring vehicle

after *Let's Sing Again*. Here he was the Southern boy transplanted to New York and having a hard time with his testy grandmother (May Robson) and others in his family (Alan Mowbray, Benita Hume) until he is befriended by the butler (Charles Butterworth) and reunited with his nanny (Louise Beavers). The many songs included Stephen Foster's classic "De Camptown Races". Kurt Neumann directed the Principal production, released by RKO Radio, from a script by Earle Snell, Harry Chandlee and William Hurlbut based on a novel by Mrs C. V. Jamison.

Stowaway This was hard-working young Shirley Temple in her fourth hit of the year. As the daughter of murdered missionaries in China, she had the nickname "Ching Ching" and her knowledge of the language helped her befriend Robert Young's tourist. She also knew how to mimic Jolson, Cantor and Astaire, and utter Charlie Chan-style aphorisms. She won the hearts of Young and Alice Faye as well as of the judge played by J. Edward Bromberg. Shunted to one side were Faye's fiancé (Allan Lane) and his overbearing mother (Helen Westley). Temple and Faye shared the musical interludes. William A. Seiter directed for 20th Century-Fox. The writers were Samuel G. Engel (story) and William Conselman, Arthur Sheekman and Nat Perrin (screenplay).

The Charge of the Light Brigade

TEN BEST-CRITICS' CHOICE

These were the films selected and the number of votes cast by 523 of America's critics polled by the *Film Daily*.

1.	*Mutiny on the Bounty* [late 1935 release]	416
2.	*Mr Deeds Goes to Town*	372
3.	*The Great Ziegfeld*	345
4.	*San Francisco*	264
5.	*Dodsworth*	254
6.	*The Story of Louis Pasteur*	250
7.	*A Tale of Two Cities*	235
8.	*Anthony Adverse*	231
9.	*The Green Pastures*	197
10.	*A Midsummer Night's Dream* [late 1935 release]	166
	Close Runners Up	
11.	*Magnificent Obsession*	149
12.	*Ah, Wilderness!*	138
13.	*Fury*	129
14.	*These Three*	106

All the top 10 were box-office successes as well.

CLOSE RUNNERS UP

15 films narrowly missed being included among the hits of the year for the month indicated: *Ah, Wilderness!* (January), *Anything Goes* (February), *Exclusive Story* (February), *The Ex-Mrs Bradford* (May), *Fury* (June), *The Gay Desperado* (November), *Little Lord Fauntleroy* (April), *Love on a Bet* (March), *The Milky Way* (February), *Petticoat Fever* (April), *Riffraff* (January), *The Singing Kid* (April), *Small Town Girl* (May), *Strike Me Pink* (January), *Three Men on a Horse* (December).

1937

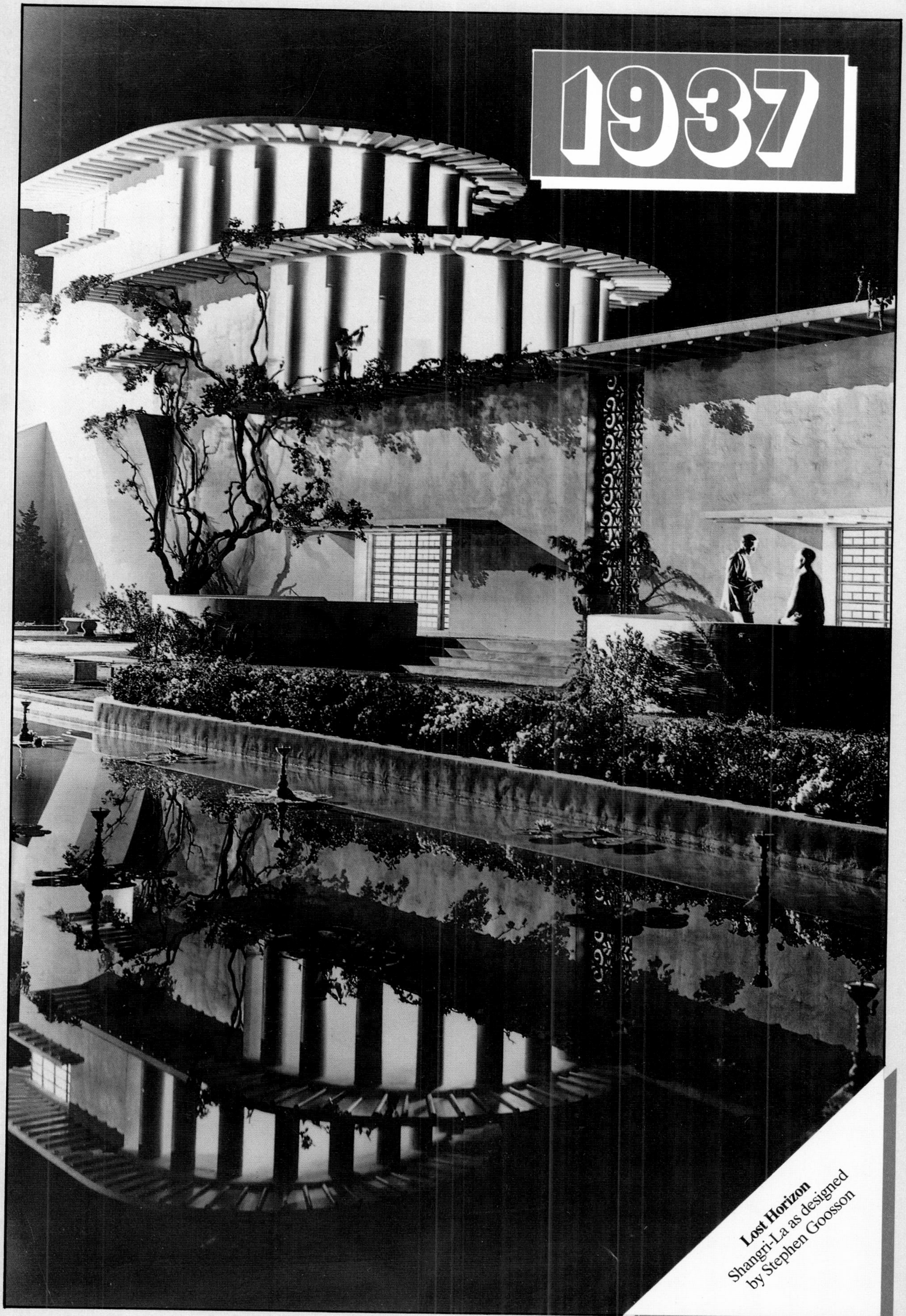

Lost Horizon
Shangri-La as designed
by Stephen Goosson

The year was a good one for the American film industry. Admissions came out at a weekly average of 88 million, the same as in 1936. World attendance was reckoned at 215 million a week. Huge amounts were now being spent on some films, more than they could reasonably hope to recover; as much as $3.8 million seems to have been lavished on Garbo's *Conquest*, which was claimed by MGM to be the costliest film ever made – it gained a very feeble response from American moviegoers but did much better overseas where it was titled *Marie Walewska*. Another expensive MGM film, *The Good Earth*, was a hit both in North America and on the foreign market, as were Paramount's *The Plainsman* and *Waikiki Wedding*, as well as Selznick's *The Prisoner of Zenda* and, after a wobbly start, Columbia's *Lost Horizon*. Other films that were stronger abroad than at home were MGM's *Camille* and *Romeo and Juliet*. One of the year's worst

"The World's Largest Motion Picture Studio"; that's the claim attached to this 5 April 1937 aerial view of the Warner Bros. lot, also the home of First National and Cosmopolitan productions. Situated north of the actual Hollywood at Burbank in the San Fernando valley, this was the original First National studio. Standing sets are just visible to the left of the sound stages. It has most recently become the Burbank Studio, shared by Warner Bros. and Columbia.

failures was the musical *High, Wide and Handsome*, on which Paramount had spent $1.8 million. Another flop was *Night Must Fall*, in which MGM indulged actor Robert Montgomery's desire to extend his range by playing a psychopathic killer who keeps his victim's head in a hatbox; his fans were horrified, but the critics applauded his work. Director Leo McCarey came a cropper with his serious study of old age, *Make Way for Tomorrow*, which only the critics liked, and he was dropped by Paramount but bounded back with the smash hit comedy *The Awful Truth* at Columbia.

Economic conditions were improving in most parts of the United States and theatre ticket prices began to rise again to offset pay increases as a result of unions gaining recognition from the companies and negotiating improved conditions.

Paramount began adding to its theatres again, bringing 400 more under its control, and other circuits expanded in response. At the same time bills were introduced in many state legislatures to prevent producer/distributors running theatres, although only one was passed and promptly challenged in the courts by Paramount. The Federal Department of Justice began taking a new interest in possible violations of the anti-trust laws.

Monogram reappeared during the year as a rival in the low-budget field to Republic, of which the original Monogram had become part. Grand National issued a second film starring James Cagney, *Something to Sing About*, before Cagney patched up his differences with Warner Bros. and called off further pictures with the independent.

The use of Technicolor for feature-length films made some definite advances during the year. David O. Selznick produced two popular films in the process, *A Star Is Born* and *Nothing Sacred*, that were big hits, although, oddly enough, the production of his that would have most benefited from colour, *The Prisoner of Zenda*, was shot in monochrome. Warner Bros. used the new Technicolor for the first time in *God's Country and the Woman*, while 20th Century-Fox shot the first Technicolor feature made in England, *Wings of the Morning*, with Henry Fonda. At the year's end, Walt Disney's eagerly awaited animation feature in Technicolor, *Snow White and the Seven Dwarfs*, made its debut to rapturous acclaim. During the year Technicolor sold shares to producers to give them a stake in the company and increase their interest in using the process.

Shirley Temple was the top box-office draw with four new pictures that brought $10 million into the coffers of 20th Century-Fox, while the studio's new discovery, Sonja Henie, skated straight into the top 10. William Powell and Myrna Loy became top favourites through the huge success of *After the Thin Man*. Robert Taylor, Bing Crosby and the Fred Astaire/ Ginger Rogers team consolidated their appeal, while longer-established Clark Gable and Gary Cooper also reaffirmed their pulling power. MGM contemplated abandoning the unfinished *Saratoga* on Jean Harlow's death but managed to finish it and ended up with the third biggest hit of the year on the American market after *Maytime* and *The Good Earth*, both also made by the studio. Universal, the only studio still losing money, had a major star find in Deanna Durbin.

STAND UP, THE UNIONS

This was the year in which the unions made a decisive stand against producer domination. The Academy of Motion Picture Arts and Sciences was no longer a tool of the bosses, and the Roosevelt administration had, in the 1935 National Labor Relations Act (popularly known as the Wagner Act), given workers new rights to organize.

In May, 6,000 members of the craft guilds – night painters, make-up men, scenic artists – went on strike demanding union recognition and closed shops from the studios. Production was quickly affected, and the number of new films starting up dropped sharply.

The Screen Writers Guild sought a working agreement with the major companies, which responded that they already had a deal with the Screen Playwrights, an organization widely regarded as a company union. This was headed by writers at MGM – James Kevin McGuinness, John Lee Mahin, Rupert Hughes – who opposed collective bargaining and considered that the Screen Writers Guild was run by Communists. The Guild petitioned the National Labor Relations Board and won the right for screenwriters to elect their representatives. The Screen Playwrights soon faded away.

The Screen Actors Guild came close to going on strike along with the craft guilds. SAG President Robert Montgomery demanded higher wages, firmer contracts and improved working conditions with a basic eight-hour working day. (Actors could be kept working up until midnight, even on Saturdays, and then resume work at 9am the next day unless it was a Sunday – and even that day was often worked on location.) The producers agreed to a 10-year contract that provided a guild shop, an increase of 10 per cent in extras' pay with a new minimum, overtime pay for lower-paid actors and changes to the "Call Bureau" system, which gave producers 24-day options on actors' services, preventing them from accepting other assignments.

The craft guilds reached a strike settlement on 10 June giving full recognition to the unions starting 1 July. Film production quickly returned to pre-strike levels.

Later in 1937, the Screen Directors Guild (whose executive committee included Howard Hawks and John Ford) was formed for collective bargaining with the studios on behalf of directors, assistant directors and unit managers. The producers argued that directors' working conditions could not be standardized and that they were already exceptionally well paid. The SDG petitioned the Federal Government to be declared a collective bargaining agency and claimed that the studios were in violation of the Wagner Act. A hearing was held in Los Angeles in August 1938. The Government found in favour of the SDG, and the producers gave in. The balance of power had shifted for good.

HITS OF THE YEAR

JANUARY

After the Thin Man

The Plainsman Alone in making big-budget westerns during this period, Paramount readily assented to Cecil B. DeMille's locating his latest historical pageant out West. He reunited the stars of *Mr Deeds Goes to Town*: Gary Cooper was Wild Bill Hickok, less wild than mild, and Jean Arthur was a spirited Calamity Jane, not quite tough enough for a man's world. James Ellison played a dashing Buffalo Bill Cody, while Anthony Quinn was among the Cheyenne warriors. Second leading lady Helen Burgess sadly died in April from lobar pneumonia. The rather elementary narrative (by Waldemar Young, Harold Lamb and Lynn Riggs) hewed to truth in closing with the murder of Hickok by Porter Hall's cowardly desperado, Jack McCall. Arthur Rosson's second-unit work provided much of the spectacle, with the stars putting in excessive hours in front of the process screen. It proved a huge success internationally, grossing well over $2.5 million.

One in a Million 20th Century-Fox launched both Sonja Henie, Olympic ice-skating champion of Norway, and a whole cycle of musicals on ice with this picture, for which a new stage with a rink was specially constructed. In the film, Sonja played the undemanding role of an Olympic ice skater – and on skates she was a star. Supporting her were Adolphe Menjou as a theatrical impresario, Don Ameche as the boyfriend and the Ritz Brothers as comedy relief spoofing Lorre, Laughton and Karloff as screen heavies. Sidney Lanfield directed from a script by Leonard Praskins and Mark Kelly. The songs were by Lew Pollack and Sidney D. Mitchell.

The Plainsman: Gary Cooper (on floor), Porter Hall (holding stool), Jean Arthur. The death of Wild Bill Hickok.

One in a Million: Introducing Miss Sonja Henie, "The Queen of the Silvery Skates".

its biggest success with Lily Pons, the French star of the Metropolitan Opera, in the second of her three films for the studio. She played the opera star who flees from her wedding ceremony and follows a swing band led by Gene Raymond to America where she becomes their singer (performing numbers by Arthur Schwartz and Edward Heyman). There was just one opera number for her stage admirers, from *The Barber of Seville*. Also seen were Jack Oakie, Mischa Auer, Frank Jenks and Lucille Ball (in her best role to date, as the jealous girlfriend of bandleader Raymond). The story by W. Carey Wonderly and Jane Murfin, previously used on *Street Girl* (1929), was revamped by Joseph A. Fields, P. J. Wolfson and Dorothy Yost. Leigh Jason directed.

Three Smart Girls The new regime at

THE RADIO BROUGHT HER TO YOUR HOME —THE SCREEN BRINGS HER TO YOUR HEART!

DEANNA DURBIN

She charmed you on Eddie Cantor's radio hour! She'll thrill you now in

3 SMART GIRLS

with
BINNIE BARNES
ALICE BRADY
RAY MILLAND
CHARLES WINNINGER
MISCHA AUER • NAN
GREY • BARBARA READ
JOHN KING
A new UNIVERSAL *picture*

2 R

Camille In what was the decade's most lavish weepie, Garbo played with exquisite delicacy the tragic lady of the camellias, Marguerite Gautier, under George Cukor's direction, and Robert Taylor was suitably young and handsome as her fervent lover. Irving Thalberg's MGM production cast Henry Daniell as her jealous protector and Lionel Barrymore as Taylor's concerned father, along with Elizabeth Allan, Jessie Ralph, Lenore Ulric, Laura Hope Crews and Rex O'Malley. Although not a runaway success in America, it could rely on Garbo's huge draw overseas. Novelist James Hilton and Frances Marion wrote the adaptation of the Alexandre Dumas story and play.

That Girl from Paris RKO Radio had

That Girl from Paris: Gene Raymond, Lily Pons, Frank Jenks, Jack Oakie, Mischa Auer.

Three Smart Girls: Deanna Durbin, Barbara Read, Charles Winninger, Nan Grey.

Universal struck lucky with the impact that Deanna Durbin, making her feature debut at age 15, had on audiences. She, Nan Grey and Barbara Read were the three sisters who have been living with their divorced mother in Switzerland and come rushing back to America when Binnie Barnes's gold-digger is about to snare their father (Charles Winninger) at the altar. In the Shirley Temple tradition, she brought her two parents back together again. Ray Milland, John King and Mischa Auer were the sisters' admirers, and Alice Brady was the gold-digger's mother. Deanna sang several numbers, including "My Heart Is Singing" and "Someone to Care for Me" (both by Gus Kahn, Walter Jurmann and Bronislau Kaper). Besides Deanna, director Henry Koster and producer Joe Pasternak, two recent refugees from Germany, also made their mark with the picture. Adele Commandini and Austin Parker wrote it. There would be a sequel, *Three Smart Girls Grow Up* (1939), while Pasternak did a virtual remake, *Three Daring Daughters* (1948) at MGM.

FEBRUARY

On the Avenue 20th Century-Fox borrowed Dick Powell from Warner Bros. to play a Broadway musical comedy writer and performer in this picture with numbers by Irving Berlin, who also collaborated on the story with William Conselman (who in turn collaborated with Gene Markey on the screenplay). When Powell's hit show mocks a prominent and wealthy New York family, the daughter (Madeleine Carroll) comes to sue and stays to love, arousing the jealousy of Alice Faye's showgirl. Songs included "I've Got My Love to Keep Me Warm" and "This Year's Kisses". The Ritz Brothers added comedy. Director Roy Del Ruth's players also included Alan Mowbray, George Barbier, Cora Witherspoon, Joan Davis and Siegfried Rumann.

One in a Million

Lloyds of London 20th Century-Fox dramatically revised British history to put some excitement into insurance. The leading role was shared between Freddie Bartholomew (top-billed), playing the boy who saves Lloyds from a serious loss, and Tyrone Power (billed fourth) as the grown-up forging a brilliant career in the insurance

Lloyds of London: Tyrone Power.

world that rests on the outcome of the Battle of Trafalgar. Madeleine Carroll was the woman Power loves, although she is married to George Sanders' aristocratic wastrel. This was the film that tested Power's appeal to audiences after several minor roles, and the favourable response made him a star. Sir Guy Standing, C. Aubrey Smith, Montagu Love and Miles Mander were some of the British contingent in Hollywood who helped evoke the proper period atmosphere. Curtis Kenyon's story was made into a screenplay by Ernest Pascal and Walter Ferris, and Henry King directed.

The Last of Mrs Cheyney Based on Frederick Lonsdale's 1925 play, this starred Joan Crawford and William Powell as two jewel thieves operating in London's *haute monde*, she masquerading convincingly as a well-bred American lady, he behaving just as impeccably as a butler. Robert Montgomery co-starred as an aristocratic cad, with Frank Morgan as a titled fool. The last work of director Richard Boleslawski (who died in production, with George Fitzmaurice completing it), the MGM picture was adapted by Leon Gordon, Samson Raphaelson and Monckton Hoffe. Previously filmed under the same title in 1929 with Norma Shearer, it was re-made as *The Law and the Lady* in 1951 with Greer Garson.

After the Thin Man

The Good Earth Things Chinese had been fascinating film-makers for some years, and a number of movies had featured evil warlords. For a change, this was a film about the real China, the life of the hard-working peasants, based on Pearl Buck's popular novel and the 1932 play version by Owen and Donald Davis (which had starred Claude Rains, Alla Nazimova and Sydney Greenstreet on Broadway). Irving Thalberg spared no cost in having art directors Cedric Gibbons and Harry Oliver reconstruct China in California (to combine with some authentic location footage shot by George Hill before his death), and the producer cast Paul Muni as the peasant who attains wealth and Luise Rainer as the patient wife he loses. Also seen in Chinese make-up were Walter Connolly, Tilly Losch, Charley Grapewin (the only recruit from the play cast). Some of Hollywood's Chinese players did participate, including Keye Luke, then more often playing Charlie Chan's number one son in Fox programmers. Thalberg wanted the sequence in which a plague of locusts devours the crops to be spectacularly effective and special effects genius A. Arnold Gillespie finally combined reversed shots of coffee grounds swirling in water for the approaching

black mass with close-ups of dead locusts moved around on plants. Talbot Jennings, Tess Slesinger and Claudine West wrote the screenplay, and Sidney Franklin was the principal director, with George Hill, Andrew Marton, Fred Niblo and Sam Wood billed as associate directors. Shooting took 120 days, and the completed picture, which ran 138 minutes, cost $2,816,000 – the most spent on a single MGM production since the silent *Ben-Hur*. Despite its huge success at home and abroad, it made a loss of $496,000 on release. For once, the producer received screen credit: "To the memory of Irving Grant Thalberg we dedicate this picture, his last great screen achievement."

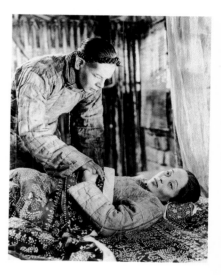

The Good Earth: Paul Muni, Luise Rainer.

MARCH

Maytime The third of the Jeanette MacDonald/Nelson Eddy romantic musicals (and MacDonald's reputed personal favourite), *Maytime* was taken from the 1917 operetta by Sigmund Romberg and Rida Johnson Young, although the story was greatly changed in Noel Langley's adaptation, and only one of the original songs, "Will You Remember", was retained. She was the American *prima donna* who becomes a favourite at the court of Napoleon thanks to her mentor and protector (John Barrymore); Eddy was the humble opera student with whom she falls in love. Like *Smilin' Through*, it was one of those films where true happiness is found in the next world. Tom Brown, Herman Bing, Lynn Carver and Rafaela Ottiano were also in the cast. Robert Z. Leonard directed for MGM, and Herbert Stothart adapted the opera selections. The May Day sequence and the finale were printed in sepia for the film's original release. It was an expensive ($1.5 million) production (running 132 minutes), but it was such a hefty money-maker that it ended up the top grossing picture of the year on a worldwide basis. MGM hoped to do even better by separating the two singers for their next films to draw in the crowds on their own.

Love is News Tyrone Power moved to top billing after *Lloyds of London* as Fox's answer to MGM's Robert Taylor in the handsome romantic lead department. This was a comedy in which Power was the reporter who tricks an interview out of Loretta Young's reclusive heiress; in revenge she turns the spotlight on Power by declaring that she has broken off her engagement to George Sanders' French count in order to marry him. After a while she decides that he really would make a good husband. Don Ameche co-starred as an irascible newspaper editor. Harry Tugend and Jack Yellen scripted from a story by William R. Lipman and Frederick Stephani. Tay Garnett directed. The same material went into service for the musical *Sweet Rosie O'Grady* (1943) and for a comedy re-make with Power again, *That Wonderful Urge* (1948).

Swing High, Swing Low Director Mitchell Leisen and cinematographer Ted Tetzlaff made a pictorially striking emotional drama with affecting performances by Fred MacMurray as the weak trumpet player and Carole Lombard as the more dominant woman he marries and then lets down. Lombard used her own voice in the singing sequences. Charles Butterworth and Jean Dixon were their married friends, and Dorothy Lamour was the exotic singer who takes MacMurray away. Virginia Van Upp and Oscar Hammerstein II wrote this latest film version of the 1927 hit play *Burlesque* by George Manker Watters and Arthur Hopkins (previously filmed as *The Dance of Life*, 1929). Paramount made the first two versions, which were withdrawn

Maytime: Nelson Eddy, Jeanette MacDonald.

from circulation when the company sold the rights to Fox for a musical re-make, *When My Baby Smiles At Me* (1948), resulting in *Swing High, Swing Low* becoming for many years one of the most elusive films of the 1930s.

Green Light Based on another inspirational medical story by Lloyd C. Douglas, the author of *Magnificent Obsession*, this Warner Bros. production (released under the First National and Cosmopolitan banners) showed that Errol Flynn could hold his own in a modern piece. He was the surgeon who takes the blame for an older man's mistake and risks his life experimenting with a cure for spotted fever. Anita Louise and Margaret Lindsay provided the romantic

complications, and Sir Cedric Hardwicke was the pontifical voice of the church. Others prominently involved were Spring Byington and Walter Abel. Frank Borzage directed from a Milton Krims screenplay.

Waikiki Wedding Bing Crosby was the press agent who dreams up a stunt to promote pineapples, and Shirley Ross was the "Pineapple Princess" who accompanies him to Hawaii. Bing sang to her the love song "Sweet Leilani" by Harry Owens. Other songs by Ralph Rainger and Leo Robin included "Blue Hawaii". Bob Burns and Martha Raye supplied the comedy support, while George Barbier, Leif Erickson and Grady

Waikiki Wedding: Shirley Ross, Bing Crosby, Martha Raye, Bob Burns.

Swing High, Swing Low: Carole Lombard, Fred MacMurray.

Sutton were also in the cast. It took four writers (Frank Butler, Don Hartman, Walter De Leon and Francis Martin) to dream up the script which Paramount gave to director Frank Tuttle.
On the Avenue

APRIL

Maytime
Marked Woman Bette Davis had been promised better scripts by Warner Bros. when she came back after her courtroom fight in England, and the studio delivered. This First National

Marked Woman: Bette Davis, Humphrey Bogart.

presentation was one of its torn-from-the-headlines tales based on the way gang buster Thomas A. Dewey smashed the prostitution racket of Charles "Lucky" Luciano. Davis played the clip-joint hostess (the word "prostitute" was inadmissible) who courageously gives evidence against the vice czar, played by Eduardo Ciannelli, even after she is scarred by his henchmen. Humphrey Bogart was the honest assistant D.A. she helps into the limelight before they go their separate ways. The commendably tough script by Robert Rossen and Abem Finkel was directed by Lloyd Bacon.
Wake Up and Live This rapid-fire satire on the world of radio created a mock feud between bandleader Ben Bernie and columnist Walter Winchell. Alice Faye came aboard as a star of the airwaves, singing several numbers by Mack Gordon and Harry Revel (including "There's a Lull in My Life" and the title tune), while Jack Haley was the mike-shy vocalist she helps make good. Patsy Kelly, Ned Sparks and Etienne Girardot also appeared. The 20th Century-Fox picture came from a script by Harry Tugend and Jack Yellen, based on a

Three of the winners: Paul Muni (sporting a beard grown for his role in *The Woman I Love*), Luise Rainer and director Frank Capra.

THE ACADEMY AWARDS

For this year only, the nominations were made by a committee of 50 from the five branches of the Academy, some of whom (like Frank Capra) were among the nominees. Capra had taken the Academy out of labour negotiations and begun to restore it to general favour. The annual prize-giving took place at the Biltmore Hotel on 4 March and was attended by over 1,500 people. The Best Picture and Best Actress Awards to *The Great Ziegfeld* and star Luise Rainer caused surprise even at the time, and it was suggested that MGM had persuaded the large number of voters on its payroll to show their loyalty (although Norma Shearer and *Romeo and Juliet* were also nominated, along with three other MGM pictures: *Libeled Lady, San Francisco* and *A Tale of Two Cities*).

The Academy persisted in presenting the Award for Best Music Score, won by *Anthony Adverse*, to the head of the studio music department, Leo F. Forbstein, instead of to the actual composer, Erich Wolfgang Korngold. *Adverse* also picked up the awards for Best Supporting Actress (a new category) (Gale Sondergaard, for her film debut), Best Cinematography (Tony Gaudio), and Best Editing (Ralph Dawson). Paul Muni was Best Actor for *The Life of Louis Pasteur*, and in the new category of Best Supporting Actor the first winner was Walter Brennan for *Come and Get It*. The Oscar for Best Director went to Frank Capra for *Mr Deeds Goes to Town*.

The Story of Louis Pasteur also won the Best Story and Best Screenplay Awards for Pierre Collings and Sheridan Gibney. Richard Day picked up the art direction Award (Best Interior Decoration) for *Dodsworth*, having won the previous year with another Goldwyn picture. Walt Disney again won the Oscar for Best Cartoon, *Country Cousin*, while "The Way You Look Tonight" by Jerome Kern and Dorothy Fields from *Swing Time* was named Best Song, and Seymour Felix won in Dance Direction for the "A Pretty Girl Is Like a Melody" number in *The Great Ziegfeld*. Special awards were made to *The March of Time* for its revolutionary approach to the newsreel and to W. Howard Greene and Harold Rosson for the Technicolor cinematography of *The Garden of Allah*. A *Crime Does Not Pay* short, *The Public Pays*, was named the winner in the two-reeler Short Subjects category.

A Star is Born: Janet Gaynor, Fredric March, Adolphe Menjou. The Oscar is a real one, awarded to Miss Gaynor in 1929.

story by Curtis Kenyon and book by Dorothea Brande. The direction was by Sidney Lanfield.

Waikiki Wedding

Internes Can't Take Money The first Doctor Kildare film, this came from Paramount who then sold the rights to MGM where the series was made. Joel McCrea played Kildare, who uses an underworld contact (Lloyd Nolan) to help Barbara Stanwyck recover her missing child, taken by her dead gangster husband. Alfred Santell directed the melodrama, which was scripted by Rian James and Theodore Reed from a story by Max Brand. In Britain it was known as *You Can't Take Money*.

A Star is Born The quintessential story of filmland, ranging from triumph to tragedy, this Selznick International production (distributed by United Artists) owed something to the earlier *What Price Hollywood?*, but its events had their true parallels in real Hollywood tragedies such as the suicide at sea of burnt-out star John Bowers while it was in production. The picture provided a vivid impression of life in the film capital with details of movie-making that rang true and settings that ranged from sound stages and studio commissaries to the Hollywood Bowl, an Academy Awards banquet at the Biltmore Hotel (where, in 1938, this film would receive an Oscar for best story), and Grauman's Chinese Theater on a gala opening night (where this picture had its world premiere on 21 April). Janet Gaynor may now seem odd casting as the young hopeful who becomes a big new star, Vicky Lester, for she fully looked her 30 years of age, but she brought her established image of wholesome innocence that suited the part (and the film revived her flagging career). Fredric March ably played the tragically flawed star Norman

Maine who couldn't handle his declining popularity, especially when contrasted with Vicky's success, and became an alcoholic. (The film gave small parts to Owen Moore and Marshall Neilan, who had wrecked their careers through drinking.) Adolphe Menjou co-starred as the considerate studio head, while Lionel Stander was the vicious publicity chief, Andy Devine the friendly assistant director and May Robson the aunt who rallies Gaynor's spirit so that she stays in Hollywood after Maine's suicide. The memorable upbeat ending (devised by John Lee Mahin) has Vicky speaking into the microphone at a premiere and identifying herself. "Hello, everybody, this is Mrs Norman Maine!" The husband and wife team of Dorothy Parker and Alan Campbell wrote the screenplay with Robert Carson from a story devised by Carson and the film's director, William A. Wellman. David O. Selznick was firmly committed to using Technicolor and worked with cinematographer W. Howard Greene, colour designer Lancing C. Holden and art director Lyle Wheeler to see that it was more subdued and natural than it had been on his previous production, *The Garden of Allah*, to avoid overwhelming the drama (even if it seems dazzling by today's standards). Along with the same producer's *Nothing Sacred*, it was one of the year's two big hits in Technicolor. In 1954, the re-make with Judy Garland and James Mason appeared.

MAY

Shall We Dance Fred Astaire and Ginger Rogers took to the floor again for another RKO musical delight, this time with music and lyrics by George and Ira Gershwin. There was a weak and familiar story (by Lee Loeb and Harold Buchman, developed by P. J. Wolfson, Allan Scott and Ernest Pagano) that gave comedy spots to Edward Everett Horton and Eric Blore. The highlight of the film was Fred and Ginger dancing for 2 minutes 40 seconds on roller skates to the tune of "Let's Call the Whole Thing Off", but there was another inventive number ("Slap That Bass") in which Fred's dancing was integrated with the movement of the equipment in a ship's engine room. Fred also performed the title routine which was a mock-classical ballet with Harriet Hoctor and with dancers in Ginger Rogers masks. With other numbers like "They All Laughed", the film was a musical treasure and a substantial profit-maker, but it didn't draw such big crowds as previous Astaire-Rogers pictures and clearly the formula was wearing thin. Mark Sandrich directed, with Hermes Pan staging the dances (except the ballet, done by Harry Losee).

A Star is Born

Wake Up and Live

Café Metropole Now that Tyrone Power and Loretta Young had shown how well they worked together in *Love Is News*, 20th Century-Fox rushed them into this Parisian frolic. He played the American playboy in Paris who, to pay off gambling debts, poses as a Russian prince in the hope of charming an American millionaire's daughter (Young) into marriage and gaining her money. Adolphe Menjou was the headwaiter at the Café Metropole who hatches the scheme, Gregory Ratoff (who wrote the story) played a real Russian prince, and Charles Winninger was the millionaire father. Jacques Deval scripted the romantic comedy and Edward H. Griffith directed.

The Prince and the Pauper Errol Flynn was back in period costume for this lavish and lengthy adaptation of the Mark Twain classic. The two lookalikes, the beggar boy and the young heir to the English throne who exchange places, were played by the Mauch twins, Billy and Bobby, and Flynn's role as the soldier of fortune who befriends the real prince was secondary, his participation solely to add box-office appeal. Claude Rains was the villainous Earl of Hertford, and others cast included Henry Stephenson, Alan Hale and British actor Eric Portman in his only Hollywood film. The film ended in a big coronation scene, which had particular appeal as the real ceremony was taking place in England this month with King George VI and attracting massive media coverage. William Keighley directed from a screenplay by the late Laird Doyle, and Erich Wolfgang Korngold provided the score.

JUNE

I Met Him in Paris Claudette Colbert was just an ordinary working girl of the '30s who saves up for five years to have a three-week spree in Paree. There she is picked up by two indolent writers, played by Melvyn Douglas and Robert Young, with whom she travels to Switzerland to test the ski slopes (Sun Valley was actually used). Lee Bowman was the fiancé Colbert left behind and Mona Barrie the wife that Robert Young forgot to mention. Following *The Gilded Lily* and *The Bride Comes Home*, this was Colbert's third successful Paramount comedy written by Claude Binyon and directed by Wesley Ruggles. The original story was by Helen Meinardi.
Slave Ship Wallace Beery was still being loaned out by MGM to 20th Century even after the company's amalgamation with Fox. He came

I Met Him in Paris: Melvyn Douglas, Robert Young, Claudette Colbert.

Captains Courageous: Freddie Bartholomew, Spencer Tracy.

novel by George S. King. The screenplay was credited to Sam Hellman, Lamar Trotti and Gladys Lehman.
Captains Courageous More marine fare, this MGM adaptation of Rudyard Kipling's famous novel put Spencer Tracy, with curled hair and a Portuguese accent, in the front rank of stardom as the simple fisherman who befriends a spoiled brat, played by Freddie Bartholomew, and teaches him the way of the sea. Melvyn Douglas was the rich father of the lost boy and Lionel Barrymore the captain of the fishing vessel that picks him up. Mickey Rooney played the captain's son. The writers were John Lee Mahin, Marc Connelly and Dale Van Every, and the director was Victor Fleming.

along with Mickey Rooney, and their first mate and cabin boy relationship recalled Beery's pictures with Jackie Cooper. Here Beery was billed after Warner Baxter in a boisterous yarn of the slave-running era, directed by Tay Garnett. Baxter was the captain who decides to chuck in the slave trade and finds himself faced with a mutiny led by Beery. Elizabeth Allan as his bride-to-be is on board at the time. George Sanders and Joseph Schildkraut were also on hand. William Faulkner extracted the screen story from a

This is My Affair: Robert Taylor, Barbara Stanwyck, Victor McLaglen.

This is My Affair The continuing off-screen romance of Barbara Stanwyck and Robert Taylor interested audiences in seeing them paired on-screen again in this 20th Century-Fox picture, whose title smacked more of a love story than the early crime-busting saga it was. Taylor was seen as a naval lieutenant dispatched on a secret mission by President McKinley to infiltrate a gang of Midwest bank robbers led by Victor McLaglen. Stanwyck's saloon songstress falls in love with him. Frank Conroy played McKinley, and Sidney Blackmer appeared as his successor, Teddy Roosevelt. Also cast were Brian Donlevy, Alan Dinehart and Robert McWade (as Admiral Dewey). William A. Seiter directed from the screenplay by Allen Rivkin and Lamar Trotti. The British release title was *His Affair*.

Saratoga: Clark Gable, Jean Harlow.

Mountain Music Paramount's slapstick musical comedy placed the Martha Raye and Bob Burns team in their own starring vehicle, a ramshackle one, which required him to have bouts of amnesia during which he regards the wide-mouthed Raye as the woman of his dreams. There was also a hillbilly feud and a murder trial involving John Howard as Burns's brother. George Hayes was a grandpappy and gabby in all but name. Raye performed in her usual abandoned style and had some lively songs written by Sam Coslow. The script came from a short story by MacKinlay Kantor, developed by John C. Moffitt, Duke Atteberry, Russell Crouse and Charles Lederer. Robert Florey was the director.

JULY

Saratoga Released a few weeks after her death, Jean Harlow's last picture was an unremarkable romantic comedy drama with a racetrack background. Clark Gable was the bookie who falls for Harlow, the daughter of a breeder who has lost all his money on bets, and Walter Pidgeon (in his first film for MGM) was the wealthy businessman to whom she is engaged. The Platinum Blonde died before completing her role and scenes were re-written to reduce her remaining dialogue while her stand-in Mary Dees and actress Geraldine Dvorak took over for several long shots, over-the-shoulder shots and shots of her face almost hidden by hats, while Paula Winslow dubbed her voice. Another unhappy event occurred when Lionel Barrymore (playing Harlow's grandfather) tripped over a lighting cable and broke his hip, which hadn't yet healed from a previous injury; as a result, he became

permanently wheelchair-bound and had to play future parts sitting down. Frank Morgan, Una Merkel and George Zucco were also in the cast. The film was written by Anita Loos and Robert Hopkins, and directed by Jack Conway. It was MGM's top-grossing picture of the year.

Wee Willie Winkie 20th Century-Fox spent a fortune on this unusual amalgam of a British-in-India action film and a Shirley Temple vehicle, and successfully widened her audience appeal. Loosely based on a Rudyard Kipling tale and scripted by Ernest Pascal and Julien Josephson (who turned the original's small boy into a girl), this made Shirley the mascot of a British regiment commanded by her crusty grandfather (C. Aubrey Smith). Besides acting out her usual role as Cupid (finding a husband for her widowed mother), she was given more important work of charming the rebels (led by Cesar Romero) and bringing about peace in the region. Her particular friend is the tough sergeant (Victor McLaglen), who allows her to drill with the troops and nicknames her Wee Willie Winkie. Director John Ford showed his affection for military tradition in his handling of the sergeant's funeral scene on a cloudy day. June Lang and Michael Whalen also appeared. For its original release, sequences were tinted sepia and blue. Reviewing the film for the British weekly *Night and Day* (an imitation *New Yorker*), Graham Greene libelled Shirley Temple and Fox by remarks that apparently suggested that her screen behaviour was sexually provocative and that were described by the judge as "a gross outrage". Fox collected £1,500 and Miss Temple £2,000, the already shaky *Night and Day* collapsed and Graham Greene

Wee Willie Winkie: Victor McLaglen, Shirley Temple.

continued to write caustic reviews for *The Spectator*.
Captains Courageous
Slave Ship
The Singing Marine After serving in the army (*Flirtation Walk*) and the navy (*Shipmates Forever*), it was inevitable that Dick Powell would be posted to the marines. In this Delmer Daves script, he was the singing marine from Arkansas who wins a talent contest. Success goes to his head for a while, and he thinks of becoming a professional singer, but after he is posted to Shanghai he returns to his senses. Harry Warren wrote the songs (five with Al Dubin, one with Johnny Mercer) and Busby Berkeley staged two dance numbers, including "Night Over Shanghai", which recalled his "Shanghai Lil" of *Footlight Parade*. Doris Weston was the girl (a change from Ruby Keeler), and she sang one of the numbers. Lee Dixon took another, leaving Powell with four, including "The Song of the Marines", which was later adopted by the Marine Corps. Ray Enright directed for Warner Bros.
Mountain Music

AUGUST

You Can't Have Everything The 20th Century-Fox musical cast Alice Faye as a young playwright, Don Ameche as the Broadway producer who turns her work into a hit musical and the Ritz Brothers as themselves performing at a nightclub. The score by Mack Gordon and Harry Revel provided a duet for Alice and Tony Martin, "Afraid to Dream". Supporting roles were taken by Charles Winninger, Louise Hovick (better known as Gypsy Rose Lee) and Arthur Treacher. Gregory Ratoff

provided the story but did not appear. Harry Tugend, Jack Yellen and Karl Tunberg turned it into a screenplay and Norman Taurog handled the direction.
Artists and Models In Paramount's musical comedy, Jack Benny dropped his customary persona to play a more conventional lead as an advertising executive who has to find the ideal girl to use in a campaign promoting the silverware manufactured by Richard Arlen's company. Contenders for the coveted job are Ida Lupino's model and Gail Patrick's socialite. There were specialty numbers from Martha Raye (in blackface), Louis Armstrong and Orchestra, Judy Canova (in her hillbilly song-and-dance act with sister Anne and brother Zeke), Kostelanetz and Orchestra, and others. The songs included "Whispers in the Dark" by Leo Robin and Frederick Hollander. Walter De Leon and Francis Martin were the credited screenplay authors (from a story by Sig Herzig and Gene Thackrey), although at least six other writers helped out. The director was Raoul Walsh. Paramount used the title – but nothing else – for a 1955 Martin and Lewis comedy, while Jack Benny starred in a titular follow-up, *Artists and Models Abroad* (1938).
Wee Willie Winkie
Saratoga
The Good Earth (Now on wider release at popular prices.)
Stella Dallas Barbara Stanwyck threw looks to the wind and gained new respect for her acting range playing the uncouth mother who marries above her station and sacrifices her own happiness for the sake of her daughter. Samuel Goldwyn had originally envisaged an older actress for this re-make of his 1925 hit (which had starred Belle Bennett), but Stanwyck made an elaborate test to win him over. This version of the Olive Higgins Prouty novel was

shaped for the screen by Victor Heerman and Sarah Y. Mason, and directed by King Vidor. Inevitably, it was John Boles who played the socially prominent husband, while Anne Shirley did the daughter. The unabashed tear-jerker won audiences over, especially in its memorable finale of the mother watching her daughter's wedding from the street outside. United Artists were the distributors of the Goldwyn output.

Stella Dallas: Barbara Stanwyck. At the end, the outsider at her own daughter's wedding.

Dead End This was a gangster film with impeccable credentials, taken by Samuel Goldwyn from Sidney Kingsley's hit play that demonstrated how slum conditions bred crime. Lillian Hellman wrote the screenplay and William Wyler directed. Joel McCrea was the idealistic architect who wants to build a better environment, Sylvia Sidney was his girl and Humphrey Bogart was the bad egg who tries to corrupt the local

Dead End: Humphrey Bogart, Billy Halop, other "Dead End kids".

Dead End: Set design by Richard Day, showing schematic juxtaposition: the service entrance of luxury apartments abuts the slums.

youth. Recruited from the Broadway cast were Marjorie Main as Bogart's mother, who slaps his face in utter disgust, and the boys (Leo Gorcey, Huntz Hall, Billy Halop, Bobby Jordan, Bernard Punsley and Gabriel Dell) who became the Dead End Kids (and later the Bowery Boys). Claire Trevor, Wendy Barrie and Allen Jenkins had other roles. Goldwyn insisted on the New York setting being re-created by art director Richard Day in an enormous studio set, where it was ably photographed by Gregg Toland even if it was never totally convincing. United Artists distributed.

Topper As young sophisticates killed in a car crash, Cary Grant and Constance Bennett returned in the flesh to liven up the existence of Roland Young's stuffy banker. Billie Burke was his nagging wife and Alan Mowbray the butler, while portly Eugene Pallette played a hotel detective. Thanks to Roy Seawright's photographic effects, Grant and Bennett appeared and disappeared at will. Thorne Smith's risqué story was necessarily toned down in the screenplay by Jack Jevne, Eric Hatch and Eddie Moran. Norman Z. McLeod directed the Hal Roach production, whose release through MGM was considerably disrupted by the hold-overs on *Saratoga*. This was the film that first demonstrated Grant's real skill as a romantic comedian. It spawned two sequels and later a television series as well as a 1979 TV movie re-make.

SEPTEMBER

Thin Ice In her second Fox skating musical, Sonja Henie's part was that of a Swiss skiing instructor who falls in love with a prince, which was Tyrone Power's department. It was another film to light on the topical theme of a commoner in love with royalty, although the story arranges for her to be ignorant of Power's standing for a while. By now, Fox had devised a special camera to follow her around on the ice, swivelling to keep up with her movements. Joan Davis scored with her comic songs as the leader of an all-girl orchestra, while Arthur

Topper: Cary Grant, Roland Young, Constance Bennett. Set design by Arthur I. Royce.

Treacher, Raymond Walburn, Siegfried Rumann and Alan Hale also acted in the film, which was directed by Sidney Lanfield from a script by Boris Ingster and Milton Sperling based on a German play by Atilla Orbok. British picturegoers saw it retitled *Lovely to Look At*.

Lost Horizon This was by far the biggest picture that Columbia had ever undertaken (costing $2 million), but Harry Cohn succumbed to his ace director Frank Capra's enthusiasm for James Hilton's novel, and no expense was spared bringing the story of Shangri-La to the screen, with Capra using his usual writer, Robert Riskin. The five outsiders who came to this hidden place of peace and happiness somewhere in the Himalayas were Ronald Colman as the wise British diplomat, John Howard as his reckless younger brother, Thomas Mitchell as a smooth-talking swindler, Edward Everett Horton as a fussy paleontologist and Isabel Jewell as a consumptive prostitute. To play the inhabitants of the earthly paradise, Capra deliberately chose less familiar faces: Sam Jaffe (then 38 but appearing as the 200-year-old High

Lost Horizon: Ronald Colman, Sam Jaffe.

Lama), Jane Wyatt (in her first major role) and Margo (as the discontented girl who is really an old woman). Stephen Goosson designed the modernistic sets, and Joseph Walker photographed the film, which had Dimitri Tiomkin's first big score. It had been road-shown at 130 minutes in the spring of 1937 and did weak business, but picked up when it went out on general release this month at popular prices and trimmed to 118 minutes. While it reportedly grossed over $2 million worldwide in its first 18 months of release, this also had to cover the cost of prints, promotion and distribution, and it failed to recoup its investment. In later reissues, and for many years on American TV, it ran only 108 minutes, but thanks to the preservation work of the American Film Institute fully complete prints have become available in recent times.

Broadway Melody of 1938 Robert Taylor, who neither sang nor danced, had the top billing in the third *Melody*. As in the 1936 edition, he played a Broadway producer, here trying to raise money for a show (what else?). Eleanor Powell was the girl whose racetrack winnings solve the problem. It was the musical numbers that counted, with Powell and George Murphy dancing (a nice number in a park, "Follow My Footsteps"), and Sophie Tucker and Judy Garland singing, the latter with the now fondly remembered "Dear Mr Gable", addressed to his portrait. The 115-minute film was written by Jack MacGowan from a story he devised with Sid Silvers; Roy Del Ruth directed; and the songs were by Nacio Herb Brown and Arthur Freed, while Dave Gould was the dance director. Binnie Barnes, Buddy Ebsen, Raymond Walburn and Robert Benchley were also featured.

Stella Dallas

The Prisoner of Zenda From Shangri-La, Ronald Colman moved to the mythical kingdom of Ruritania,

The Prisoner of Zenda: Madeleine Carroll, Ronald Colman.

playing the Englishman on holiday who is persuaded to stand in for the kidnapped heir to the throne who looks exactly like him. Colman was used to dual roles, having played them previously in *The Magic Flame* (1927) and *The Masquerader* (1933). The story was familiar from Anthony Hope's novel, the stage adaptation by Edward Rose and earlier film versions, but David O. Selznick's production was in a class of its own. Madeleine Carroll played the princess; Douglas Fairbanks Jr was the dashingly villainous Rupert of Hentzau; Raymond Massey was the leader of the conspiracy; and C. Aubrey Smith, Mary Astor and David Niven all had good roles. From its spectacular duel between Colman and Fairbanks to the tender parting scene between Colman and Carroll (the princess must marry the king and lose the Englishman she has come to love), the picture flowed with splendid assurance, having been refined in the usual process of sneak previews to its final length of 101 minutes. It benefited from the exceptional skills of cinematographer James Wong Howe, art director Lyle Wheeler and composer Alfred Newman. John Cromwell was the director (although George Cukor shot the final version of the renunciation scene), and John L. Balderston scripted (with input from Wells Root and Donald Ogden Stewart). The distributor was United

One Hundred Men and a Girl: Deanna Durbin, Leopold Stokowski.

Artists. It was so perfectly done that MGM didn't tamper with it on obtaining the re-make rights and released an almost exact copy in 1952 starring Stewart Granger.

One Hundred Men and a Girl With national unemployment disturbingly on the rise again, Hans Kraly's story of a young singer played by Deanna Durbin who finds work for one

hundred unemployed musicians had topical appeal to add to its other advantages. Durbin's tactic was to bulldoze the celebrated Leopold Stokowski into accepting the hundred men, who included her widowed father (Adolphe Menjou), as an orchestra for him to conduct. Alice Brady and Eugene Pallette were a wealthy couple, and Mischa Auer was inimitably himself. The lighthearted whimsy was written by Bruce Manning, Charles Kenyon and James Mulhauser, while the team of director Henry Koster and producer Joe Pasternak had again hit exactly the right note of pleasant escapism and firmly established Deanna Durbin as Universal's top money-maker.

OCTOBER

Life Begins in College The Ritz Brothers were promoted to starring status in this football musical comedy in which they – as college tailors allowed to take the field in the big match – won the game with their antics. Joan Davis, Tony Martin, Gloria Stuart, Nat Pendleton and Fred Stone all contributed to the merriment under William A. Seiter's direction. 20th Century-Fox's writers were Darrell Ware (story), and Karl Tunberg and Don Ettlinger (screenplay). Songs came from Lew Pollack and Sidney D. Mitchell.

The Prisoner of Zenda

Music for Madame Opera tenor Nino Martini starred in this musical comedy, a Jesse L. Lasky production released by RKO Radio. Between his miscellany of songs there was a story (credited to Robert Harari and Gertrude Purcell) in which he becomes the dupe of jewel thieves who work while he sings at a wedding. The leading lady's role went to Joan Fontaine, appearing as a serious-minded composer. Others participating were Alan Mowbray as a musical maestro, Alan Hale, Erik Rhodes and Lee Patrick. John Blystone directed. Martini decided against a Hollywood career after this picture.

Stage Door Katharine Hepburn and Ginger Rogers were two contrasting types in a boarding house full of stagestruck ladies who also included Eve Arden, Lucille Ball, Andrea Leeds, Ann Miller, Gail Patrick and ageing Constance Collier, praying for a comeback. Hepburn was the smug rich girl and Rogers her down-to-earth, wisecracking room-mate, while Andrea Leeds was the overly-sensitive hopeful who cracked up under the strain. Adolphe Menjou had the only substantial male role as a philandering producer. Director Gregory La Cava deftly handled the large cast. The RKO Radio film had its origins in the

Stage Door: Ginger Rogers, Katharine Hepburn.

Broadway hit of 1936 by Edna Ferber and George S. Kaufman, but it was heavily altered in the screen adaptation by Morrie Ryskind and Anthony Veiller.

The Life of Emile Zola Warner Bros. followed up the success of *The Story of Louis Pasteur* with another historical biopic in which Paul Muni played another bearded Frenchman who fought for his beliefs, and worked with the same director, William Dieterle. The film was largely concerned with the Dreyfus case and raised discreetly but still daringly the very relevant issue of anti-Semitism. Joseph Schildkraut played the falsely accused army officer; Gale Sondergaard appeared as his wife; Robert Barrat was the real villain, Esterhazy; Gloria Holden took the role of Zola's wife; Erin O'Brien-Moore was Nana, the disreputable subject of Zola's famous novel; and Morris Carnovsky made his screen debut as Anatole France. Heinz Herald and Gina Herczeg created the story and wrote the screenplay with Norman Reilly Raine. It was the most acclaimed film of the year and brought both prestige and mild profits to the studio.

NOVEMBER

The Awful Truth The colossal success of this witty comedy with Irene Dunne and Cary Grant more than compensated Columbia for the financial shortcomings of *Lost Horizon.* The two stars played a divorced couple who maintain a link through Grant's right to visit their joint pet, a terrier called Mr Smith (played by Asta of the *Thin Man* films). Vina Delmar's script (from the 1922 play by Arthur Richman, already filmed twice) and Leo McCarey's direction developed many uproarious sequences of situational and slapstick comedy, but the film's ultimate strength was the way it brought out the tender regard underlying the farcical complications that ultimately reunites the couple. Ralph Bellamy was the stuffy other man and Cecil Cunningham his Aunt Patsy, while Alexander D'Arcy and Joyce Compton had wonderful moments. Columbia later turned it into a musical called *Let's Do It Again* (1953) with Jane Wyman and Ray Milland.

Ali Baba Goes to Town Eddie Cantor tried his luck at 20th Century-Fox after terminally disagreeing with Sam Goldwyn on future projects. His new material recalled *Roman Scandals* as he dreams his way back to the Arabian nights while working as an extra on a Hollywood movie. As adviser to a Sultan (Roland Young), he dodges around harems and institutes a New Deal programme that puts his life in danger from political rivals. Tony Martin, June Lang, Louise Hovick (later Gypsy Rose Lee), Virginia Field and Douglas Dumbrille gave support. The film ended with glimpses of top Fox stars like Shirley Temple, Sonja Henie and Tyrone Power at a gala premiere. David Butler directed.

Harry Tugend and Jack Yellen scripted from a story by Gene Towne, Graham Baker and Gene Fowler. The songs were mostly by Mack Gordon and Harry Revel.

Double Wedding MGM put William Powell and Myrna Loy in tandem again in a zany comedy (written by Jo Swerling from a Ferenc Molnar play) in which he was a bohemian painter whose campaign to wed Loy's prim and proper dress designer takes the devious form of wooing her sister (Florence Rice). John Beal was the other man in the finale promised by the film's title. Jessie Ralph and Edgar Kennedy were also involved. It was one of the films produced by Joseph L. Mankiewicz while direction was by Richard Thorpe.

The Perfect Specimen Errol Flynn in this Warner Bros. comedy was not entirely the perfect choice to play the protectively reared son of a wealthy family who is taken out of his cocoon into the real world by Joan Blondell's vivacious newspaper reporter. In one scene Flynn displayed his physique in the boxing ring, which pleased his female following. Also in the cast were May Robson, Hugh Herbert, Edward Everett Horton, Dick Foran, Beverly Roberts and Allen Jenkins. A story by Samuel Hopkins Adams was the inspiration for the movie, which was written by Norman Reilly Raine, Lawrence Riley, Brewster Morse and Fritz Falkenstein and directed by Michael Curtiz. It was released as a First National picture.

The Firefly In this latest lengthy and lavish MGM operetta, Jeanette MacDonald was partnered by Allan Jones (who introduced the song "The Donkey Serenade", written for the

The Firefly: Jeanette MacDonald, Allan Jones.

The Awful Truth: Irene Dunne, Asta, Cary Grant. The wife attempts to conceal the evidence of her hidden gentleman visitor from her ex-husband.

film). Very freely drawn from Rudolf Friml and Otto A. Harbach's stage production (first seen in 1912), it relocated the story in the Spain of the Napoleonic era and offered MacDonald as a café singer and Spanish Mata Hari who falls in love with Jones, a nobleman and spy for France. Warren William was a general who coveted MacDonald almost as much as she coveted his secret dispatches. Ogden Nash did the script adaptation, and Frances Goodrich and Albert Hackett wrote the screenplay. The director's chair was occupied by Robert Z. Leonard.

Nothing Sacred This well-titled comedy offered Carole Lombard masquerading as a tragic heroine doomed to die of radium poisoning (a temporary diagnostic error by her local physician, Charles Winninger), and Fredric March as the newshound who exploits her apparent predicament to sell papers and restore himself to favour with his apoplectic editor, Walter Connolly. In one scene, March is bitten in the leg by a kid as a sample of small-town hospitality; in another he socks Lombard on the jaw to get her into better shape to maintain her pretence under examination by Siegfried Rumann's eminent consultant. Ben Hecht wrote it from a story by James H. Street (with uncredited assists from Dorothy Parker, Budd Schulberg and Ring Lardner Jr); William Wellman directed for David O. Selznick. It was shot in Technicolor and released by United Artists. Martin and Lewis starred in a 1954 remake, *Living It Up*.

DECEMBER

The Awful Truth
Nothing Sacred
Navy Blue and Gold The only new film to cut through the customary pre-Christmas slump, this was also the most successful of a number of concurrent Annapolis salutes by different studios. Lacking major stars and relying on its subject matter to whip up interest, it was nevertheless an A feature, as attested by its important director (Sam Wood) and length (94 minutes), but one that didn't have too much riding on it so that it could be used to keep the theatres going while people's minds were on Christmas shopping. In fact,

TEN BEST-CRITICS' CHOICE

A new record total of 531 critics sent in ballots to *The Film Daily*, voting on the films released from 1 November 1936 to 31 October 1937. Their votes were cast as follows:

1.	*The Life of Emile Zola*	453
2.	*The Good Earth*	424
3.	*Captains Courageous*	380
4.	*Lost Horizon*	325
5.	*A Star Is Born*	287
6.	*Romeo and Juliet* [1936 release]	251
7.	*Stage Door*	235
8.	*Dead End*	197
9.	*Winterset*	165
10.	*The Awful Truth*	160
	Close Runners Up	
11.	*Lloyds of London*	154
12.	*One Hundred Men and a Girl*	152
13.	*The Prisoner of Zenda*	146
14.	*Camille*	121
15.	*Maytime*	121
16.	*Conquest*	107

In the top 10, only *Winterset* was cold-shouldered by the mass audience.

CLOSE RUNNERS UP

The following 17 films came close to being included among the hits of the year for the month indicated: *Alcatraz Island* (November), *The Bride Wore Red* (October), *Call It a Day* (May), *Champagne Waltz* (February), *A Day at the Races* (June), *Easy Living* (July), *Fifty Roads to Town* (May), *Gold Diggers of 1937* (February), *History Is Made at Night* (April), *The King and the Chorus Girl* (April), *Parnell* (June), *The Road Back* (June), *Seventh Heaven* (March), *Sing Me a Love Song* (January), *Submarine D-1* (November, December), *There Goes My Girl* (June), *Wife, Doctor and Nurse* (October).

it had more popular appeal than Garbo's big-budget *Conquest*, which it followed into release. It was full of routine material (script by George Bruce from his novel) about three buddies at the Naval Academy from different walks of life: the brilliant but lazy Robert Young, the poor but eager James Stewart and the wealthy Tom Brown. Florence Rice was the girl and Lionel Barrymore was a retired football coach, with Paul Kelly, Billie Burke and Samuel S. Hinds also seen. James Stewart had the best acting opportunity and handled it so effectively that MGM began to realize his potential and, just as importantly for his future, director Frank Capra took note of what he was capable of doing emotionally.

1938

This wasn't the best of years for Hollywood as admissions fell back three million to 85 million a week in the United States, and profits slumped at all the studios. The good news was that the one loss-maker, Universal, had reduced its losses from the previous year and the Walt Disney organization had great cause for rejoicing as *Snow White and the Seven Dwarfs* became the biggest grossing picture by far of the decade (and remained so; *Gone with the Wind* opened at the end of 1939 but made its fortune in the 1940s). *Alexander's Ragtime Band* was the second great hit of the year, while *Test Pilot, In Old Chicago, The Hurricane, The Adventures of Robin Hood, Marie Antoinette, Love Finds Andy Hardy* and *Boys Town* were other top grossers, with *Angels with Dirty Faces* and *Sweethearts* joining them at the end of the year. Also late in the year, Universal's reissue double-bill of *Dracula* plus *Frankenstein* showed more drawing power than most of its new releases.

Mickey Rooney became a big sensation during the year, while the most important newcomer was John Garfield. Exhibitors in the United States named as the top box-office stars Shirley Temple, Clark Gable, Sonja Henie, Mickey Rooney, Spencer Tracy, Robert Taylor, Myrna Loy, Jane Withers, Alice Faye and Tyrone Power, but it was *Variety*'s reckoning that only Gable and Temple were among the very top draws internationally where Garbo, Gary Cooper, Paul Muni, Jeanette MacDonald, Charles Boyer, Deanna Durbin, Errol Flynn and Claudette Colbert held greater sway than the other eight most popular at home.

Foreign films continued to compete artistically with Hollywood. The American critics raved over *La Grande Illusion* and *The Lady Vanishes*. Academy Award nominations for Best Picture went to *La Grande Illusion, Pygmalion* and *The Citadel*.

NO SEX PLEASE, WE'RE AMERICAN

In the Spring of 1938, the Motion Picture Producers and Distributors Association became concerned about a wave of "questionable" movies that were being launched on the American market, mostly without Production Code Administration seals of approval. While films lacking the seal could not be booked into the theatre chains owned by the major studios without attracting a fine of $25,000, they did prove attractive to many independent theatres, which were being hurt by a product famine and the trade recession and which found that daring films on sexual subjects could attract huge audiences when promoted heavily.

With scenes of actual childbirth, *The Birth of a Baby* was a feature-length semi-documentary professionally made at a cost of $50,000 for the American Committee on Maternal Welfare by the Christie company in Hollywood (whose normal specialty was comedy shorts). It was not originally intended for showing in theatres but public interest was fuelled by a pictorial feature in *Life* magazine, and the film did colossal business in city centre theatres in Detroit, Denver, Omaha, Indianapolis, and elsewhere. The issue of *Life* magazine was banned in many areas, and there was considerable uproar at *The Birth of a Baby* being shown as entertainment.

Other films that were causing concern dealt with nudism: in *The Unashamed*, an attractive secretary lures her husky employer to a nudist camp where a runaway heiress spoils her plans. And there were dramas about the danger of syphilis: *Damaged Lives*, directed by Edgar G. Ulmer, and *Damaged Goods*, a production with established Hollywood actors (Pedro de Cordoba, Esther Dale and others) about a man afflicted with v.d. who gives the disease to his new-born child.

There were pictures warning about white slave traffic, such as *Slaves in Bondage*, a Hollywood production with known players like Donald Reed and Wheeler Oakman, and films demonstrating the danger of drugs, such as *Assassin of Youth* about marijuana. There were dramas about the danger of lesbianism, such as *Children of Loneliness*, "inspired by *The Well of Loneliness*", with a cautionary story introduced by a doctor (whose literature was on sale after the show) in which a girl narrowly avoids becoming a lesbian by falling for a fullback and a gay artist commits suicide. And there was even a film called *The Love Life of a Gorilla*. It got to the point

This is not the Hedy Lamarr that American audiences would see. A scene from *Extase* (*Ecstasy*) (1933).

where the New York Censor Board revoked the permit that allowed showings of a two-reeler made in 1921 about social diseases called *Animated Diagrams of the Human Body*.

A rather different category was that of foreign films that were well regarded in their country of origin but were too frank to pass the American censors. Jacques Deval's *Club de Femmes* was one, starring Danielle Darrieux as an unwed mother in a women's hostel where lesbianism and procurement for prostitution were depicted. The film opened in New York after changes that turned the Darrieux character into a married woman and converted the lesbian relationship into one of sisterly solicitude.

The most celebrated case concerned Gustav Machaty's *Extase* (*Ecstasy*) which was banned in New York and finally opened there after a long court battle in 1940, seven years after it was made. It, too, was doctored so that its lovers were married and other daring details were eliminated or toned down.

MADE IN ENGLAND

The American film companies had been actively involved in British production for some years because their distribution organizations established there were legally obliged to handle a percentage of domestically-made pictures. Many companies, like MGM, simply bought low-budget "quota quickies" to meet this requirement or produced cheap pictures themselves. Other companies, like RKO Radio, encouraged the production of A films that might do well on the British and Empire market; RKO formed Associated Radio with Basil Dean and had a huge local success with Gracie Fields' first film, *Sally*

Director King Vidor, Robert Donat and Ralph Richardson outside Stage 5 at Denham during production of *The Citadel* (1938).

in Our Alley. These films were not intended for release in the United States. However, United Artists found that its British productions from Alexander Korda's London Films could also perform well at the American box-office, and *Drums* (originally called *The Drum*) was a case in point in 1938.

20th Century-Fox had made *Wings of the Morning* (1937) in Britain in three-colour Technicolor. The period costume tale might just as well have been shot in Hollywood as it displayed few signs of its British origins.

In 1937, Metro-Goldwyn-Mayer started production at Denham studios on films that would, in effect, have dual nationality. They would deal with British subjects in a way that would make them popular with audiences on both sides of the Atlantic. Top producer Michael Balcon was signed up to head production. Robert Taylor starred in *A Yank at Oxford*, which cost $900,000, including the expense of establishing a production centre in England. Balcon resigned because of the interference from New York and Hollywood, and another leading British producer, Victor Saville, took over.

The Citadel was next to be filmed, starring Robert Donat. The two pictures were made to American standards, with Hollywood directors, cameramen, editorial supervision and technical procedures. Both were shown in America before they opened in Britain and were very popular with American audiences who simply regarded them as Hollywood pictures shot in England.

British audiences looked on them as lavishly-made British pictures. *A Yank at Oxford* was second only to *Snow White and the Seven Dwarfs* as the biggest success of 1938 in British cinemas. *The Citadel* was one of the two top money-makers of 1939. MGM would have even greater success with its third British-made production, *Goodbye Mr Chips*, when Robert Donat took the Academy Award for Best Actor. It also purchased *Pygmalion* for release in the United States in 1939 and had producer Gabriel Pascal do some re-takes and new dubbing to bring it up to "American standards".

Other companies were impressed enough to plan their own major productions. Warner Bros., which had long made quota quickies at a loss, considered starring Paul Muni in a biopic about the newsman Reuter and Claude Rains in a re-make of *Disraeli*. Columbia contemplated a production of a Cary Grant comedy. 20th Century-Fox envisaged four major productions. MGM itself had plans to make numerous films including *A Yank at Eton*, *Rage in Heaven* and *National Velvet* in Britain after a thriller called *Haunted Honeymoon*. Production of the latter was scheduled to start the day after Britain declared war on Germany. Although the film was made in England a while later, World War II put an end to Hollywood's large-scale invasion of the British Isles.

However, after the war, the big studios all shot major productions in England, and MGM became the most active Hollywood company in British production, setting up its own studio at Borehamwood, Hertfordshire.

ARE THEY WORTH IT?

In May, Harry Brandt, New York exhibitor and spokesman of the Independent Theatre Owners of America, lashed out at the huge salaries being paid to stars who had, he alleged, lost their box-office appeal. According to one source, he was smarting from the low takings he had experienced with *Bringing Up Baby*, one of the year's worst flops. His article in the obscure *Independent Film Journal* was headed "Box-Office Poison", and it declared: "Among those players whose dramatic ability is unquestioned, but whose box-office draw is nil, can be numbered Mae West, Edward Arnold, Greta Garbo, Joan Crawford, Katharine Hepburn and many, many others." Fred Astaire was another victim of Brandt's wrath.

The uproar was intensified when *Time* magazine publicized the remarks and put them in the public arena, contacting the stars for their comments. Katharine Hepburn bravely responded: "If I weren't laughing so hard, I might cry." Mae West had the best comeback: "Why, the independent theatre owners call me the mortgage lifter. When business is bad, they just re-run one of my pictures. The box-office business in the entire industry has dropped off 30 per cent. The only picture to make real money was *Snow White and the Seven Dwarfs*, and that would have made twice as much if they'd had me play Snow White."

There was actually nothing new about Brandt's onslaught. Star salaries had been heavily criticized 16 years before and would be again (Brando in *Superman*). Fortunately, just about all of Brandt's victims not only survived but did very nicely, thank you, in the years ahead. Even Marlene Dietrich, who was apparently being paid by Paramount *not* to make films, quickly bounded back with *Destry Rides Again* at Universal in 1939, and Katharine Hepburn set her own terms for making *The Philadelphia Story* in 1940.

HITS OF THE YEAR

JANUARY

Happy Landing Sonja Henie pursues Cesar Romero's amorous bandleader back to the States after he crashlands near her Norwegian village. His aide Don Ameche is told to take care of her, and he turns her into a skating star. It was a good enough excuse for some elaborate skating numbers and for some songs from Ethel Merman as Romero's tempestuous girlfriend. El Brendel appeared as a Swiss bandleader. Milton Sperling and Boris Ingster wrote the screenplay and Roy Del Ruth directed for 20th Century-Fox.

Wells Fargo Paramount again put its money on big-budget westerns and assigned director Frank Lloyd to another sprawling historical saga – the building of the famous express service – that was long enough in footage (115 minutes) but surprisingly short on action. The husband and wife team of Joel McCrea and Frances Dee played husband and wife on screen where his devotion to the company breaks up their marriage. Others on board included Ralph Morgan, Mary Nash, Johnny Mack Brown and Porter Hall, while Frank McGlynn made one of his many appearances as Abraham Lincoln. The writers were Paul Schofield, Gerald Geraghty and Frederick Jackson, from a story by Stuart N. Lake, and Howard Estabrook (the screenwriter of *Cimarron*) was, interestingly, the associate producer.

Rosalie Separated from Jeanette MacDonald (while she made *The Firefly*), Nelson Eddy was paired instead with Eleanor Powell in this film version of one of Florenz Ziegfeld's great hits, dating from 1928. Eddy was rather old to be playing a West Point cadet and Powell wasn't the most believable Balkan princess, here attending Vassar. Cole Porter provided new songs (including "In the Still of the Night") and Powell devised an elaborate tap-dancing number across big drums. Ray Bolger did some further hoofing, newcomer Ilona Massey sang one number, Frank Morgan played the king of the Balkan country, and Jerry Colonna and Billy Gilbert handled the humorous element. William Anthony McGuire, who had written the stage version of *Rosalie* with Guy Bolton, did the screenplay, and W. S. Van Dyke II directed for MGM.

The Hurricane With source material in a novel by the authors of *Mutiny on the Bounty*, Charles Nordhoff and James Norman Hall, and scope for as spectacular a climax as *San Francisco*, producer Samuel Goldwyn could afford to take a chance on starring the virtually unknown Jon Hall (said to be a cousin of co-author Hall) and the rising Dorothy Lamour (who had demonstrated her worth in a sarong in the minor *The Jungle Princess* at Paramount). They looked most attractive as recently married natives on a South Sea island whose happiness is shattered when a cruel governor (Raymond Massey) imposes a six-

Wells Fargo: Frances Dee, Mary Nash, Ralph Morgan, Joel McCrea, unbilled, Johnny Mack Brown.

The Hurricane: Dorothy Lamour, Jon Hall.

month jail sentence on the innocent young man. C. Aubrey Smith as a priest, Mary Astor as the governor's wife, Thomas Mitchell as an alcoholic doctor and John Carradine as a sadistic guard were also prominent. Director John Ford worked with his favourite writer of the period, Dudley Nichols, while Oliver H. P. Garrett was credited for the adaptation and Stuart Heisler was billed as associate director. James Basevi created the powerful 20-minute climactic hurricane sequence at a cost of $400,000. Alfred Newman's score contributed substantially to the mood. With its strong visual emphasis and story of fundamental appeal, this was a huge success not only in the US but especially on the foreign market. United Artists were the distributors.

True Confession One of the period's many madcap comedies, this required Carole Lombard, playing an inveterate liar, to confess to a murder she didn't commit so that she can be defended by her straitlaced attorney husband (Fred MacMurray) and do his career some good. In addition to John Barrymore as a drunken blackmailer and Una Merkel as Lombard's confidante, the characters included Edgar Kennedy's detective and Porter Hall's prosecutor. It was the fourth teaming of Lombard and MacMurray and a further collaboration between writer Claude Binyon and director Wesley Ruggles for Paramount. A French play by Louis Verneuil and George Berr was the basis of the film. The re-make with Betty Hutton was called *Cross My Heart* (1945).

FEBRUARY

Snow White and the Seven Dwarfs Premiered on 21 December 1937 and now moving into general release, Walt Disney's animated feature became not only by far the most popular picture of the year but the most successful launched in the decade bar only *Gone with the Wind*. It had taken four and a half years to make and gone many times over its original budget to cost $1.67 million, and there had always been the alarming possibility that moviegoers might not want to sit still for a cartoon feature, but the skill of the huge Disney team (under supervising director David Hand) in bringing the characters of Grimm's fairy tale to life (and, in particular, the distinctive characteristics given to the dwarfs) enthralled audiences. (In Britain, the wicked Queen was considered so frightening that children were allowed to see the film only in the company of adults.) *Snow White* was also a musical feast, thanks to the eight catchy songs in its 83 minutes of running time ("Whistle While You Work", "Someday My Prince Will Come", "Heigh-Ho", etc.). The film used the multiplane camera to move backward and forward and to shoot through several layers of drawings to give a greater sense of depth and more complex images. It was another triumph for Technicolor, which provided 789 prints for circulation by RKO Radio in America at a cost of $700,000. The production brought in rentals of over $5 million in the United States alone in the 18 months of release before it was withdrawn (to be reissued in 1940). This huge figure was helped by the stiff terms imposed: 50 per cent of the take, no flat fee rentals, a minimum admission price of 15¢, and no double-billing (hence more shows daily). (Many of RKO's established outlets baulked at the terms, but other theatres were more than ready to step in.) It took a further $3 million on its first release abroad; in London alone, it ran at one West End cinema for nine months where it racked up 819,000 admissions, and it grossed at least $1 million in Britain. In Paris it had an astounding seven-month premiere run. Disney forged ahead with more animated features, and others started work on rival productions.

The Goldwyn Follies And Sam Goldwyn plumped for the new Technicolor for this lengthy (115 minute) revue in which the cine-mogul hoped to equal the stage efforts of Ziegfeld. He was the third big independent producer (after David O. Selznick and Walter Wanger) to take up Technicolor. This picture became known as *Goldwyn's Folly* because of the many discarded scripts, the hefty $2 million budget (the use of Technicolor was partly responsible) which prevented the film showing a profit, and the disorganized result.

There was a slight plot centered on a film producer (Adolphe Menjou), and there was a juvenile romance (conducted partly in song by Kenny Baker and a dubbed Andrea Leeds), but the film was really a string of production numbers featuring top talents of stage, opera and radio. There were the Ritz Brothers, radio favourites Edgar Bergen and Charlie McCarthy (in their screen debut), ballerina Vera Zorina, Bobby Clark and Ella Logan from musical comedy, Helen Jepson and Charles Kullman from the Metropolitan Opera, and the Met's American Ballet Company under George Balanchine, plus of course the Goldwyn Girls. The extravaganza featured the last work of George Gershwin including the hit song "Love Walked In" (he died before completing his task and Vernon Duke wrote further songs; all the lyrics were by Ira Gershwin). Ben Hecht took credit for the script (augmented by Sam Perrin and Arthur Phillips) and George Marshall directed the United Artists release. What with the financial loss and scathing reviews, it was the first and last of what Goldwyn had once envisaged as a series, and it was the last time Goldwyn used Technicolor until *Up in Arms* (1944).

The Buccaneer Donning a French accent, Fredric March seemed to relish his swashbuckling role of the brazen pirate Jean Lafitte in Cecil B. DeMille's adventure. The showman director lavishly re-staged the Battle of New Orleans, in which Lafitte helped the American side against the British in the War of 1812, and had other spectacular scenes, including the opening destruction of the White House. Franciska Gaal was the Dutch girl who loved him and Margot Grahame the society belle he loved, Akim Tamiroff was his sidekick, while

Hugh Sothern portrayed Andrew Jackson with Walter Brennan as the general's orderly. The 124-minute-long Paramount release had an episodic script delivered by Edwin Justus Mayer, C. Gardner Sullivan and Harold Lamb (working from a novel by Lyle Saxon). DeMille's last work, released in 1958, was a new production of the story, directed by Anthony Quinn, who played one of Lafitte's henchmen in this first version.
Happy Landing
The Hurricane

MARCH

Snow White and the Seven Dwarfs
Mad about Music Deanna Durbin's third feature gave her the choice role of a film star's daughter pent up in a Swiss boarding school who invents a famous explorer father, then recruits Herbert Marshall to play the part and convince her dubious friends. Deanna sang Gounod's "Ave Maria" with the Vienna Boys Choir. She also performed, while bicycling along, "I Love to Whistle" (by Jimmy McHugh and Harold Adamson) with Cappy Barra's Harmonica Band. The cast included Gail Patrick (as her vain mother), Jackie Moran (as a schoolboy), Arthur Treacher, William Frawley and Helen Parrish. Norman Taurog directed for producer Joe Pasternak and Universal. The writers were Bruce Manning and Felix Jackson, working from a story by Marcella Burke and Frederick Kohner. 1957's *The Toy Tiger* with Jeff Chandler was a remake.
A Yank at Oxford MGM's British-made production had begun life as an idea by John Monk Saunders in 1934 and over the years some 30 writers (including F. Scott Fitzgerald) had struggled to develop a screenplay, although only seven of them participated in the final writing credits (Malcolm Stuart Boylan, Walter Ferris, George Oppenheimer, Leon Gordon, Sidney Gilliat, Roland Pertwee, Michael Hogan) and were credited differently on American prints from British ones (with Pertwee omitted). Robert Taylor starred as the brash American who is at first ridiculed and finally respected by the Brits at Oxford. It helped him create a tougher image as well as show off his physique on the running track and in the climactic boat race with Cambridge. Maureen O'Sullivan played the girl he romances, while Vivien Leigh made a telling appearance as the promiscuous wife of a don. Lionel Barrymore played Taylor's father in scenes shot in Hollywood. Besides Vivien Leigh, other British players included Edmund Gwenn, Griffith Jones and

A Yank at Oxford: Vivien Leigh, Robert Taylor, Griffith Jones.

Edward Rigby. Jack Conway directed. In Britain, the film ran 115 minutes. In America, it was shortened to 100 minutes. It was a big success in both countries.
Rebecca of Sunnybrook Farm The popular children's story by Kate Douglas Wiggin (last filmed in 1932 with Marian Nixon) was barely recognizable after writers Karl Tunberg and Don Ettlinger had finished re-shaping it into a vehicle for Shirley Temple, playing a child who

Rebecca of Sunnybrook Farm: Bill "Bojangles" Robinson, Shirley Temple.

realizes her show business ambitions despite her aunt's objections, thanks to a talent scout neighbour played by Randolph Scott. The 10-year-old star

had a more mature hairstyle and performed a medley of her previous song hits. She also teamed again with Bill "Bojangles" Robinson for a dance routine. Gloria Stuart, Helen Westley, Jack Haley, Phyllis Brooks, Slim Summerville and William Demarest lent support. Allan Dwan directed for 20th Century-Fox.
Bluebeard's Eighth Wife In a now celebrated instance of "meeting cute", Gary Cooper and Claudette Colbert came together in a department store on the French Riviera, he wanting to buy the top of a pair of pajamas, she the bottom. It was the first collaboration of writers Billy Wilder and Charles Brackett (working from a French play by Alfred Savoir, revised for Broadway in 1921 by Charlton Andrews and filmed in 1923 with Gloria Swanson). The Paramount picture was directed by Ernst Lubitsch. Gary Cooper was odd casting as a millionaire who has had seven wives and intends to make Colbert's Frenchwoman his eighth. Edward Everett Horton was her impoverished father (who persuades her to marry for the money), and David Niven was Cooper's secretary.
The Adventures of Tom Sawyer David O. Selznick spent nearly $1.5 million on a new version of the Mark Twain classic, last filmed in 1930, and found that this was more money than the market for a children's film could possibly return. The producer cast the unknown Tommy Kelly in the title role after a well-publicized talent hunt, and chose two little-knowns already in Hollywood – Jackie Moran (also appearing in *Mad About Music*) for Huck Finn and Anne Gillis for Becky, the small girl who is lost in the

THE ACADEMY AWARDS

The Biltmore Hotel was again the venue for the tenth year of Academy Awards. The night was 10 March (delayed a week because of widespread flooding), and the number of people entitled to vote had increased dramatically from around 1,000 to around 15,000, making the results far more democratic than hitherto. The voting in most categories had been opened to non-Academy members with "established qualifications in all branches of productions", which meant the members of guilds and included 12,000 registered extras. The winners were known shortly before the start of the proceedings. *The Life of Emile Zola* won the Best Picture award. To widespread surprise, Luise Rainer was honoured as Best Actress for the second year running, this time for *The Good Earth*. (Other nominees had been Greta Garbo for *Camille*, Janet Gaynor for *A Star Is Born*, Irene Dunne for *The Awful Truth* and Barbara Stanwyck for *Stella Dallas*.) Both Spencer Tracy (Best Actor for *Captains Courageous*) and Alice Brady (Best Supporting Actress for *In Old Chicago*) were unable to attend for medical reasons, but Joseph Schildkraut was there as Best Supporting Actor for *The Life of Emile Zola*.

Leo McCarey was named Best Director for *The Awful Truth*. *The Life of Emile Zola* also won Oscars for Heinz Herald, Geza Herczeg and Norman Reilly Raine (Best Screenplay). Walt Disney triumphed yet again in the Best Cartoon category, not for the achievement of *Snow White and the Seven Dwarfs* because the cartoon category was for shorts only, but for *The Old Mill*. *Snow White* could have been nominated for Best Picture; but it was only nominated in the Best Score category, losing to *One Hundred Men and a Girl*, which had no composer credit: Leopold Stokowski was responsible for all the music but studio department head Charles Previn received the Award. In the Best Song category, Harry Owens won for "Sweet Leilani" from *Waikiki Wedding*, thanks, it was thought, to the extras' voting. The result was rather an embarrassment when the Gershwins had been nominated for *Shall We Dance?*, and the rules were promptly changed to exclude the extras from voting for the Best Song next year.

Other winners included: William Wellman and Robert Carson (Best Original Story, *A Star Is Born*); Karl Freund (Best Cinematography, *The Good Earth*); W. Howard Greene (Special Award, a plaque, for the Best Colour Cinematography, *A Star Is Born*); Stephen Goosson (Best Interior Decoration, *Lost Horizon*); Thomas Moulton (Best Sound Recording, *The Hurricane*); and Gene Havlick and Gene Milton (Best Editing, *Lost Horizon*).

story culminating in the fire that destroyed Chicago in 1871. There was a comparable setting in the low-life saloon district with a cabaret entertainer in a leading role. Jean Harlow had been set for this (on loan-out from MGM) at the time of her death, and Alice Faye inherited the part in which she is the singing star who opens her own establishment in partnership with an unscrupulous charmer played (in a change of image) by Tyrone Power. Don Ameche was his honest brother who becomes mayor after Power doublecrosses Brian Donlevy's political boss. They were the sons of Mrs O'Leary (played by Alice Brady), whose cow overturns a lantern to start the fateful blaze. The film was written by Lamar Trotti and Sonya Levien from a novel by Niven Busch, and mostly directed by Henry King; the fiery climax (which lasted 20 minutes, cost $750,000, had sets blazing on the backlot for three days, and called out in vain for Technicolor) was directed by H. Bruce Humberstone with the special effects arranged by Fred Sersen, Ralph Hammeras and Louis J. Witte. The total cost of the picture was put at $1.8 million, but it was one of the year's top grossers. The film had a special run in Los Angeles at the end of 1937, qualifying it for Academy Award consideration as one of that year's releases. It was nominated for Best Picture (the only Fox production among 10 nominees) and in several other categories, and went into general release soon after the results were announced, hoping to benefit from Oscar victories. Its major success came with Alice Brady's Oscar for Best Supporting Actress. 30 minutes of footage was cut for later reissue and has never been found again.

Test Pilot: Clark Gable, Spencer Tracy.

Test Pilot Another of MGM's big pictures with irresistible three star value and aerial spectacle, this had Clark Gable as a daring, egotistical test pilot, Spencer Tracy as his devoted mechanic and Myrna Loy as the farmer's daughter who marries Gable and finds his way of life hard to

caves with Tom at the scary climax. Under the direction of Norman Taurog (well experienced with handling children), they were acceptable but none of the three had much of a subsequent career. May Robson, Walter Brennan and Victor Jory took the leading adult roles, and Jory made a striking villain. Technicolor became available for shooting the film at the last minute and most of the colour was invested in the costumes rather than the sets, which had been prepared for monochrome photography. This

resulted in cameramen James Wong Howe and Wilfred M. Cline providing a less vibrant, more subdued look. William Cameron Menzies did the production design. Selznick recruited George Cukor to do over some of the scenes after previews, before passing the film to United Artists for release.

APRIL

In Old Chicago Recalling MGM's success with the epic destruction of *San Francisco*, 20th Century-Fox hoped to match it with a very similar

take. Starkly dramatic at times, the film was vigorously directed by Victor Fleming and written by Vincent Lawrence and Waldemar Young from a story by Frank Wead. Lionel Barrymore appeared as the kindly head of the aircraft company.
The Girl of the Golden West Jeanette MacDonald and Nelson Eddy were reunited in MGM's film of the 1905 David Belasco stage melodrama (last brought to the screen in 1930). Its storyline had MacDonald's saloon proprietor in love with Eddy's dashing bandit and loved by Walter Pidgeon's sheriff. Sigmund Romberg and Gus Kahn wrote a score for the film, which was supplemented by Gounod's "Ave Maria", sung by MacDonald (audiences were also hearing Deanna Durbin perform it in *Mad About Music*). Leo Carrillo was the outlaw's sidekick, and Buddy Ebsen, Monty Woolley and H. B. Warner also pitched in. Robert Z. Leonard directed from a screenplay by Isabel Dawn and Boyce DeGaw, and it was released in sepia.
Mad about Music
Snow White and the Seven Dwarfs
The Adventures of Tom Sawyer

MAY

Test Pilot
The Adventures of Robin Hood
Warner Bros. spent a record sum of $2 million on this Technicolor adventure and spent it so that it showed to great advantage. Like *The Prisoner of Zenda* it was an exhilaratingly good example of the swashbuckling movie, thanks particularly to effective casting, dashing direction and a vigorous score. Errol Flynn was the daring outlaw of Sherwood Forest (for

In Old Chicago: Alice Brady, Tyrone Power, Alice Faye.

which Bidwell Park at Chico, California, stood in), Olivia De Havilland was Lady (not Maid) Marian, and Basil Rathbone and Claude Rains were powerful villains as Sir Guy of Gisbourne and Prince John respectively. Shooting was not without its troubles with the original director William Keighley yielding to Michael Curtiz after the studio felt that a more robust hand was needed. The climactic duel between Flynn and Rathbone (working under fencing master Fred Cavens) was one of the very best of its type, fully comparable to *Zenda* and better than their earlier set-to in *Captain Blood*. Others in the cast were Alan Hale as Little John (a part he had played in Douglas Fairbanks' very different *Robin Hood* of 1922), Eugene Pallette as the rotund Friar Tuck, Patric Knowles as Will Scarlet, Melville Cooper as the spineless Sheriff of Nottingham and Ian Hunter as good King Richard.

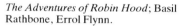
The Adventures of Robin Hood; Basil Rathbone, Errol Flynn.

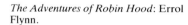
The Adventures of Robin Hood: Errol Flynn.

Norman Reilly Raine and Seton I. Miller wrote the script, and Erich Wolfgang Korngold was persuaded to write what became one of his most memorable scores. The movie, which opened with the Warner Bros. crest in medieval trimmings, was released as a First National picture.
In Old Chicago
Vivacious Lady Ginger Rogers was the lady, or rather the showgirl, who marries a young college professor played by James Stewart, and the problem was how to break it gently to his parents (Charles Coburn and Beulah Bondi). It was a thin situation humour, but engagingly acted and enabling Stewart to display a gift for comedy under George Stevens' deft direction. Also around were Frances Mercer as Stewart's blueblood fiancée and James Ellison as a college pal.

Vivacious Lady: James Stewart, Ginger Rogers.

P. J. Wolfson and Ernest Pagano wrote the RKO Radio picture from a novelette by I. A. R. Wylie.

JUNE

Three Comrades This adaptation of an Erich Maria Remarque best seller related the post-war experiences in their homeland of three former German soldiers played by Robert Taylor, Franchot Tone and Robert Young, and their friendship with Margaret Sullavan's doomed tubercular fraulein. Director Frank Borzage played up the tender and tragic romance between Taylor and Sullavan and blurred the political issues that led to the proto-Nazi Robert Young being killed in a riot. The foursome were re-united in spirit for an up-beat, sentimental ending. MGM's film was produced by Joseph L. Mankiewicz and written by Edward E. Paramore Jr and F. Scott Fitzgerald. It is now famous for Fitzgerald's complaint to Mankiewicz over the re-writing of his dialogue: "I am utterly miserable at seeing months of work and thought negated . . . Oh, Joe, can't producers ever be wrong?"

Three Blind Mice A pleasantly handled romantic comedy, this concerned three gold-diggers from Kansas who come to California in search of wealthy husbands. The girls were played by Loretta Young, Marjorie Weaver and Pauline Moore, and the men they latched on to were Joel McCrea, David Niven and Stuart Erwin. It was written for 20th Century-Fox by Brown Holmes and Lynn Starling from a play by Stephen Powys (Mrs Guy Bolton) and directed

by William A. Seiter. Later re-makes were *Moon Over Miami* (1941) and *Three Little Girls in Blue* (1946), while it also resembles *How to Marry a Millionaire* (1953).

Holiday In this tender but tonic romantic comedy, Cary Grant was the happy-go-lucky figure with an un-American disinterest in wealth who liberates Katharine Hepburn's unhappy rich girl from her stifling existence. Doris Nolan and Lew Ayres played Hepburn's sister and brother who are unprepared or unable to gamble with Grant's philosophy of life. Edward Everett Horton and Jean Dixon were Grant's eccentric pals. Philip Barry's 1928 play had already become a successful 1930 movie (with Horton in the same role as he played

Holiday: Katharine Hepburn, Cary Grant.

here), but this version for Columbia Pictures eclipsed it with a sensitive adaptation by Donald Ogden Stewart and masterful direction by George Cukor. *Free to Live* was its title for British release.

The Adventures of Robin Hood

JULY

Having Wonderful Time RKO Radio's comedy about a holiday romance at a camp in the Catskills starred Ginger Rogers and Douglas Fairbanks Jr, with Peggy Conklin, Lucille Ball, Lee Bowman, Eve Arden and Richard "Red" Skelton (his screen debut) joining in the frolics. The film was based on a 1937 Broadway hit by Arthur Kober in which the characters were all Jews, but when Kober adapted his work for the screen they became Gentiles in order to widen its appeal. The ethnic flavour was generally held to have been the play's best feature, but audiences clearly found the movie version ideal escapist fare for the time of year. Alfred Santell directed, with uncredited additional work by George Stevens.

Always Goodbye 20th Century-Fox gave Barbara Stanwyck another story of mother love and sacrifice to cash in on her success in *Stella Dallas*. She was the mother whose illegitimate son is adopted by a wealthy businessman (Ian Hunter) whom she succeeds in marrying after he is widowed. Herbert Marshall was her doctor friend and Lynn Bari the other woman who almost married Hunter. The studio didn't have to reach far for the material – it was a remake of *Gallant Lady*, a Twentieth Century production with Ann Harding, released as recently as 1934. Kathryn

Scola and Edith Skouras re-fashioned the Gilbert Emery and Douglas Doty story for its new outing, and Sidney Lanfield directed.

Cowboy from Brooklyn A Dick Powell musical comedy with more of an emphasis on the humour, this cast him as a drifter who can't stand animals but who works on a dude ranch and sings for the guests. A press agent (Pat O'Brien) launches him on a radio and movie career. The leading ladies were Priscilla Lane and Ann Sheridan, and other men were Dick Foran, Johnny Davis and Ronald Reagan. Earl Baldwin wrote it from a play by Robert Sloane and Louis Pelletier Jr. and Lloyd Bacon directed. Songs in the Warner Bros. picture came from Johnny Mercer working with Richard Whiting ("Ride, Tenderfoot, Ride") and Harry Warren (title number).

The Shopworn Angel In this re-make of the 1928 film with Nancy Carroll and Gary Cooper, Margaret Sullavan portrayed the hard-bitten showgirl who is idolized by James Stewart's naïve young soldier and eventually succumbs to his charm and sincerity. Walter Pidgeon was her draft-dodging lover. Waldo Salt scripted from a Dana Burnet story and H. C. Potter directed the sentimental story for MGM.

The Amazing Dr Clitterhouse In a rather bizarre comedy melodrama, Edward G. Robinson appeared as the eminent psychologist who gets carried away by his researches into the criminal temperament when they lead him to take over command of a band of jewel thieves and finally to murder Humphrey Bogart, its deposed leader. Claire Trevor was the gangster's moll, Donald Crisp a police inspector, while Gale Page and Allen Jenkins were also prominent. John Huston and John Wexley adapted the play by Barré Lyndon (a London stage hit, less successful on Broadway) and Anatole Litvak directed for Warner Bros.

Love Finds Andy Hardy With this, the fourth of MGM's pictures about the lives of the small-town Hardy family, the series really took off at the box-office (preceding films had been *A Family Affair* in 1937, and *You're Only Young Once* and *Judge Hardy's Children* in 1938). Here 15-year-old Andy (Mickey Rooney) has female trouble with three young ladies on his hands: Ann Rutherford as his regular girlfriend, Lana Turner as a pal's girl entrusted to his keeping, and Judy Garland as the new girl next door who can sing (she is given three numbers to perform). Andy has the by now customary heart-to-heart discussion with his father (Lewis Stone), here over his amorous difficulties. Other regulars were Cecilia Parker (as Andy's sister), Fay Holden (as Mrs

Hardy) and Betsy Ross Clarke (as Aunt Milly). Aurania Rouverol first invented the characters in a 1928 Broadway hit called *Skidding*, Vivien R. Bretherton later wrote stories about them, and William Ludwig devised the screenplay for this film, which George B. Seitz directed at MGM.

AUGUST

Alexander's Ragtime Band A sensational hit everywhere and the most successful film of the year after *Snow White*, the 20th Century-Fox musical tribute to ragtime devised by Irving Berlin smashed all the attendance records at the Roxy in New York, drawing 29,614 patrons on its opening Friday (5 August) and 192,520 in its first week. The lavishly-made, $2 million production reunited the three stars, director and one of the writers of Fox's previous smash, *In*

Alexander's Ragtime Band: Tyrone Power, Alice Faye.

Love Finds Andy Hardy: Judy Garland, Mickey Rooney.

Old Chicago. It told the story of Tyrone Power's bandleader, Alice Faye's star singer and Don Ameche's pianist across nearly three turbulent decades, and was a musical feast drawing on 26 Berlin numbers, three of them (including "Now It Can Be Told") written especially for the movie. Ethel Merman, Jack Haley, Jean Hersholt, Helen Westley and John Carradine had subsidiary roles. Henry King directed from a screenplay by Kathryn Scola, Lamar Trotti and Richard Sherman.

Love Finds Andy Hardy

The Crowd Roars Robert Taylor took another of his more "manly" roles as a boxer who is soured on life after he accidentally kills an opponent. He becomes a pawn of Edward Arnold's racketeer, but redeems himself through love for the man's daughter (Maureen O'Sullivan). Frank Morgan was Taylor's alcoholic partner, and further casting included Lionel Stander, William Gargan, Jane Wyman and Nat Pendleton. MGM's picture was directed by Richard Thorpe and written by George Bruce, Thomas Lennon and George Oppenheimer. Mickey Rooney starred in the 1947 remake, *Killer McCoy*.

Letter of Introduction Adolphe Menjou was the ageing movie star reluctant to admit that he is old enough to have a grown-up daughter, Andrea Leeds was the aspiring actress unaware that he is her father, and George Murphy was the boyfriend who misunderstood their relationship. Universal's romantic melodrama, written by Sheridan Gibney and Leonard Spigelgass from a story by Bernice Boone, was directed by John M. Stahl. A big hit were ventriloquist Edgar Bergen and Charlie McCarthy as themselves in their first film since

the Parisian visitor to the Casbah who falls in love with Charles Boyer. He is the celebrated jewel thief who has already taken refuge there, and so has no cause to say "Come with me to the Casbah", the line so often misattributed to this picture. It was a close re-make of the French picture *Pépé Le Moko* (1936) with Jean Gabin and Mireille Balin, even retaining the tragic ending. Sigrid Gurie was the discarded Algerian girlfriend who betrays the thief out of jealousy; Joseph Calleia was the detective who waits patiently for his prey to leave the sanctuary; and Gene Lockhart was a slimy informer. John Howard Lawson and James M. Cain wrote this version (Henri Jeason did the Gallic original from the novel by Detective Ashelbé)

The Texans: Raymond Hatton, Walter Brennan, Randolph Scott.

Letter of Introduction: Eve Arden, Adolphe Menjou, Charlie McCarthy, Edgar Bergen, Andrea Leeds.

Goldwyn Follies, and they were joined by the bucktoothed Mortimer Snerd, the hayseed dummy with unruly hair who irks Charlie. Others on view were Rita Johnson, Ann Sheridan, Eve Arden and Ernest Cossart.

The Amazing Dr Clitterhouse

The Texans A rare grade A western (once again from the Paramount stable), this was a re-make of the 1924 *North of 36*, re-using some of the epic footage from that silent film. Randolph Scott was the Southerner in the turbulent post-Civil War period who undertakes the arduous cattle drive from Texas to Kansas that opens up the Chisholm Trail and who is accompanied by the herd's pretty part-owner, Joan Bennett. With trouble from Indians, carpetbaggers, blizzards, brush fires and mutinous cowhands, the film packed in plenty of incident, not overlooking the Ku Klux Klan and the completion of the transcontinental railroad. Walter Brennan took part (as he would in a later account of the same trail drive, *Red River*), and also on hand were Robert Cummings, Raymond Hatton and Robert Barrat. This adaptation of Emerson Hough's novel was the work of Bertram Millhauser, Paul Sloane and William Wister Haines. James Hogan directed.

Algiers Walter Wanger's production introduced Hedy Lamarr to American audiences after she had become notorious for her nude appearance in the much banned and censored Czech film *Ecstasy*. James Wong Howe's photography and Irene's costumes ensured that even dressed she made a powerful impact as

Algiers: Charles Boyer, Hedy Lamarr.

and John Crowmell directed (following in the footsteps of Julien Duvivier). There was a further musical remake with Tony Martin and Yvonne de Carlo, *Casbah* (1948).

SEPTEMBER

Marie Antoinette Norma Shearer returned to the screen for the first time in two years portraying the Austrian princess who becomes the Queen of France and dies at the guillotine during the Revolution. Tyrone Power played the Swedish count who becomes her lover and tries to save her. John Barrymore was the weary Louis XV, Robert Morley (in his very first film) was the unfortunate Louis XVI who cannot consummate his marriage to Marie, Joseph Schildkraut was a cunning duke, Gladys George made a vulgar Madame DuBarry and Joseph Calleia was a keen Revolutionary. This was the movie that Shearer's husband, Irving Thalberg, had been preparing for her

Marie Antoinette: Henry Stephenson, Norma Shearer. Costumes by Adrian.

at the time of his death, the one that Marion Davies had been so anxious to star in. MGM spared no expense (other than colour) in making the sumptuous historical spectacle, although the original director, Sidney Franklin, was replaced for working too slowly and the fast-shooting W. S. Van Dyke, nicknamed "One Shot Woody", then pushed it through in only 10 weeks. Even so, it was the costliest picture of the year, assertedly requiring $2.8 million, and (at 160 minutes) the longest. The expense showed in the lavish settings by Cedric Gibbons and William A. Horning, the glittering costumes designed by Adrian and Giles Steele, and the huge numbers in the ballroom, theatre and riot scenes. Claudine West, Donald

Ogden Stewart and Ernest Vajda wrote the picture from the book by Stefan Zweig. It was the only 1938 release to be initially road-shown, with twice daily separate performances at advanced prices. In New York, MGM whipped up extra

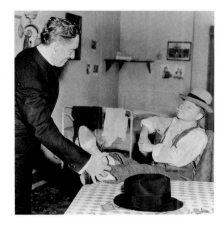

Boys Town: Spencer Tracy, Mickey Rooney.

interest by creating an historical exhibition at the Astor which drew 200,000 visitors before the film opened there. Worldwide, it performed creditably enough at the box-office to justify its cost.

Boys Town Having effectively played a priest in *San Francisco*, Spencer Tracy emerged as a top MGM star with this story about a real Nebraska priest, Father Flanagan, who established a correctional home just west of Omaha to help abandoned children avoid lives of crime ("No boy is bad, if given a chance!"). Mickey Rooney greatly enhanced his popularity as the priest's most difficult case. Other adult roles went to Henry Hull, Leslie Fenton

Four Daughters: Priscilla Lane, John Garfield.

and Edward Norris, while among the numerous boys were Bobs Watson, Jimmy Butler, Frankie Thomas, Mickey Rentschler and Sidney Miller. The film's story was by Eleanore Griffin and Dore Schary, the screenplay by Schary and John Meehan. Norman Taurog, the established director of boys pictures, capped everything with this one.

Four Daughters The sensation of *Four Daughters* was John Garfield, the Broadway star of *Having Wonderful Time*. In his film debut (apart from some extra work), he demonstrated his skill at playing likable heels as the brash, embittered big city misfit who disrupts life in the home of a music professor (Claude Rains). Priscilla Lane appeared as the youngest daughter who falls for him; her three sisters were played by Rosemary Lane and Lola Lane (Priscilla's own sisters) and Gale Page. Jeffrey Lynn was a decent, normal young man who wasn't nearly as interesting to audiences as Garfield's tragic figure. Frank McHugh, May Robson and Dick Foran were also featured. Michael Curtiz handled the direction of the Warner Bros. picture, written by Julius J. Epstein and Lenore Coffee from a story by Fannie Hurst. Frank Sinatra starred in the musical remake, *Young in Heart* (1954).

Three Loves Has Nancy They were Robert Montgomery as a novelist, Franchot Tone as a publisher and Grady Sutton as her elusive fiancé. In MGM's mildly ingratiating comedy, Nancy was played by Janet Gaynor, and she was in no rush to become romantically involved after being jilted at the altar by Sutton. (In reality, Gaynor fell in love with her studio dress designer, Gilbert Adrian, married him in 1939 and retired from acting for many years.) Undoubtedly reinforced by the film's producer, comedy author Norman Krasna, the

Carefree: Fred Astaire. Number: "Since They Turned Loch Lomond into Swing".

writing team officially consisted of Bella and Samuel Spewack, George Oppenheimer and David Hertz (working from a story by Lee Loeb and Mort Braus). Richard Thorpe directed.

My Lucky Star It was Sonja Henie on skates again with an impressive *Alice in Wonderland* ballet. There was a romantic contest between Cesar Romero (as her department store employer who sends her to college to advertise his sportswear) and handsome British newcomer Richard Greene in his second starring role (as the teacher she meets there). Joan Davis and Buddy Ebsen provided some humour along with Arthur Treacher. Harry Tugend and Jack Yellen wrote the 20th Century-Fox picture from a story by Karl Tunberg and Don Ettlinger, and Roy Del Ruth directed.

Carefree After a gap of over a year, Fred Astaire and Ginger Rogers weren't as popular as they used to be. RKO Radio had seen takings plummet when Fred starred without Ginger in *A Damsel in Distress*, and the studio hoped that its prize team would recover lost ground, but *Carefree* didn't do well enough to recover its lavish budget. Fred wanted a more substantial characterization to perform, but it was a bit surprising to see him as a Freudian psychiatrist. In the script by Allan Scott and Ernest Pagano from a story by Dudley Nichols and Hagar Wilde, he falls in love with Ginger Rogers as a patient who can't make up her mind whether or not she wants to marry stuffy lawyer Ralph Bellamy (Hollywood's quintessential "other man"). Mark Sandrich again directed. There was an Irving Berlin score that had only one real hit tune, "Change Partners". Astaire's dancing routines included a memorable number with golf clubs and balls, and the specialty piece "The

Yam" with Ginger. In this, their eighth film together, Fred kissed Ginger for the first time in a long clinch at the end of the slow-motion "I Used to Be Colour Blind" number.
Alexander's Ragtime Band
Algiers

OCTOBER

You Can't Take it With You Who could resist a family that doesn't

You Can't Take It With You: Donald Meek, James Stewart, Jean Arthur, Samuel S. Hinds, Halliwell Hobbes.

believe in paying income tax and puts into practice the notion that everybody should do exactly what they want to do? George S. Kaufman and Moss Hart invented such a household for their huge Broadway success of 1936, which cost Columbia the record sum of $250,000 to acquire the film rights. It was money well spent, for the studio's ace director Frank Capra and regular adaptor Robert Riskin delivered a smash hit when they re-created its infectious good humour on screen. Jean Arthur was the girl who taught her well-off beau James Stewart to relax and have fun before introducing him to her madcap family, headed by Lionel Barrymore. Edward Arnold was Stewart's stuffy banker father who came to dinner and learned to unbend and enjoy life again. Members of the eccentric group also included Ann Miller, Mischa Auer, Spring Byington, Samuel S. Hinds, Donald Meek and Dub Taylor.
Boys Town
That Certain Age Deanna Durbin was allowed to grow up a bit in this, her fourth feature film for Universal. (Audiences didn't want to see her too grown up, though, and an adverse reaction to kissing scenes at previews cued their deletion.) Bruce Manning's script (from a story by F. Hugh Herbert) made Deanna into the 15-

year-old daughter of a newspaper publisher who falls for Melvyn Douglas's man-of-the-world war correspondent, much to the despair of Jackie Cooper as the boy of her own age with a mad crush on her. John Halliday and Irene Rich portrayed Deanna's parents. She had several songs by Harold Adamson and Jimmy McHugh including the hit "My Own". Producer Henry Koster had Edward Ludwig direct Durbin on this occasion.

Too Hot to Handle Clark Gable was quickly re-teamed with Myrna Loy after their strong rapport in *Test Pilot* in this MGM comedy adventure. He and Walter Pidgeon were rival newsreel cameramen, and she was an aviatrix who persuades them to look for her brother missing in the Amazon jungle. It was a bracingly irreverent, episodic affair, often in savagely bad taste (as when Gable calmly fakes shots of bombing atrocities). Walter Connolly, Leo Carrillo and Virginia Weidler also made spicy contributions. Laurence Stallings and John Lee Mahin based their screenplay on a story by Len Hammond, and Jack Conway directed.
Four Daughters
Stablemates When the strong response to this racing story was added to the popularity of the Andy Hardy films and *Boys Town*, it was clear that Mickey Rooney had suddenly become one of MGM's biggest attractions. Here he was teamed with Wallace Beery in a variation on the formula of *The Champ*. Beery played a former veterinarian who has become a drunken racetrack tout but reforms under the influence of Mickey's young jockey who has a promising horse that needs medical attention. (Pint-sized Mickey was well-suited to playing jockeys and had done so before in 1936's *Down the Stretch* and 1937's *Thoroughbreds Don't Cry*.) Leonard Praskins and Richard Maibaum wrote it from a story contributed by actor Reginald Owen and William Thiele. Sam Wood directed, and some of the other cast members were Margaret Hamilton, Marjorie Gateson and Minor Watson.

NOVEMBER

Men With Wings Director and aerial enthusiast William A. Wellman made the first flying movie in Technicolor and his third in the process after *A Star Is Born* and *Nothing Sacred*. It was part of an aviation cycle that included *The Dawn Patrol, Wings of the Navy, Tail Spin* and *The Flying Irishman*. Robert Carson's script concerned two pioneer flyers (Fred MacMurray and Ray Milland) and the woman (Louise Campbell) they both

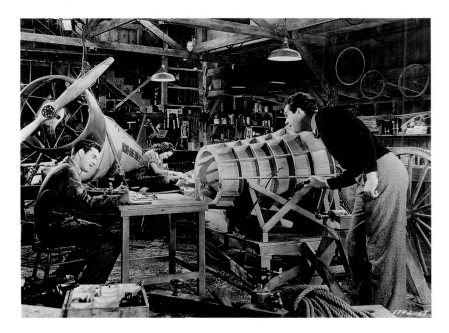

Men With Wings: Ray Milland, Louise Campbell (rear), Fred MacMurray.

love, and how one of them settles down and the other keeps on flying until it kills him. Also cast were Andy Devine, Lynne Overman, Walter Abel, Porter Hall and (as MacMurray's character at age 10) Donald O'Connor. Wellman also produced for Paramount and Wilfrid Cline handled the extensive and demanding aerial photography (W. Howard Greene did the ground shooting), while Paul Mantz and Frank Clarke did the principal flying.

Suez Having successfully dramatized the insurance business with Tyrone Power, 20th Century-Fox put him to work in an entertainment about the building of the Suez Canal that swept aside many inconvenient historical facts. Power was the Frenchman, Ferdinand de Lesseps, who in reality was in his fifties and a model of propriety, but here became a dashing young lover who was dispatched to Egypt by Napoleon (Leon Ames) to break up his relationship with a woman (Loretta Young) that the future Emperor covets for himself. Annabella was the perky French girl he meets out there who becomes his devoted ally as he struggles to realize his dream of building the canal. A desert hurricane provided a spectacular interlude. Joseph Schildkraut, J. Edward Bromberg, Henry Stephenson and (as Benjamin Disraeli) Miles Mander were also seen. Philip Dunne and Julien Josephson wrote the screenplay from

Suez: Tyrone Power, Annabella.

a story by Sam Duncan, and Allan Dwan directed (with Otto Brower in charge of the second unit). The film was initially released in sepia.

The Citadel MGM's second British-made production was based on A. J. Cronin's novel and starred the internationally popular Robert Donat as the dedicated young doctor who works hard on a cure for tuberculosis in a Welsh mining community and temporarily succumbs to the lure of the big money to be made in fashionable London consulting circles. Rosalind Russell was assigned to play his supportive wife and broaden its American appeal (English actress Elizabeth Allan had been originally cast and successfully sued MGM for breach of contract), but the rest of the players consisted of British talent: Ralph Richardson, Emlyn Williams, Rex Harrison, Penelope Dudley-Ward, Francis L. Sullivan, Mary Clare, Cecil Parker and others. The writers were the British Ian Dalrymple and Americans Frank Wead and Elizabeth Hill (with British actor/playwright Emlyn Williams contributing additional dialogue). There was a British producer, Victor Saville, and an American director, King Vidor. The cinematographer, Harry Stradling, was also American. The film opened in America two months before it was seen in London. It had a phenomenal success in Britain, but it was gratifyingly popular in America, too.

If I Were King Ronald Colman clearly relished the opportunity to play the impudent poet and vagabond François Villon in Preston Sturges' spirited adaptation of Justin Huntly McCarthy's historical play of 1901. Basil Rathbone was almost unrecognizable as the sly and cackling

If I Were King: Ronald Colman, Ellen Drew, Basil Rathbone, Alena Lloyd.

monarch, Louis XI, who grants Villon the power to rule France and is given a lesson in winning over the people. Frances Dee was the regal lady of Villon's affections and Ellen Drew the adoring commoner who sadly never has a chance. The direction went to the experienced hands of Frank Lloyd. The play had previously been seen on film in 1920 with William Farnum (who had a small role as a general in this version) and in 1926 (as *The Beloved Rogue*) with John Barrymore. (There was also a musical adaptation, *The Vagabond King*, filmed by Paramount in 1930 with Dennis King and re-filmed with Oreste in 1956.)

Brother Rat Titled after the term of friendly address used by cadets to each other at the Virginia Military Institute, this Warner Bros. comedy (a First National production) was taken from the Broadway smash hit by two of the Institute's graduates, Fred F. Finkelhoffe and John Monks Jr. It introduced to the screen the stand-out of the play's cast, Eddie Albert, as a secretly married cadet. He was joined by two of the studio's promising new players, Wayne Morris and Ronald Reagan, as other cadets, while

Priscilla Lane, Jane Wyman and Jane Bryan played the girls in their lives. William Keighley was the director, and the script came from Richard Macaulay and Jerry Wald. The play's authors wrote a film sequel, *Brother Rat and a Baby* (1940), and the original was re-made musically as *About Face* (1952).

Angels With Dirty Faces Back at Warner Bros., James Cagney really got into his stride playing the tough

criminal who feigns cowardice on the way to the electric chair to disillusion the kids who hero-worship him. Pat O'Brien was the parish priest who puts him up to the grand gesture, and the

Angels With Dirty Faces: James Cagney, Pat O'Brien and the Dead End kids – left to right: Bobby Jordan, Billy Halop, Huntz Hall (behind Cagney), Gabriel Dell (behind O'Brien), Bernard Punsley (foreground), Leo Gorcey.

youngsters were played by the Dead End Kids. Humphrey Bogart and George Bancroft were shifty villains, and Ann Sheridan was the girl. Rowland Brown's story was turned into a screenplay by John Wexley and Warren Duff, and Michael Curtiz handled the direction. It was Warners' biggest hit of the year after *Robin Hood.*

You Can't Take It With You

The Cowboy and the Lady Gary Cooper was well cast as the rodeo rider who married the aristocratic daughter (Merle Oberon) of a politician with White House aspirations (Henry Kolker). In his honest, direct fashion he tears a strip off the smart set who find him amusing. The film was mild stuff, despite the efforts of a great many writers (of whom only S. N. Behrman and Sonya Levien received screen credit). (It was very similar to Cooper's 1931 *I Take This Woman* with Carole Lombard.) Legend has it that the well-known writer-director Leo McCarey sold Samuel Goldwyn the title and idea for the film, which he improvised on the spur of the moment, and then refused to have anything more to do with such a worthless project (he shared credit for the story with Frank R. Adams). It fell to H. C. Potter to occupy the director's chair (with some additional work by Stuart Heisler). The United Artists release also featured Walter Brennan and Fuzzy Knight as fellow cowboys, and Harry Davenport as the lady's understanding uncle.

Stablemates

DECEMBER

Angels With Dirty Faces

Out West with the Hardys Lewis Stone's Judge Hardy took the family to Arizona to help an old friend in a legal dispute over the water rights on her ranch. Cecelia Parker's Marian Hardy falls in love with Gordon Jones's cowpoke, and Mickey Rooney's boastful Andy is thoroughly out-smarted by Virginia Weidler's 11-year-old cowgirl who can out-shoot, out-ride and out-rope him. It was the fifth in the series, the third this year, and Rooney's ninth film of 1938. George B. Seitz directed MGM's production, which was written by Kay Van Riper, Agnes Christine Johnston and William Ludwig.

The Cowboy and the Lady

The Dawn Patrol This Warner Bros. picture was a close re-make of the 1930 production, re-using much of its flying footage and retaining the original script, only slightly revised by one of its writers, Seton I. Miller, in collaboration with the new director, Edmund Goulding. Errol Flynn inherited the Richard Barthelmess

role as the British flyer who is put in command and tortured by the responsibility of sending young pilots to almost certain death in World War I. David Niven played the fellow pilot whose friendship he loses. Basil Rathbone was the first flight commander who is thankful to hand over to Flynn. Others in an all-male cast were Donald Crisp, Melville Cooper, Barry Fitzgerald, Morton Lowry and Carl Esmond. It seemed a very down-beat film for the period (if somewhat topical with a new European war threatening) but Flynn's box-office appeal and its celebration of heroism saw it through.

Sweethearts For its first complete feature in three-strip Technicolor, MGM presented Jeanette MacDonald and Nelson Eddy as feuding performers who are starring in the Victor Herbert operetta *Sweethearts*

on Broadway. This provided a means for retaining the melodies like the title number and "Pretty as a Picture" from the original 1913 show, while dumping its out-moded story (the original lyrics went too, replaced with new ones by Bob Wright and Chet Forrest). The husband and wife writing team of Dorothy Parker and Alan Campbell supplied a breezy tale of producer Frank Morgan conspiring to keep his two stars from going to Hollywood by sowing marital discord. W. S. Van Dyke II directed, Oliver Marsh and Allen Davey handled the colour cinematography, and supporting players included Florence Rice, Ray Bolger, Mischa Auer, Reginald Gardiner and young Terry Kilburn. It was MGM's second biggest grosser of the 1938–9 season, behind only *Boys Town.*

The Citadel

1939

Stagecoach
Claire Trevor,
John Wayne

The last year of the decade is generally regarded in retrospect as Hollywood's *annus mirabilis*, a year in which an enormous number of memorable pictures appeared, most of them popular enough at the time to figure in the Hits of the Year, but one or two, like *Of Mice and Men*, not finding such great favour.

It was the year in which both *The Wizard of Oz* and *Gone with the Wind* appeared. Both were launched with promotion budgets of $250,000 and went down well, but *The Wizard of Oz* still showed a loss on first release. *Gone with the Wind* opened in the last half of December, providing a fitting climax to the decade. *The Wizard of Oz* is widely regarded, thanks to its enormous television audiences, as the most seen film of all time, and *Gone with the Wind* remains, in relative terms, the biggest grossing picture of all time. One was made by MGM, the other by David O. Selznick and released by MGM. The studio had the biggest number of money-makers overall, with 1938 releases like *Boys Town, Sweethearts, Too Hot to Handle* and *Marie Antoinette* still bringing in huge sums and the new Andy Hardy pictures, a new Thin Man adventure, *The Adventures of Huckleberry Finn*, the British-made *Goodbye Mr Chips!* and *Pygmalion, The Women, Idiot's Delight, Babes in Arms* and *Ninotchka* all scoring well among its 1939 output. MGM ended the decade as it had began, and it remained the champion among studios, with its parent company Loew's making more than twice the profits of its nearest competitor, 20th Century-Fox. All the studios were making money in this year's results except for Columbia, which broke even, and RKO, which made a small loss for the first time since the financial year ending in 1934. One of the small independents, Grand National, went into receivership.

The abundance of artistically great pictures did not, however, result in increased attendances. In fact, attendances were thought to be slipping during the year itself. However, as they remained at the same estimated weekly average of 88 million as in 1938, a late recovery may well have taken place. (The figures mean that the 11 million theatre seats in the United States were each being occupied on average 8 times weekly.) Certainly the year ended well because, apart from *Gone with the Wind* becoming the hottest attraction ever known, there was the debut of *The Hunchback of Notre Dame* at the Radio City Music Hall with that theatre's biggest day ever and the opening of *Swanee River* at the Roxy in New York with a record-breaking weekend attendance of 89,207.

Political subjects remained largely absent from the screen despite the worsening situation in Europe. MGM did put out *Idiot's Delight*, but it was Warner Bros. which courageously attacked the Nazi influence in America in *Confessions of a Nazi Spy*, despite political pressure and threats from Germany (although the spy trials that provided the evidence on which the film was based had taken place in 1937).

Hollywood had to face up to the loss of foreign markets as a result of the outbreak of war in Europe. This resulted in belt-tightening at all the major studios. MGM dropped its plans to film an epic *Quo Vadis* and made no haste to renew its lapsed contract with Greta Garbo, whose appeal was mainly outside America. There were fears that the $50 million that Hollywood earned in Britain each year might be blocked now that the country was engaged in war with Germany. One solution to the general

This publicity photograph shows the guarded set during production of *Confessions of a Nazi Spy* at Warner Bros. One wonders if the sound stage being used was really made so obvious.

problem was to cultivate the Latin American market more assiduously.

The big companies also faced anti-trust suits because of their domination over first-run theatres, and they had to agree in February not to acquire any more outlets without the permission of the Federal Anti-Trust Division.

British films continued to exert an appeal, especially when released by major American companies. Paramount had *Jamaica Inn* and *The Beachcomber* (known in its country of origin as *Vessel of Wrath*) from Charles Laughton and Erich Pommer's Mayflower Productions. MGM had the above-mentioned *Pygmalion* and its own production of *Goodbye Mr Chips!*. Besides *Jamaica Inn*, director Alfred Hitchcock had audiences enthralled by *The Lady Vanishes*. Even a film with as pure a British cast and subject as *The Four Feathers* did big business in towns as far apart as Kansas City, Boston, Cleveland, Pittsburgh and Washington, proving that there was no blanket prejudice against English pictures on the part of theatre owners or moviegoers.

The Four Feathers had the advantage of being shot in Technicolor, and this the year when colour suddenly became a box-office asset, as demonstrated by the appeal of the westerns *Jesse James* and *Dodge City* while *The Wizard of Oz* and *Gone with the Wind* would hardly have been the same pictures without their use of all the hues of the rainbow. Monochrome was still very much in evidence of course, and Bette Davis raised her standing to appear for the first time in the exhibitors' top 10 box-office draws thanks primarily to *Dark Victory* and *The Old Maid*, which in their turn would surely not have been the same had they appeared in Technicolor. Errol Flynn, too, was a newcomer to the top 10, although the Technicolor picture he made with Bette Davis, *The Private Lives of Elizabeth and Essex*, was not among the year's hits.

HITS OF THE YEAR

JANUARY

Jesse James A boom in sagebrush sagas was underway with *Jesse James* the first to arrive and one of three smash hits. 20th Century-Fox's romantic depiction of the notorious outlaw's life had sympathetic portrayals from Tyrone Power as Jesse and Henry Fonda as his brother Frank, and a storyline that justified their actions as revenge on a railroad for the brutal activities of its representative played by Brian Donlevy. Jesse's death, shot in the back, was retained, but Henry Hull's newspaper editor gave the film an upbeat ending with his eulogy. This was, surprisingly, the first western made in the new full Technicolor (cinematographer: W. Howard Greene), although it had been used on several outdoor subjects that were near-westerns. On location in Missouri, stuntman Cliff Lyons was paid a record sum to take two horses on a 75ft downward plunge into a lake, a fall that killed both animals and resulted in a court case against Fox brought by the Missouri Humane Association. Nancy Kelly, Randolph Scott, Slim Summerville, J. Edward Bromberg, John Carradine (as Jesse's assassin, Bob Ford), Jane Darwell and Donald Meek made up the principal players. Nunnally Johnson wrote the screenplay and produced. Henry King directed. There would be a sequel (*The Return of Frank James*, 1940) and a re-make (*The True Story of Jesse James*, 1957).

Jesse James: Tyrone Power.

Kentucky Another Technicolor success for 20th Century-Fox, this was a story of feuding and horse racing with a Kentucky Derby climax. Loretta Young and Richard Greene were the lovers from opposing families, and Walter Brennan was the fiery old-timer who won't let bygones be bygones. John Tainter Foote and Lamar Trotti wrote it, and David Butler directed, with other players including Karen Morley and Douglass Dumbrille.

Sweethearts
The Dawn Patrol
Stand Up and Fight MGM contributed this action-packed road-versus-rail drama to the western cycle. It starred Wallace Beery as the stagecoach operator who feuds with Robert Taylor's two-fisted railroad pioneer. Charles Bickford was a villainous slave-runner, aided by Barton MacLane, and Florence Rice was the heroine. The screenplay by James M. Cain, Jane Murfin and Harvey Ferguson (from a story by Forbes Parkhill) was directed by W. S. Van Dyke II.

Trade Winds Director Tay Garnett wrote the story to use a filmed record of his recent, extended travels in the Far East. In the screenplay developed by Dorothy Parker, Alan Campbell and Frank R. Adams, Fredric March's detective pursued Joan Bennett's murder suspect halfway around the world, with the travel footage used in back projection. The Walter Wanger production, released by United Artists, had comic relief supplied by Ralph Bellamy and by Ann Sothern, whose performance inspired MGM to give her the title role in *Maisie*.

Idiot's Delight MGM had been sitting on the rights to Robert E. Sherwood's 1936 hit play, which had starred Lunt and Fontanne. Following the European crisis of late September 1938 (when Chamberlain flew to Munich), the studio rushed the story into production with an adaptation by the author. It starred Clark Gable as the song-and-dance man travelling with a troupe of girls in Europe as World War II threatens to break out. He meets Norma Shearer as a blonde-wigged Russian countess who seems to be a girl he knew back in Omaha. Major issues were debated through the contrived presence of Edward Arnold's munitions king, Charles Coburn's research scientist and Burgess Meredith's pacifist. Joseph Schildkraut also appeared as a local army officer. Clarence Brown directed. The film was prophetic in concluding with the outbreak of war.

FEBRUARY

Gunga Din It was not just the frontier days of the Old West that attracted audiences, as the huge success of this stirring adventure of British soldiers fighting another kind of Indian on the North-west Frontier demonstrated. It was in the tradition of *The Lives of a Bengal Lancer* and *The Charge of the Light Brigade* and rousingly directed by George Stevens from a screenplay by Joel Sayre and Fred Guiol and a story by Ben Hecht and Charles MacArthur, not forgetting the poem by Rudyard Kipling. Cary Grant, Victor McLaglen and Douglas Fairbanks Jr were the lusty trio of sergeants, Joan Fontaine was the girl who wanted to break up the team by marrying Fairbanks, and Eduardo Ciannelli was the fanatical leader of the insurgent Thuggees. Sam Jaffe had, in the title role of the gallant native water-bearer, another memorable part to compare with his High Lama of *Lost Horizon*, even if the character's enthusiasm to serve his white masters now grates a little. Alfred Newman contributed a stirring score, and Joseph H. August handled

Idiot's Delight: Clark Gable's song-and-dance man sings "Puttin' on the Ritz".

the excellent camerawork. Costing $1,915,000 and taking 104 days to shoot with as many as 900 extras (the outdoor locations were done at Lone Pine, north of Los Angeles at the foot of Mount Whitney), *Gunga Din* was RKO Radio's most expensive picture ever, but it was money well spent and soon recovered. The story was transferred to the American West in a comedy remake, *Sergeants Three* (1961).
Idiot's Delight
Jesse James
Honolulu MGM's South Seas musical romance had Robert Young as a film

star trading places with a Hawaiian pineapple grower who looks exactly like him, and Eleanor Powell as a dancer with whom he falls in love. Powell performed an elaborate hula number, and Gracie Allen, as her zany partner, did an impersonation of Mae West in a musical sequence with the King's Men as the three Marx Brothers. George Burns was the film star's agent, while Rita Johnson and Sig Rumann were also cast. Edward Buzzell directed from a script by Herbert Fields and Frank Partos, while the songs were by Gus Kahn and Harry Warren.

Gunga Din: Cary Grant, Victor McLaglen, Douglas Fairbanks Jr.

THE ACADEMY AWARDS

To atone for its gaffe of the previous year, the Academy had Shirley Temple present Walt Disney with a very special Oscar, flanked by seven miniature Oscars on steps, for *Snow White and the Seven Dwarfs*. The Disney organization also won as usual the Oscar for the Best Short Cartoon, *Ferdinand the Bull*. Among other Special Awards at the banquet on 23 February were those made to Deanna Durbin and Mickey Rooney for their outstanding record as juvenile players.

You Can't Take It With You was honoured as Best Picture of 1938, and Frank Capra took his third Academy Award for Best Director. There were other repeat winners, too: Spencer Tracy as Best Actor the second year running for *Boys Town*, Bette Davis as Best Actress for *Jezebel* and Walter Brennan as Best Supporting Actor for *Kentucky*. Fay Bainter had two chances of success, as a nominee for Best Actress in *White Banners* and for Best Supporting Actress in *Jezebel*, and the latter did the trick for her.

The British production of *Pygmalion* won two writing awards for Adaptation and Screenplay, the latter given to George Bernard Shaw. *Boys Town* brought an Academy Award to Eleanor Griffin and Dore Schary for Original Story. Joseph Ruttenberg picked up the Oscar for Cinematography for *The Great Waltz*, while colour cinematography was recognized in a Special Award to Oliver Marsh and Allen Davey for *Sweethearts*. *The Adventures of Robin Hood* made winners out of Erich Wolfgang Korngold for Best Original Score, Carl Jules Weyl for Interior Decoration and Ralph Dawson for Best Film Editing. In the musical field, the song "Thanks for the Memory", sung by Bob Hope and Shirley Ross in *The Big Broadcast of 1938*, won for Leo Robin and Ralph Rainger, and Alfred Newman received the first award in the new category of Best Score, referring to musical direction, for *Alexander's Ragtime Band*. Newman had also been nominated in the Best Original Score category for *The Cowboy and the Lady* but lost to Korngold.

Sir Cedric Hardwicke watches Spencer Tracy and Bette Davis admiring their latest Oscars.

MARCH

Love Affair Irene Dunne and Charles Boyer were two cynical people who had a shipboard romance followed by a trial separation. The complications to their reunion had elements of both tragedy and suspense when the woman is crippled in an accident, a particularly severe punishment for an immoral past. Director Leo McCarey devised the story with Mildred Cram and shot the picture in sequence without a finished script (Delmer Daves and Donald Ogden Stewart were the credited screenwriters). Thanks to the experienced hand of McCarey and the sincerity of the two stars, the picture moved assuredly from light romance to poignant drama. Maria Ouspenskaya took the important part of Boyer's mother with Astrid Allwyn, Lee Bowman and Maurice Moscovitch providing further support in the RKO Radio picture. McCarey remade it at 20th Century-Fox as *An Affair to Remember* (1957) with Cary Grant and Deborah Kerr.

You Can't Cheat an Honest Man This was W. C. Fields as hard-up circus owner Larson E. Whipsnade sharing the comedy limelight with Edgar Bergen and his partners Charlie McCarthy and Mortimer Snerd. Fields wrote what passed for a story under his Charles Bogle alias and George Marion Jr, Richard Mack and Everett Freeman turned in the screenplay. Fields drew most laughter in disrupting life at the mansion of the wealthy Bel-Goodie family with tasteless stories and dynamic ping pong. As stuffy socialites were Mary Forbes, Thurston Hall and John Arledge, while Constance Moore appeared as Fields's lovely daughter. George Marshall was the Universal picture's ringmaster.

Stagecoach John Ford's western was enthusiastically reviewed but didn't catch on with the public as much as several others in the boom, probably because it lacked star names and was somewhat misleadingly advertised to play down its genre setting ("Two women on a desperate journey with seven strange men", "Nine oddly assorted strangers . . ."). In fact, John Wayne was then associated with five-day B westerns and his name was more of a hindrance, while the director (billed as "John *The Hurricane* Ford") and producer (Walter Wanger) were given more prominence than the cast. Ford had almost got Samuel Goldwyn to back this long-cherished project, but he had refused the producer's suggestion of Gary Cooper and Marlene Dietrich as the leads and insisted on Wayne and Claire Trevor instead, rightly confident of making new stars. He shot the film so economically (at a cost

Love Affair: Charles Boyer, Irene Dunne, Maria Ouspenskaya.

lead horse of the coach team and doubling for John Wayne as he goes forward to retrieve the fallen reins. This was the first of Ford's films to use the majestic Monument Valley setting in southern Utah. It was distributed by United Artists. There was a re-make in 1966.

Midnight Paramount continued to supply the sophisticated European society comedy. Claudette Colbert was the American, stranded penniless in Paris, who is engaged by John Barrymore's wealthy aristocrat to masquerade as a Hungarian princess and distract lecherous playboy Francis Lederer from his pursuit of Mary Astor as Barrymore's wife. Complication: Don Ameche's Hungarian taxi-driver falls for Colbert and butts in, pretending to be her

of only $222,000, most of the scenes with the principals being done inside the studio), that it was still highly profitable. The screenplay by Dudley Nichols (from a story by Ernest Haycox) created nine distinctive characters bound together on the stagecoach journey, and they were memorably played by Claire Trevor (the "bad" woman), John Wayne (outlaw), John Carradine (gambler), Thomas Mitchell (drunken doctor), Andy Devine (driver), Donald Meek (whisky drummer), Louise Platt (pregnant "good" woman), George Bancroft (sheriff) and Berton Churchill (crooked banker). The spectacular stuntwork in the chase scene across the salt flats was done by Yakima Canutt, playing the Indian who leaps from his mount onto the

Midnight: Francis Lederer, Mary Astor, Rex O'Malley, Claudette Colbert, John Barrymore.

husband. It was ingeniously scripted by Charles Bracket and Billy Wilder (from a story by Edwin Justus Mayer and Franz Schulz), and smoothly directed by Mitchell Leisen.

APRIL

Dodge City Warner Bros. sent its top leading man Errol Flynn out west as an Irish adventurer who tames a wide-open cattle town. The boisterous production was the second smash hit of the western cycle, offering

Stagecoach: Donald Meek, John Wayne, Andy Devine, Claire Trevor, George Bancroft, Louise Platt, Francis Ford (foreground), Tim Holt (rear), Thomas Mitchell (foreground), Berton Churchill (behind), John Carradine (rear).

Technicolor and loads of action, including a cattle stampede, a massive bar-room brawl and a climactic shoot-out on board a moving train. The leading ladies were Olivia de Havilland as the good girl and Ann Sheridan as the good "bad" girl who works in a saloon. Alan Hale and Guinn (Big Boy) Williams were Flynn's saddlemates, Frank McHugh ran the local newspaper and Bruce Cabot and Victor Jory dispensed the villainy. Michael Curtiz directed with characteristic dash from a stolid Robert Buckner screenplay. Sol Polito and Ray Rennahan handled the Technicolor camerawork, and Max Steiner provided the sonorous score. The film was given a huge send-off at the modern Dodge City with a world premiere in all three of the town's theatres on 1 April, and Flynn, Sheridan, Alan Hale, Priscilla Lane and Buck Jones made personal appearances.

The Story of Vernon and Irene Castle In the final picture that Fred Astaire owed RKO Radio on his contract, the studio attempted to recover the popularity of his partnership with Ginger Rogers by putting them into a more dramatic framework, portraying two ballroom legends of the pre-war era and reconstructing the dances they performed. It was an opportunity to flood the screen with the music of a bygone time and hopefully emulate the success of *Alexander's Ragtime Band*. One of *Alexander*'s writers, Robert Sherman, was engaged to write the script from an adaptation by Oscar Hammerstein II and Dorothy Yost of the published memoirs of Irene Castle (who retained various approvals over the finished picture). H. C. Potter directed, Hermes Pan created the dance ensembles, and Edna May Oliver (as the team's agent), vaudeville star Lew Fields (as himself), Walter Brennan, Etienne Girardot and Janet Beecher were also in the cast. Vernon Castle's death in a flying accident during World War I provided an unavoidably tragic conclusion, although it was softened by a ghostly Fred dancing with Ginger one more time. The film was a costly production with its large number of dance sequences (including the "Whirlwind Tour" number across a map of the United States) and its parade of songs, but its appeal wasn't quite strong enough to put it in profit on first release and it was the last Fred and Ginger film at RKO.

Three Smart Girls Grow Up In this sequel to Universal's 1937 hit, Deanna Durbin took an interest in her older sisters' love lives and found them suitable husbands in Robert Cummings and William Lundigan. Father was again Charles Winninger and Nan Grey re-appeared as one of

Dodge City: Bruce Cabot, Errol Flynn, Alan Hale.

Dark Victory: Bette Davis, George Brent.

the sisters, while Helen Parrish took over as the other. The film had Deanna's biggest song hit, "Because" (by Edward Teschemacher and Guy D'Hardelot), as well as "The Last Rose of Summer". She was back with her old director Henry Koster and writers Felix Jackson and Bruce Manning. There would be another sequel: *Hers to Hold* (1943).

Dark Victory The original play by George Brewer and Bertram Bloch had been a flop on Broadway in 1934. David O. Selznick had tried to work out a way of filming it and failed – who'd want to see a woman going blind with a fatal brain tumour? Garbo had turned it down years before and Selznick had decided terminal illness was better treated for laughs (*Nothing Sacred*). The rights were sold to Warner Bros. where Casey Robinson did an adaptation, Edmund Goulding directed it and Bette Davis had audiences weeping buckets as she changed from being a spoiled little rich girl into a woman of rare courage. George Brent played the physician who marries her, Humphrey Bogart was an Irish groom

and Geraldine Fitzgerald made her American debut as the secretary-companion, a character cleverly invented for the film. Ronald Reagan and Henry Travers also appeared. It was the start of a wonderful year for Bette.

Midnight

The Story of Alexander Graham Bell Or how Don Ameche came to invent the telephone. (His last name became the jocular slang word for telephone, as in "Give me a call on the ameche".) He was seen as the teacher of the deaf whose struggles to perfect a device to transmit the human voice telegraphically are finally successful. He receives encouragement from Loretta Young as his deaf girlfriend. Henry Fonda was a little oddly cast, providing moments of levity as Bell's loyal but unimaginative assistant. Other parts went to Charles Coburn, Gene Lockhart, Spring Byington and Loretta Young's real-life sisters, Sally Blane, Polly Ann Young and Georgiana Young, playing her sisters on screen. It was the first screen biography of an inventor, and his

The Story of Alexander Graham Bell: Henry Fonda, Don Ameche.

Union Pacific: Robert Preston, Barbara Stanwyck, Joel McCrea.

Canadian origins were glossed over. Following sharp protests, scenes were added for its release north of the border showing Bell's homestead and the memorial erected in his honour. Lamar Trotti wrote the 20th Century-Fox picture from a story by Ray Harris, and Irving Cummings directed. British audiences saw it retitled *The Modern Miracle*.
Love Affair

MAY

Union Pacific Cecil B. DeMille's epic about the construction of the first transcontinental railroad was the third western smash hit of the year. Joel McCrea led as the overseer for the Union Pacific who fights Indians and saboteurs *en route* to the linking point with the Central Pacific. Barbara Stanwyck was the tomboy postmistress, Robert Preston (in his first big role) the likable gambler who joins the bad guys but atones for his mistake in the end, Brian Donlevy was the principal heavy, and Akim Tamiroff and Lynne Overman provided some comic relief. Arthur Rosson's second unit filmed most of the action sequences, including an exciting Indian raid on a train, and provided much footage for back projection behind the stars in the studio. DeMille shot the closing ceremony, of the driving of the golden spike where the two railroads meet, at Canoga Park, near Hollywood. The writers were Walter De Leon, C. Gardner Sullivan and Jesse Lasky Jr, working from a novel by Ernest Haycox. Not to be outdone by the *Dodge City* send-off, the film had been

launched in epic style with a world premiere on 28 April at three theatres in Omaha, Nebraska, linked to the 70th anniversary celebrations of the Union Pacific, and 200,000 visitors packed the city. Stanwyck, Donlevy, Robert Preston, Lynne Overman, George Raft and Lloyd Nolan were among the stars on hand, along with DeMille himself. The celebrities had come out on a special Union Pacific train, which had left Los Angeles five days before, making publicity stops along the way.
Dark Victory
Rose of Washington Square 20th Century-Fox's third teaming of Tyrone Power and Alice Faye was a show-biz story from the New York of the 1920s with plenty of scope for famous melodies of the period. She played the singer who becomes a Ziegfeld star; he played the scoundrel she can't live without. Al Jolson completed the star line-up as an entertainer who loves her, while William Frawley and Joyce Compton had key supporting roles. Faye ended up singing "My Man" (by Channing Pollock and Maurice Yvain) so movingly that Power willingly goes to jail to make amends. Obvious similarities to the lives of Fanny Brice and Nicky Arnstein enabled both of them to sue Fox for invasion of privacy and collect modest settlements. Nunnally Johnson wrote and produced (from a story by John Larkin and Jerry Horwin), while Gregory Ratoff directed.
The Hardys Ride High Thinking they've inherited a fortune, the Hardy family moves into a large mansion. The usual cast (Lewis Stone, Mickey Rooney, Ann Rutherford *et al*) was supplemented by Virginia Grey, John King, Halliwell Hobbes,

Minor Watson and others. The director was, as usual, George B. Seitz, while the same writers (Kay Van Riper, William Ludwig, Agnes Christine Johnson) had penned the previous entry in MGM's series. There would be two more released during 1939.
Confessions of a Nazi Spy The Warner brothers' first feature film had been *My Four Years in Germany* (1918), a documentary-like account of German bestiality and how America became involved in World War I. This time the Warners bravely decided to be ahead of events in making the first Hollywood film to come out against the Germany of Adolf Hitler. Edward G. Robinson's patient government investigator unearths Nazi spying and recruiting activities among the German-American population of the United States. It was filmed in semi-documentary technique on closed sets, using a voice-over commentary, maps and newsreel extracts, and it pulled no punches in showing the Nazis as the enemy of America and democracy. Characterization was crude but effective, with Francis Lederer as the egocentric dupe of the Nazi menaces played by George Sanders and Paul Lukas. James Stephenson appeared as the Scotland Yard man who begins the investigation in Scotland. Warner Bros. kept the names of actors playing Hitler, Goebbels and Goering secret to shield them from reprisals and made special security arrangements to

Confessions of a Nazi Spy: George Sanders.

safeguard the premiere from sabotage. Cast member Wilhelm Von Brincken changed his name to William Vaughn for billing on this picture. The script was by Milton Krims and John Wexley from a book by Leon G. Turrou, and the direction was by Anatole Litvak. The First National (Warner Bros.) picture did big business in cities as far apart as Boston, Detroit, Buffalo and San

Francisco. Its foreign returns were clipped by bans from countries professing a political neutrality (Holland, all of Scandinavia, Switzerland) and by South American countries friendly with Hitler like Argentina and Brazil.

Only Angels Have Wings Howard Hawks' compelling study of an enclosed community of flyers transporting the mail over the Andes expressed his pre-occupation with characters' behaviour under stress, their concern to live with self-respect and die with dignity. It had something of *The Dawn Patrol* but was more abstract in setting and introduced women into the group. Cary Grant was the flight manager who has to send men up in atrocious conditions, and Jean Arthur was the showgirl who learns to fit in. Richard Barthelmess (in his first film in three years) was the flyer trying to live down a past mistake, Thomas Mitchell the old pilot called Kid whose eyesight is failing, and Rita Hayworth (showing her potential for the first time) the old flame of Grant's who soured him on women and unexpectedly reappears in his life, while Noah Beery Jr, Allyn Joslyn, John Carroll and James Millican were other airmen and Sig Rumann the Dutchman who owns the ramshackle airline. It was Hawks' own story (screenplay by Jules Furthman), and he directed and produced for Columbia. Though a late addition to the aviation cycle, it gave the studio one of its two big hits of the year.

JUNE

Juarez The third of the Warner Bros. historical biopics starring Paul Muni and directed by William Dieterle, this served as a timely reminder of a past fight for a democratic way of life against a foreign dictator. Barely recognizable under extensive make-up to give him a strong bone structure and a dark, Indian complexion, Muni portrayed the honest and principled Benito Juarez, the Mexican president who opposes the harsh rule of France's Napoleon III (Claude Rains). Brian Aherne was Napoleon's puppet, Maximilian, the hapless new Emperor of Mexico, hoping to rule peacefully but caught between the two sides, and Bette Davis appeared as his wife, driven to madness by grief at his eventual fate. The biggest difficulty for writers Wolfgang Reinhardt, Aeneas MacKenzie and John Huston was in uniting its story of Juarez with the rest of the film, as Juarez and Maximilian never actually met. The script was based in part on a book by Bertita Harding and a play by Franz Werfel. The big star line-up also included John Garfield, miscast as the

Juarez: Paul Muni. Juarez looks down on the body of the adversary he never met, Emperor Maximilian.

fiery revolutionary general who serves Juarez, while support came from Donald Crisp, Joseph Calleia, Gale Sondergaard, Gilbert Roland and a reputed 1,180 other players. Erich Wolfgang Korngold composed the score. *Juarez* was released in the slack summer period as part of Warners' established policy of providing exhibitors with substantial attractions at this time, and the wordy, worthy and long (130 minutes) movie proved both a popular and prestige success, if hard put to recover all its considerable production costs.

Only Angels Have Wings

JULY

Goodbye Mr Chips! In the third of MGM's British productions, Robert Donat starred as the gentle schoolmaster whose career at a public school is shown over a period of nearly sixty years. Greer Garson (her screen debut) co-starred as the wife who rejuvenates Chips before dying in childbirth, and Paul von Hernreid (soon Paul Henreid) was the German whose friendship is interrupted by the Great War. Terry Kilburn and John Mills were prominent among the pupils. The unashamedly sentimental picture was a faithful adaptation of James Hilton's celebrated story (published in 1934), written by R. C. Sherriff, Claudine West and Eric Maschwitz, and directed by Sam Wood, with a *tour de force* performance by Donat, seen in four different make-ups at the ages of 24, 40, 60 and 83. Victor Saville produced

Goodbye Mr Chips! Robert Donat.

the picture, which was opened cautiously by MGM in the United States but soon proved to be a smash hit in cities everywhere, often doubling the normal takings in big theatres. A musical re-make with Peter O'Toole was released in 1969.

Man About Town Jack Benny had the lead in Paramount's musical comedy as the Broadway producer putting on a show in London and making his singing star Dorothy Lamour jealous by the attention he gives to British wives Binnie Barnes and Isabel Jeans. Edward Arnold and Monty Woolley were the aggrieved husbands, and Eddie "Rochester" Anderson did his familiar stint as Benny's manservant. Dorothy Lamour succeeded Betty Grable when appendicitis forced her out of the co-starring role. Betty still contributed one lively song number, "Fidgity Joe", while Dorothy delivered the other songs, on her own

Man About Town: Edward Arnold, Jack Benny.

(notably "Strange Enchantment") and with Phil Harris. Direction was by Mark Sandrich and the screenplay by Morrie Ryskind from a story that he, Allan Scott and Zion Myers wrote.
Daughters Courageous Warner Bros. took the cast of *Four Daughters* – John Garfield, Claude Rains, Jeffrey Lynn, Frank McHugh, Dick Foran and, as four daughters, Priscilla Lane, Rosemary Lane, Lola Lane and Gale Page – and put them in another small-town story under the same director, Michael Curtiz, but this time with a lighter mood. They played different characters – if only because Garfield had died in the earlier film – and Fay Bainter and Donald Crisp also appeared. Rains as the wandering father and Garfield as a happy-go-lucky confidence trickster were kindred spirits who hate a settled existence, and Priscilla Lane was the daughter who falls for Garfield's cocky charm. Julius J. and Philip G. Epstein wrote the picture (released under the First National banner) from the popular 1935 Broadway presentation *Fly Away Home* by Dorothy Bennett and Irving White, which was filmed again in 1942 as *Always in My Heart* with Walter Huston.
Second Fiddle Spoofing the search for an actress to play Scarlett O'Hara, this musical comedy from 20th Century-Fox had Tyrone Power as a studio publicity chief who discovers Sonja Henie's Minnesota schoolteacher and promotes a romance between her and Rudy Vallee's leading man while falling in love with her himself. Sonja skated while Rudy Vallee and Mary Healy sang six Irving Berlin songs. Edna May Oliver and Lyle Talbot lent support. Harry Tugend wrote it from a George Bradshaw story and Sidney Lanfield directed.
Andy Hardy Gets Spring Fever In the second of three 1939 additions to the MGM series, Mickey Rooney's Andy falls in love with his high school drama

teacher (Helen Gilbert) while writing himself the leading role in a class play. W. S. Van Dyke II was the director of this episode, written by Kay Van Riper.

AUGUST

The Wizard of Oz In 1938 MGM acquired the rights to L. Frank Baum's classic story, published in 1900, expecting a demand for fantasy subjects in the wake of *Snow White and the Seven Dwarfs*. Shirley Temple was sought for the leading role of Dorothy before it was given to contract player Judy Garland. She was then 16 but convincingly acted younger as the lonely Kansas farm girl who imagines the wonderful world of Oz. It was MGM's second major use

The Wizard of Oz: Judy Garland, Jack Haley, Ray Bolger.

The Wizard of Oz: Judy Garland, Ray Bolger. On the yellow brick road.

of the new Technicolor process, which was cleverly reserved for the fantasy world with the framing sequence set on a dreary prairie landscape filmed in black and white (and originally printed in sepia). The shrewd musical adaptation improved considerably on the original story, relating Dorothy's Kansas acquaintances to the characters she meets in Oz and refining Dorothy's final line to create a strong close ("Oh, Aunt Em, there's no place like home"). Besides Judy's Dorothy, the film abounded in memorable characters: Ray Bolger's Scarecrow, Jack Haley's Tin Woodsman, Bert Lahr's cowardly lion, Frank Morgan's bulbous-cheeked Wizard, Margaret Hamilton's Wicked Witch of the West and Billie Burke's fluttery Good Witch, as well as 124 midgets playing the Munchkins – and not forgetting Toto the dog. The splendidly zippy Oz songs by Harold Arlen and E. Y. Harburg like "We're Off to See the Wizard" (with dance direction by Bobby Connolly) were preceded by Judy Garland's serious solo "Over the Rainbow". MGM spared no expense in creating the highly artificial yet satisfyingly fanciful land of Oz, a combination of art direction (Cedric Gibbons and William A. Horning), cinematography (Harold Rosson) and special effects (A. Arnold Gillespie). King Vidor directed (without credit) the Kansas sequences, while Victor Fleming directed most of the rest before being switched to *Gone with the Wind*. Noel Langley, Florence Ryerson and Edgar Allan Woolf did the screenplay. The film went over budget, costing $2,777,000 to make (with another $250,000 spent on a campaign, concentrating on colour ads in magazines, to launch it). Its drawing power was insufficient to put

it in profit on first release, but its enduring appeal, especially on TV, has made it very probably the most popular film of all time.

Stanley and Livingstone 20th Century-Fox's stirring tribute to the British explorer and missionary, Dr David Livingstone (played by Sir Cedric Hardwicke), cast Spencer Tracy as the American newspaperman, Henry M. Stanley, who spends nine months tracking him down deep in the heart of Africa and is himself inspired by the man's compassion and dedication. The film contrasted the greatness of Livingstone with the small minds of the geographers in comfortable clubs in London and brought out the vastness and loneliness of the African continent. Otto Brower took a unit to shoot background footage in British East Africa, which was skilfully integrated with the work of the principal actors under director Henry King in Hollywood. Richard Greene and Nancy Kelly received co-star billing with Tracy for enacting a dispensable romantic sub-plot, Walter Brennan played a garrulous expedition guide, Charles Coburn and Henry Hull were newspaper editors and Henry Travers was a British consular agent overcome by the Dark Continent. The script was by Julien Josephson and Philip Dunne (from a story outline by Hal Long and Sam Hellman) and gave Tracy one of the decade's longest monologues: a 412-word speech to the Royal Geographical Society, answering charges of fraud over his claim to have met Livingstone.

Bachelor Mother This sharp and inventive comedy had Ginger Rogers' store assistant, dismissed on Christmas Eve, being mistaken for the mother of an abandoned baby, and David Niven, as the store owner's son who befriends her, finding himself regarded as the father. It was written by Norman Krasna and directed by Garson Kanin at RKO Radio. Charles Coburn was the store owner, Frank Albertson a rival for Rogers' hand in love. The picture was suggested by a 1935 Austrian film, *Kleine Mutti*, scripted by Felix Joachimson, who took story credit under his Hollywood name of Felix Jackson. RKO did a musical re-make with Debbie Reynolds, *Bundle of Joy* (1956).

When Tomorrow Comes The stars of *Love Affair* were quickly reunited by Universal in another romantic sob-story. Irene Dunne is the waitress who falls for Charles Boyer's concert pianist, but happiness cannot be theirs as he is married to a woman (Barbara O'Neil) who has lost her mind. John M. Stahl directed and Dwight Taylor wrote it from a story by James M. Cain. It was remade as *Interlude* (1956) with June Allyson and Rossano

Stanley and Livingstone: Spencer Tracy, Sir Cedric Hardwicke.

Brazzi. According to Cain, the original movie also used, without permission, material from his novel *Serenade*, which was also seen on film in 1956.

Each Dawn I Die James Cagney and George Raft top-lined this vigorous prison melodrama. Cagney was the crusading journalist who goes to jail on a frame-up, and Raft was the racketeer serving a life sentence who befriends Cagney and clears his name. A thwarted jailbreak made for an exceptionally violent climax. Jane Bryan was the girl Cagney left behind, and George Bancroft was the fair-minded warden. William Keighley directed the Warner Bros. picture, scripted by Norman Reilly Raine, Warren Duff and Charles Perry from a novel by Jerome Odlum. For showing in Britain, a preface was added stating that conditions depicted in the film had no parallel in His Majesty's prisons. . . .

The Star Maker After Bing and a baby (in the very recent *East Side of Heaven*), it was "99 kids and Bing!" in a Paramount musical suggested by the career of vaudeville impresario Gus Edwards. Crosby portrayed an entertainer (daringly married for a change, to Louise Campbell in the first reel) who hits the big time when he trains kids and forms them into song-and-dance acts. Songs by Johnny Burke and James V. Monaco (including "An Apple for the Teacher") decorated the slim narrative by Frank Butler, Don Hartman and Art Caesar (from a story by Caesar and William Pierce). Roy Del Ruth directed the players, who included new singing star Linda Ware,

Ned Sparks, Laura Hope Crews and Walter Damrosch conducting the Los Angeles Philharmonic.

SEPTEMBER

The Rains Came And 20th Century-Fox had a field day with special effects in this lavish adaptation of Louis Bromfield's 1937 novel set in India. Tyrone Power appeared in a skin dye as the dedicated Hindu doctor and future leader who has a love affair with a British Lord's wife, played by Myrna Loy (in a shocking change of image from her recent parts). George Brent (as an alcoholic wastrel), Brenda Joyce (as a missionary's daughter), Nigel Bruce (as the cuckolded aristocrat), H. B. Warner and Maria Ouspenskaya (as the local Maharajah and wife), Marjorie Rambeau (as a social climber), Henry Travers (as a clergyman) and the ever-versatile Joseph Schildkraut (as the Maharajah's secretary) were also in the powerful cast. The story culminates in an earthquake and flood, which provided a spectacular sequence reminiscent of the conclusions of *San Francisco* and *The Hurricane*. To this was added an outbreak of plague, which enabled Myrna Loy to atone for her immorality by nursing the victims and becoming fatally contaminated herself, leaving Power to wed the more suitable Brenda Joyce, a rare instance of permitted miscegenation on screen. The writing team of Philip Dunne and Julien Josephson had another success to follow *Suez* and *Stanley and Livingstone*. The director was Clarence Brown in his only talkie away from MGM. There was a re-make: *The Rains of Ranchipur* (1955).

The Women And not a man in sight.

The Crawford character is no match for the film's group of so-called friends, of whom she says: "There's a word for you ladies but in polite society it's only used around kennels!" There was Rosalind Russell displaying a gift for low comedy as the worst gossip of the bunch, Mary Boland as a much-married countess, Paulette Goddard as a chorus girl and Joan Fontaine as a newly-wed patching up her marriage (by phone). In an attempt to enhance the film's appeal, an irrelevant fashion show (dresses here and throughout by Adrian) was inserted in Technicolor, helping make the film exceptionally long at 134 minutes. Anita Loos and Jane Murfin wrote the adaptation, and George Cukor again demonstrated his skill at directing women. There was to be a musical re-make: *The Opposite Sex* (1956).

The Rains Came: Maria Ouspenskaya, Tyrone Power.

That, plus its pungent display of cattiness, formed the distinctiveness and huge appeal of the Clare Boothe comedy, which opened on Broadway at the end of 1936. MGM's film version expanded the action to feature 135 women but still excluded men. (For the record, there had been an earlier all-female film, Paramount's *The Mad Parade*, released in 1931, about eight women serving in World War I. Evelyn Brent was the star.) *The Women* brought together for one scene two of the studio's top stars – Norma Shearer as the devoted wife and Joan Crawford as the tough salesgirl carrying on with her husband.

The Women: Paulette Goddard, Mary Boland, Norma Shearer.

The Old Maid: Marlene Burnet, Miriam Hopkins, Bette Davis.

The Old Maid In a late return to the mother-love genre of handkerchief drama, Warner Bros. gave Bette Davis a memorable part as the woman whose illegitimate child is brought up by her sister (Miriam Hopkins) and doesn't even know on the day of her marriage that her fusspot old maid aunt is really her mother. Skilful scripting by Casey Robinson (from the Zoë Akins play based on Edith Wharton's novel) and direction by Edmund Goulding plus a marvellously controlled performance by Davis kept some bite in the blatant tear-jerker. George Brent (the father killed in the Civil War), Jane Bryan (the grown-up daughter), Donald Crisp (the family doctor), Louise Fazenda, James

Beau Geste: Robert Preston, Gary Cooper, Ray Milland.

Stephenson and Jerome Cowan also performed.

Beau Geste Paramount had a strong line-up in Gary Cooper, Ray Milland and Robert Preston as the three Geste brothers who join the Foreign Legion, with Brian Donlevy as the vicious, scar-faced drill sergeant, Susan Hayward (in her first important, though still small, role) as the girl the trio left behind, and 13-year-old Donald O'Connor as Cooper's Beau Geste in the childhood prologue. Memorable was the opening sequence of the fort in the desert with its rows of dead legionnaires at the embrasures, from which a warning shot is fired at the relief column. P. C. Wren's 1925 novel of brotherly love and honour (last filmed in 1926 with Ronald Colman) was admirably brought to life by Robert Carson's adaptation and William Wellman's spirited direction. There would be a re-make in 1966.

In Name Only RKO Radio's weepie had Cary Grant as the disillusioned

In Name Only: Charles Coburn, Carole Lombard, Maurice Moskovitch, Cary Grant.

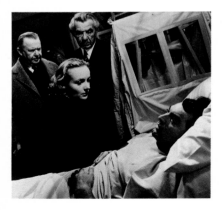

husband of a cold, venomous and selfish wife (Kay Francis) who married him for his money and position. Carole Lombard co-starred as the young widow he desperately wants to marry, and she and Grant gave some feeling to the hackneyed triangle story. John Cromwell directed and Richard Sherman wrote it from a Bessie Brewer novel. Charles Coburn and Helen Vinson had the top supporting roles.

The Star Maker

OCTOBER

Babes in Arms A new type of puttin'-on-a-show musical starring Mickey Rooney and Judy Garland, this brashly energetic MGM offering had its origins in a 1937 Rodgers and Hart Broadway production. Under Busby Berkeley's direction, the young stars played descendants of vaudevillians. They lead a bunch of kids demonstrating what they can do by creating a show of their own and reaffirming America as a land of opportunity. Mickey was bigheaded and irrepressible with keen imitations of Lionel Barrymore and Clark Gable, while Judy especially scored singing "I Cried For You", and they teamed up well for the song "Good Morning" (both numbers by Nacio Herb Brown and the film's producer Arthur Freed, which replaced several deleted Rodgers and Hart ones). June Preisser, Betty Jaynes and Douglas McPhail were other youngsters performing exuberantly, while Charles Winninger, Ann Shoemaker, Guy Kibbee and Henry Hull represented the older generation. Jack McGowan and Kay Van Riper wrote the screenplay. 1941's *Babes on Broadway* re-teamed Mickey, Judy and Busby Berkeley for more of the same.

Mr Smith Goes to Washington Frank Capra's latest picture was a smash hit that held up remarkably well on extended runs thanks to the enthusiastic word of mouth. James Stewart made the breakthrough to front-rank stardom, superbly playing the shy, idealistic young senator who stubbornly refuses to be the stooge of a crooked party machine and eventually, after a gruelling filibuster on the Senate floor, wins the day. It had echoes of *Mr Deeds Goes to Town* – especially in the repeat casting of Jean Arthur as the cynical figure who first wounds the hero but ultimately inspires him to victory – but it was none the worse for that. In the dark days of war in Europe it had an intensely relevant message about the need to be watchful and not take freedom for granted and to defend it against all odds. Claude Rains co-starred as a dignified senator who is really corrupt, Edward Arnold was the political boss, Guy Kibbee appeared as a bought Governor, Beulah Bondi played Stewart's mum, Thomas Mitchell was a political reporter and cowboy star Harry Carey Sr was the avuncular vice-president whose encouragement makes Senator Smith's victory possible. The original story was by Lewis R. Foster, the screenplay by Sidney Buchman.

Hollywood Cavalcade 20th Century-Fox's Technicolor musical was a fond evocation of tinseltown's early days, made when it was still possible to re-assemble the original silent comics: Eddie Collins, Hank Mann, Heinie Conklin, James Finlayson and Snub Pollard returned to playing Keystone Kops (producer Mack Sennett played himself), while cross-eyed Ben Turpin appeared as the bartender and Chester Conklin as the sheriff in a western sequence. Buster Keaton and Al Jolson made guest appearances, Keaton throwing a custard pie into Alice Faye's face and Jolson re-creating the sound revolution singing "Kol Nidre" from *The Jazz Singer*. In

Mr Smith Goes to Washington: Claude Rains, James Stewart.

the actual leads were Don Ameche as a film director making a star out of Faye and, never finding the time to marry her, losing her to Alan Curtis. An Ernest Pascal screenplay from a story by Hilary Lynn and Brown Holmes was based on an idea by Lou Breslow. Irving Cummings directed, although Mal St Clair handled the reconstructions of early sound comedy under Sennett's supervision.
The Women
The Old Maid

NOVEMBER

Mr Smith Goes to Washington
Drums Along the Mohawk This hugely successful historical drama focused on the lives of farmers in the Mohawk Valley before and during the American Revolution and starred Claudette Colbert and Henry Fonda as a couple who lose their crop and cabin and almost their lives to hostile Indians. Playing other pioneers were Edna May Oliver, Eddie Collins, John Carradine, Dorris Bowden, Jessie Ralph, Arthur Shields and Ward Bond. Photographed in Technicolor by Bert Glennon and Ray Rennahan, the film was a triumph for the process, and had some unforgettable images of Fonda being pursued on foot by three Indians, silhouetted against a sunset. Lamar Trotti and Sonya Levien wrote the screen adaptation of Walter D. Edmonds' novel. It was Ford's first picture in colour and his second with Fonda after the less popular *Young Mr Lincoln*, released earlier in 1939.

Drums Along the Mohawk:
Edna May Oliver, Ward Bond, Henry Fonda, Claudette Colbert.

Star and director then made it three in a row with *The Grapes of Wrath*.
Another Thin Man The third entry in the series, after a gap of three years, this offered Nick (William Powell) and Nora (Myrna Loy), now blessed with an infant son (William Anthony Poulsen), paying a visit to the New York estate of an armaments manufacturer (C. Aubrey Smith) whose life is threatened. Three murders ensue. Leading man Powell's own life had been threatened by the discovery of cancer (passed off as a minor illness at the time) and he had been off-screen for 18 months. Audiences were thrilled to have him and the series back. Dashiell Hammett provided the screen story, while the movie had the same writing

team (Frances Goodrich, Albert Hackett) and director (W. S. Van Dyke II) as its predecessors. Behaving suspiciously in it were Ruth Hussey, Sheldon Leonard and Tom Neal, while Otto Kruger and Nat Pendleton represented the heavy hand of the law.
Ninotchka "Garbo laughs" said MGM's advertising. She had before, but never so scintillatingly. This was her first comedy, and it made fun of her customary aloofness by presenting her as a stern Russian official sent on a mission to Paris where she is thawed out by Melvyn Douglas's playboy and learns to laugh. Like her compatriots (Sig Rumann, Felix Bressart, Alexander Granach), she eventually

Ninotchka: Greta Garbo, Melvyn Douglas.

decides to settle in the fun-loving West. Ina Claire as a grand duchess and Bela Lugosi as a commissar were also seen. Billy Wilder, Charles Brackett and Walter Reisch fashioned Melchior Lengyel's story into a script, which director Ernst Lubitsch handled with his famous light touch. *Silk Stockings* was the 1957 musical re-make.

First Love Deanna Durbin was finally allowed her first on-screen kiss with newcomer Robert Stack. She was cast as the orphan who goes to live with a wealthy uncle (Eugene Pallette), is ignored by his scatterbrained wife (Leatrice Joy) and snubbed by his bitchy daughter (Helen Parrish). Deanna's songs included "Amapola" and "Home Sweet Home". Henry Koster again guided her through her paces, while Lionel Houser and Bruce Manning wrote the Universal picture for producer Joe Pasternak.

The Roaring Twenties: Humphrey Bogart, James Cagney, Abner Biberman.

The Roaring Twenties A bustling anthology of the stock situations of the gangster films of the '30s, this presented James Cagney, Jeffrey Lynn and Humphrey Bogart as three war-time comrades who go their different ways after a spell in the rackets: Lynn becomes the crusading District Attorney, Bogart the unscrupulous big-time racketeer and Cagney the man in between – at first Bogart's partner, later a humble taxi-driver, and finally the one who sacrifices his life doing the right thing. Priscilla Lane was the girl he loved in vain, Gladys George the nightclub dame who loved him and provides the now-classic closing line and epitaph – "He used to be a big shot" – as he lies dead on church steps. Raoul Walsh directed the Warner Bros. picture from a screenplay (by Richard Macaulay, Jerry Wald and Robert Rossen) based on a story by celebrated columnist Mark Hellinger (who spoke the narration). The montages (including the expressionistic treatment of the Wall Street Crash) were the work of Don Siegel.

Gulliver's Travels

DECEMBER

Another Thin Man
Ninotchka
Gulliver's Travels The success of *Snow White and the Seven Dwarfs* had encouraged Paramount to commission this animated version of the Swift classic from the Fleischer Studios, which supplied it with the Popeye cartoons. It was made at specially established studios at Miami, Florida, under the direction of Dave Fleischer, and became, two years later, the second feature-length cartoon, rushed to completion for the Christmas market. Although the settings were well created, the Swiftian satire and much of the story was abandoned, while undemanding, one-dimensional characterizations were substituted. Songs were introduced, by Paramount's regular team of Leo Robin and Ralph Rainger. The public response was not in the *Snow White* league but positive enough to encourage another feature, *Hoppity Goes to Town* (1941).

The Hunchback of Notre Dame This lavish $1.8 million production of the Victor Hugo story (last filmed with Lon Chaney in 1923) provided a vivid recreation of the bustling Middle Ages and a remarkable performance by Charles Laughton as the deformed bellringer of Notre Dame who comes to the aid of Maureen O'Hara's ill-treated gypsy girl. It was a triumph of Hollywood craftsmanship, happily appreciated (despite its often grim story) by audiences who rewarded RKO Radio with a handsome profit. William Dieterle directed from the screenplay by Bruno Frank and Sonya Levien. Joseph H. August photographed, Alfred Newman wrote the score, and the art director was Al Herman, credited with department

head Van Nest Polglase, while set decoration was done by Claude Carpenter working under Darrell Silvera. A strong supporting cast included Cedric Hardwicke, Edmond O'Brien (his screen debut), Thomas Mitchell, Harry Davenport, Walter Hampden, Alan Marshall and George Zucco as well as 83-year-old Etienne Girardot in his final role as the king's physician. RKO claimed that an all-time record high of 3,500 extras were used. Fifteenth-century Paris was recreated on the studio's 88-acre ranch in the San Fernando valley.

That's Right – You're Wrong A vehicle for the screen debut of popular radio bandleader and comic Kay Kyser, this retained his airwave format from the programme "Kollege

The Hunchback of Notre Dame: Charles Laughton.

of Musical Knowledge" of combining swing music with a slapstick quiz show. Director David Butler, with William Conselman, devised a story of sorts that had Kyser and band in Hollywood, hoping to make a picture despite the opposition of Adolphe Menjou's producer and the dithering of two writers (played by Edward Everett Horton and Hobart Cavanaugh). Conselman and James V. Kern were the actual writers of this RKO Radio picture, which also featured Lucille Ball as a glamorous film star, May Robson and Dennis O'Keefe.

Destry Rides Again Marlene Dietrich made a dazzling comeback, letting her hair down in Universal's year-end addition to the western boom. Someone felt, shrewdly, that after so many straight westerns the time was ripe for a good parody. But the storyline (from Max Brand's novel) was strong enough to serve a conventional western (as it had for a 1932 Universal production with Tom Mix), and it remained satisfying in its own right. James Stewart co-starred as the deceptively mild, apparently gun-shy deputy who helps the stooge of a sheriff (Charles Winninger) clean up a town. Dietrich was a saloon singer,

Destry Rides Again: James Stewart, Marlene Dietrich. The final shootout – the bad girl must pay the price and is fatally wounded.

giving her some memorable numbers to perform including "See What the Boys in the Back Room Will Have". She was the good-bad girl contrasted

with an insipidly proper Irene Hervey. Brian Donlevy contributed zestful villainy, supported by Samuel S. Hinds' crooked judge. Mischa Auer added some broad comedy, while Una Merkel engaged Dietrich in a lively bar-room brawl. Felix Jackson revised the original novel and wrote the screenplay with Henry Myers and Gertrude Purcell. The director was George Marshall. For Jackson and producer Joe Pasternak, it was another success to set beside their work with Deanna Durbin. The studio returned to the story for *Frenchie* (1950) and *Destry* (1955).

Gone With the Wind The most expensive and most eagerly awaited production of the decade made its debut on 15 December at Loew's Grand in Atlanta. By the end of the year it was playing at eight theatres in six cities. (President Roosevelt saw it with his family at the White House on 26 December.) Its real release came at the end of January and in early February 1940 when it opened all over America. Margaret Mitchell's massive first book was published in 1936, and the film rights were bought by David

Gone With the Wind: Clark Gable, Vivien Leigh.

O. Selznick before its phenomenal popularity became evident. In the same year, the producer engaged playwright and occasional screenwriter Sidney Howard to write the script (he died in a farm accident in August 1939). Intense interest developed among the book's readers and every actress in Hollywood as to who would play Scarlett O'Hara. Clark Gable quickly became the popular choice to play Rhett Butler and was secured from MGM, but only in a deal by which that company distributed the picture, financed half the costs and shared half the profits. As Selznick was contracted to United Artists until 1939, this meant a delay in making the picture. Having Gable, Selznick determined on a new face to play Scarlett, and finally settled on Vivien Leigh, a well-established British actress familiar to American audiences for her work in *A Yank at Oxford* and others. Leslie Howard and Olivia de Havilland took the other principal roles, and the key supporting parts went to Thomas Mitchell, Hattie McDaniel, Butterfly McQueen, Victor Jory, Evelyn Keyes, Ann Rutherford, Rand Brooks, Laura Hope Crews, Harry Davenport, Ona Munson and Paul Hurst. Victor Fleming took the director credit, having replaced George Cukor (who began the picture) and being temporarily replaced himself (after exhaustion set in) by Sam Wood. The film's visual magnificence stemmed from William Cameron Menzies' unifying production design, Lyle Wheeler's art direction, Ernest Haller's Technicolor cinematography, Jack Cosgrove's special effects and Walter Plunkett's costumes. Max Steiner's score was equally memorable. *Gone with the Wind* provided unsurpassed spectacle in vivid colour and was also unusually bold and even shocking in some of its storytelling, having Gable cry in one scene, and daring to use the proscribed word "damn" in Rhett's last line to Scarlett as he leaves her and she asks what will she do: "Frankly, my dear, I don't give a damn." (There is more emphasis on *give* than *damn*, no doubt to soften the impact.) The film ran an unprecedented 220 minutes plus intermission. It was budgeted at $2.85 million and ended up costing $3.8 million. Admission cost a minimum of

70¢ (when the average was still 23¢) but everyone had to see it, and MGM took in $22 million from its first release on the North American market alone. Frequent reissues have upped this total to $76.7 million (according to *Variety*'s figures). It has

been overtaken by 21 other films, the earliest being 1965's *The Sound of Music*, but if the figures are adjusted to allow for inflation it easily remains the biggest box-office hit of all time, without even adding its earnings from television and video.

TEN BEST-CRITICS' CHOICE

There were 542 critics casting votes on the top 10 films for the annual poll organized by the *Film Daily*. The top 10 and other films attracting more than 100 votes were:

1.	*Goodbye, Mr Chips*	472
2.	*Mr Smith Goes to Washington*	433
3.	*Pygmalion* [British]	349
4.	*Wuthering Heights*	283
5.	*Dark Victory*	280
6.	*The Women*	254
7.	*The Wizard of Oz*	244
8.	*Juarez*	216
9.	*Stanley and Livingstone*	213
10.	*The Old Maid*	166
	Close Runners Up	
11.	*Stagecoach*	153
12.	*Young Mr Lincoln*	152
13.	*Babes in Arms*	135
14.	*Love Affair*	128
15.	*Union Pacific*	112
16.	*On Borrowed Time*	111

Only *Young Mr Lincoln* was a box-office disappointment.

CLOSE RUNNERS UP

Demonstrating substantial big city appeal, 20 more movies were nearly included among the hits of the year for the months indicated: *The Adventures of Huckleberry Finn* (March), *Dust Be My Destiny* (October), *Fifth Avenue Girl* (September), *The Hound of the Baskervilles* (April), *Invitation to Happiness* (June), *It's a Wonderful World* (June), *Lady of the Tropics* (September), *Made for Each Other* (March), *Maisie* (July), *The Man in the Iron Mask* (August), *Man of Conquest* (May), *On Borrowed Time* (July), *The Real Glory* (October), *Swanee River* (December), *They Made Me a Criminal* (January), *Topper Takes a Trip* (January), *Tower of London* (December), *Wings of the Navy* (February), *Wuthering Heights* (April), *Yes, My Darling Daughter* (March).

BIBLIOGRAPHY

Basten, Fred E., *Glorious Technicolor, The Movies' Magic Rainbow*, A. S. Barnes, South Brunswick, New Jersey, and New York, 1980

Baxter, John, *Stunt, The Story of the Great Movie Stunt Men*, Macdonald, London, 1973

Belafonte, Dennis (with Marill, Alvin H.), *The Films of Tyrone Power*, Citadel Press, Secaucus, New Jersey, 1979

Bodeen, DeWitt, and Ringgold, Gene, *Chevalier, The Films and Career of Maurice Chevalier*, Citadel Press, Secaucus, New Jersey, 1973

Bookbinder, Robert, *The Films of Bing Crosby*, Citadel Press, Secaucus, New Jersey, 1977

Bronner, Edwin J., *The Encyclopedia of the American Theatre 1900–1975*, A. S. Barnes & Co., San Diego and New York, 1980

Croce, Arlene, *The Fred Astaire and Ginger Rogers Book*, Galahad Books, New York, 1972/W. H. Allen, London, 1972

Curtis, James, *James Whale*, Scarecrow Press, Metuchen, New Jersey and London, 1982

Dickens, Homer, *The Films of Gary Cooper*, Citadel Press, New York, 1970

Dooley, Roger, *From Scarface to Scarlett, American Films in the 1930s*, Harcourt Brace Jovanovich, New York and London, 1981

Eames, John Douglas, *The MGM Story, The Complete History of Fifty Roaring Years*, Octopus, London, 1975

Eyles, Allen, *James Stewart*, W. H. Allen, London, 1984/Stein and Day, New York, 1984

Geist, Kenneth L., *Pictures Will Talk, The Life and Films of Joseph L. Mankiewicz*, Charles Scribner's Sons, New York, 1978

Gomery, Douglas, *The Hollywood Studio System*, Macmillan, London, 1986

Haver, Ronald, *David O. Selznick's Hollywood*, Secker & Warburg, London, 1980

Jacobs, Jack, and Braum, Myron, *The Films of Norma Shearer*, A. S. Barnes, South Brunswick and New York, 1976

Jewell, Richard B. (with Harbin, Vernon), *The RKO Story*, Octopus Books, London, 1982

Katz, Ephraim, *The International Film Encyclopedia*, Macmillan, London, 1979

Knowles, Eleanor, *The Films of Jeanette MacDonald and Nelson Eddy*, A. S. Barnes, South Brunswick, New Jersey, and New York, 1975

Marill, Alvin H., *Samuel Goldwyn Presents*, A. S. Barnes, South Brunswick, New Jersey, and New York, 1976

Marx, Samuel, *Mayer and Thalberg, The Make-Believe Saints*, W. H. Allen, London, 1976

Milne, Tom, *Rouben Mamoulian*, Thames & Hudson/British Film Institute, London, 1969

Munden, Kenneth W. (Executive Editor), *The American Film Institute Catalog of Motion Pictures Produced in the United States, Feature Films 1921–1930*, R. R. Bowker, New York and London, 1971

Osborne, Robert, *Academy Awards Illustrated*, ESE, La Habra, California, 1969

Parish, James Robert, *The Fox Girls*, Arlington House, New Rochelle, New York, 1971

Parish, James Robert, *The RKO Gals*, Ian Allan, London, 1974

Parish, James Robert, *The Paramount Pretties*, Arlington House, New Rochelle, New York, 1972

Parish, James Robert, and Stanke, Don E., *The Leading Ladies*, Arlington House, New Rochelle, New York, 1977

Parish, James Robert (with Mank, Gregory W.), *The Hollywood Reliables*, Arlington House, Westport, Connecticut, 1980

Quirk, Lawrence J., *The Films of Fredric March*, Citadel Press, New York, 1971

Quirk, Lawrence J., *The Films of Robert Taylor*, Citadel Press, Secaucus, New Jersey, 1975

Roddick, Nick, *A New Deal in Entertainment, Warner Brothers in the 1930s*, British Film Institute, London, 1983

Stanley, Robert, *The Celluloid Empire, A History of the American Motion Picture Industry*, Hastings House, New York, 1978

Swindell, Larry, *The Last Hero, A Biography of Gary Cooper*, Robson Books, London, 1981

Tuska, Jon, *The Films of Mae West*, Citadel Press, Secaucus, New Jersey, 1973

Who wrote the movie and what else did he write?, Academy of Motion Picture Arts & Sciences and the Writers Guild of America, West, Los Angeles, 1970

Wiley, Mason, and Bona, Damien, *Inside Oscar, The Unofficial History of the Academy Awards*, Columbus Books, Bromley, England, 1986

Winchester, Clarence (editor), *The World Film Encyclopedia*, Amalgamated Press, London, 1933

INDEX OF FILM TITLES

Numbers in **bold** type indicate major references

INDEX OF FILM TITLES

ACKNOWLEDGEMENTS

The following were used as primary sources of information: *Variety; Motion Picture Herald; Motion Picture Daily; Film Daily Yearbook.*

Other periodicals were of value, particularly *Films in Review* and *Focus on Film.*

The key books consulted (and others recommended) are listed in the select Bibliography on page 157.

My grateful thanks to the British Film Institute's Information and Documentation Department for full access to its resources, to the London office of *Time* (Michael Brunton), and to Alvin H. Marill in New York.

This book is illustrated with publicity photographs and other publicity material mostly obtained from the Stills Library of the National Film Archive, London, and originally issued by British Lion, Columbia, First National, Fox (later 20th Century-Fox), General Film Distributors, Ideal, Metro-Goldwyn-Mayer, Paramount, Radio (later RKO Radio), United Artists, Universal, Warner Bros. and other organizations.